History of Multicultural Education, Volume IV

Policy and Policy Initiatives

History of Multicultural Education

Edited by Carl A. Grant and Thandeka K. Chapman

History of Multicultural Education, Volume IV

Policy and Policy Initiatives

Edited by

Carl A. Grant
University of Wisconsin, Madison

Thandeka K. Chapman
University of Wisconsin, Milwaukee

Routledge
Taylor & Francis Group

NEW YORK AND LONDON

First published 2008
by Routledge
270 Madison Ave, New York, NY 10016

Simultaneously published in the UK
by Routledge
2 Park Square, Milton Park, Abingdon, Oxon OX14 4RN

Routledge is an imprint of the Taylor & Francis Group, an informa business

© 2008 Taylor & Francis

Typeset in Sabon by
RefineCatch Limited, Bungay, Suffolk

Library of Congress Cataloging in Publication Data
History of multicultural education / edited by Carl A. Grant and Thandeka K. Chapman.
    p.cm.
Includes bibliographical references and index.

ISBN 978-0-8058-5439-8 (hardback, volume i : alk. paper) – ISBN 978-0-8058-5441-1 (hardback, volume ii : alk. paper) – ISBN 978-0-8058-5443-5 (hardback, volume iii : alk. paper) – ISBN 978-0-8058-5445-9 (hardback, volume iv : alk. paper) – ISBN 978-0-8058-5447-3 (hardback, volume v : alk. paper) – ISBN 978-0-8058-5449-7 (hardback, volume vi : alk. paper)

1. Multicultural education–United States.   I. Grant, Carl A.   II. Chapman, Thandeka K.
LC1099.3.H57 2008
370.1170973–dc22   2008016735

ISBN10: 0–8058–5445–2 (hbk)
ISBN10: 0–415–98889–6 (set)

ISBN13: 978–0–8058–5445–9 (hbk)
ISBN13: 978–0–415–98889–6 (set)

CONTENTS

PREFACE TO THE SIX-VOLUME SET

How we came to this work

We were invited by a large publishing house to create a multi-volume set on what we are calling the history of multicultural education. A change within the organizational structure of the publishing house resulted in the discontinuation of the initial project. However, over the course of the last seven years, the project was embraced by a second publishing house that later merged with our first publishing home. Our 360 degree turn has been both a professional challenge and an amazing opportunity. The project has grown and expanded with these changes, and given us the opportunity to work with many different people in the publishing industry.

We relate this series of events for multiple reasons. First we want to encourage new scholars to maintain their course of publication, even when manuscripts are not accepted on the first or second attempt to publish. Second, we would like to publicly thank Naomi Silverman and Lawrence Erlbaum Associates for throwing us a necessary lifeline for the project and for their vision concerning this project. Lastly, we would also like to thank Routledge Press for warmly welcoming us back to their publishing house and providing ample resources to support the publication of the six-volume set.

What we got out of it and what we saw

Over the course of six years, we have worked to complete these volumes. These volumes, separately or as a set, were marketed for libraries and resources rooms that maintain historical collections. For Thandeka it was an opportunity to explore the field of multicultural education in deep and multifaceted ways. For Carl, it was a bittersweet exploration of things past and an opportunity to reflect on and re-conceptualize those events and movements that have shaped multicultural education. Collectively, the time we spent viewing the articles, conceptualizing the volumes, and writing the introductions was also a meaningful chance to discuss, critique, lament, and celebrate the work of past and present scholars who have devoted time to building and expanding the literature on equity and social justice in schools.

Looking across journals and articles we noticed patterns of school reform that are related to political and social ideas that constantly influence and are influenced by the public's perceptions of the state of education and by professionals working in the field of education. We would also like to recognize authors who have made consistent contributions in journals to multicultural education. These authors have cultivated lines of inquiry concerning multicultural education with regard to teachers, students, parents, and classroom events for decades. Although we would like to list these scholars, the fear of missing even one significant name keeps us from making this list.

Moreover, we recognize that a good deal of the significant work in the field was not published in journal articles or that articles were greatly altered (titles, tone, examples, word choice) to suit the editors and perceived constituents of the journal. There are many stories that are told between the lines of these articles that may go unnoticed by readers who are less familiar with the field, such as the difficulty authors had with finding publication outlets, and questions and criticism from colleagues about conducting research and scholarship in the areas of multicultural education. Although these pressures cannot be compared across groups, scholars of color, white scholars, men and women all felt marginalized because they chose to plant their careers in the rich but treacherous soil of multicultural education.

Just as we can see career patterns, we also saw patterns of journals that were willing to publish articles that focused on multicultural education. While many journals have created an *occasional* special issue around topics of equity, social justice, and students of color, there are journals that have consistently provided outlets for the work of multicultural scholars over the past three decades.

Our hopes for the use of the volumes

We began this project with the desire to preserve and recount the work conducted in multicultural education over the past three decades. As scholars rely more heavily on electronic resources, and funding for ERIC and other national databases is decreased, we are concerned that older articles (articles from the late 60s thru the early 80s) that may never be placed in this medium would eventually be lost. The volume set is one attempt to provide students, teacher educators, and researchers with a historical memory of debates, conceptualizations, and program accounts that formed and expanded the knowledge-base of multicultural education.

GENERAL INTRODUCTION TO THE VOLUMES

Multicultural education's rich and contested history is more than thirty years old; and is presently having an impact on the field of education, in particular, and society in general. It is time to provide a record of its history in order that the multiple accounts and interpretations which have contributed to the knowledge base, are maintained and documented. Whereas this account is not comprehensive, it nevertheless serves as a historically contextualized view of the development of the field and the people who have contributed to the field of multicultural education.

The paradigm of multicultural education as social reconstruction asserts the need to reform the institutional structures and schooling practices that maintain the societal status quo. These reforms are fashioned by socially reconstructing the ways that educators and politicians approach issues of equity and equality in our public schools. Multicultural education has become the umbrella under which various theoretical frameworks, pedagogical approaches, and policy applications are created, shared, critiqued, and implemented through on-going struggles for social justice in education. These campaigns for educational reform influence and benefit all citizens in the United States.

As a movement, multicultural education has brought forth an awareness of and sensitivity to cultural differences and similarities that continues to permeate the highest institutional infrastructures of our nation. Although the movement is rooted in struggles for racial equality, multicultural education readily includes physical disabilities, sexual orientation, issues of class and power, and other forms of bias affecting students' opportunities for academic and social success. The inclusion of other forms of difference beyond skin color is one way that multicultural education acknowledges diversity in a myriad of forms and dismantles the assumptions of homogeneity within racial groups.

The purpose of this set of volumes on the history of multicultural education is to locate, document, and give voice to the body of research and scholarship in the field. Through published articles spanning the past thirty years, this set of books provides readers with a means for knowing, understanding, and envisioning the ways in which multicultural education has developed; been implemented and resisted; and been interpreted in educational settings. By no means consistent in definition, purpose, or philosophy, multicultural education has influenced policy, pedagogy, and content in schools around the United States and the world. In addition, it has stimulated rigorous debates around the nature and purpose of schooling and how students and teachers should be educated to satisfy those purposes.

This set of volumes draws attention to how scholars, administrators, teachers, students, and parents have interpreted and reacted to various political and social events that have informed school policy and practices. Each volume in the set documents and tells a story of educators' attempts to explicate and advocate for the social and academic needs of heterogeneous and homogeneous communities. Through their struggles to achieve access and equity for all children, different scholars have conceptualized the goals, roles, and participants of multicultural education in numerous ways. Through the academic arena of scholarly publications, and using diverse voices from the past thirty years, the *History of Multicultural Education* acknowledges the challenges and successes distinguished through struggles for equity in education.

Methods for collecting articles and composing the volumes

It is because of the multifaceted nature of multicultural education that we have taken multiple steps in researching and collecting articles for this volume set. Keeping in mind the many ways in which this set of volumes will enrich the study and teaching of education, we have approached the task of creating the texts using various methods. These methods reflect the spirit of inclusion intrinsic to scholarship in multicultural education and respect for diversity in the academic communities that promote and critique multicultural education. This was a multiple step process that included the following stages of data collection.

In the Spring of 2000, we began collecting articles using an electronic data bank called the *Web of Science*. This program allows the Editors to discover the number of times articles have been referenced in a significant number of refereed journals. We submitted proper names, article titles, and subject headings to create lists of articles that have been cited numerous times. The number of citations gave us an initial idea of how frequently the article had been cited in refereed journals. Using the *Web of Science* we established a list of articles, which because of their extensive referencing, have become seminal and historical works in the field of multicultural education. The authors cited in these pieces generated the names of over forty scholars who are both highly recognized or not immediately recognized for their scholarship in the area of multicultural education.

To extend the breadth and depth of these volumes, we returned to the *Web of Science* and used various subject headings to uncover other articles. The articles found in our second round of searching were also highly referenced by various scholars. The two searches were then cross-referenced for articles and authors. Through this process we attempted to reveal as many significant articles that dealt with multicultural education as possible. Some articles are foundational pieces of literature that have been copiously cited since their publication, while other articles represent a specific area of scholarship that has received less attention. For example, articles specific to early childhood and middle school education were not as easily identified as conceptual pieces that articulated various aspects of multicultural education.

The *Web of Science* program has some limitations. Articles that were published in less mainstream or more radical journals may not appear. The creation of a list of articles based solely on this program begs the questions of "What knowledge is of most worth?" and "How do we validate and acknowledge those significant contributions that have been marginalized in educational discourses?"

As multicultural educators, we were cautious not to re-instantiate those very discourses and practices that marginalize academic conversations. Therefore we used other educational and social science databases and traditional library-stack searches to present a more comprehensive set of texts that represent the field of multicultural education. For example, the reference sections in the first two searches were cross-referenced for articles that may not have appeared on-line. These articles were manually located, assessed, and used for their reference pages as well.

The main program limitation that haunted us was the lack of articles from the late 1960s and early 1970s that appeared in the electronic searches. We realized that educational research is lacking a comprehensive knowledge of its history because many scholars only cite articles written in the last ten to fifteen years when reporting their findings in academic journals. The lack of citations from the early years of multicultural education scholarship forced us to take a third approach to researching articles.

Using the ERIC files from 1966–1981 and manually sifting through bounded journals from the 1960s and 1970s, we were able to uncover other significant articles to include in the volumes. The decision to include or exclude certain articles rested primarily on the editors and other scholars who reviewed earlier drafts of the introductions to each volume and the references cited for that volume. We used the feedback from these scholars to complete our search for articles.

The volumes are a reflection of the field of research in multicultural education as well as a reflection of the community of scholars who contribute to the discourse(s) concerning issues of equity and equality in public schools. Our concern with shouldering such an awesome responsibility and our desire to include the voices from the many communities of multicultural education scholarship lead us to the final approach to finding quality articles. We solicited the opinions of over twenty multiculturalists. We asked them to choose the articles they believed belong in the volumes and suggest articles or areas that were not represented. Several scholars such as Sonia Nieto, Carlos Ovando, and Christine Sleeter answered our request and provided us with valuable feedback.

Polling various academic communities made the project a more inclusive effort, but also served as a tool to communicate the work of multicultural scholars. We appreciated the opportunity to engage with other scholars during the creation of these volumes. The multi-step research methodology for this project strengthens and enhances the finished product, making the volumes a valuable contribution to the field of education. This set of volumes, because it represents the voices of many scholars, is a spirited set of articles that reflects the tenets of multicultural education, its history, its present, its ideas for the future, and the people who believe in equity and social justice for all citizenry.

Features of the volumes

Each volume in the set includes a diverse group of authors that have written in the field of multicultural education. The array of work is based on the article's contribution to educational scholarship; they represent well-known and lesser-known points of view and areas of scholarship. The volumes do not promote one scholar's vision of multicultural education, but include conflicting ideals that inform multiple interpretations of the field.

Many of the articles from the early 1970s and 1980s are difficult for students to obtain because technology limits the number of years that volumes can be accessed through web databases. Volumes in the set provide students with access to the foundational articles that remain solely in print. Students and veteran scholars doing historical research may be especially interested in the volumes because of the rich primary sources.

The volumes are delineated by six subject groupings: *Conceptual Frameworks and Curricular Content, Foundations and Stratifications, Instruction and Assessment, Policy and Governance, Students and Student Learning,* and *Teachers and Teacher Education.* These six, broadly defined areas reflect the diversity of scholarship dealing with issues of equity and social justice in schooling. The articles illustrate the progression of research and theory and provide a means for readers to reflect upon the changes in language and thought processes concerning educational scholarship. Readers also will see how language, pedagogical issues, policy reforms, and a variety of proposed solutions for equity attainment have been constructed, assimilated, and mutated over the thirty year time period.

Volume I: Conceptual Frameworks and Curricular Issues

The articles in this volume illustrate the initial and continued debates over the concepts, definitions, meanings, and practices that constitute multicultural education. The authors articulate how best to represent the history and citizens of the United States, what types of content should be covered in public schools, and the types of learning environments that best serve the needs of all students. For example, this volume shows how multicultural education challenged the representations of people of color that are presented or ignored in textbooks. Conversely, articles that challenge conceptions of multicultural education are also included. Content wars over the infusion of authors of color, the inclusion of multiple historical perspectives, and an appreciation for various scientific and social contributions from people of color that reflect challenges to Eurocentric knowledge and perspectives are presented in this volume.

Volume II: Foundations and Stratifications

This volume presents theoretical and empirical articles that discuss the institutional factors that influence schooling. Issues such as the historical configurations of schools, ideologies of reproduction and resistance, and administrative structures that often maintain imbalances of power and equity in schools are discussed. In addition, articles explicating the various ways that students and educational opportunities are racially and socio-economically stratified are present in this volume.

Volume III: Instruction and Assessment

The articles in this volume elucidate general pedagogical approaches and specific instructional approaches with consideration given to content areas and grade level. Diverse instructional practices and the relationships between students and their teachers are discussed. Although content and pedagogy are difficult to separate, the work in this volume addresses the dispositions of the teacher and his/her awareness of learning styles, and his/her ability to incorporate aspects of students' culture and community affiliations into pedagogy. Also included in this volume are theories and models of multicultural assessment tools that reflect the needs of diverse learning communities.

Volume IV: Policy and Policy Initiatives

This volume on policy and governance explores the effects of federal and state mandates on school reforms dealing with equity in education. The articles in this volume show how educational organizations and associations have attempted to influence and guide school policy, instructional practices, and teacher-education programs. In addition, the volume presents articles that discuss how interest groups (e.g., parents and concerned teachers) influence enactments of education policy in schools.

Volume V: Students and Student Learning

This volume on "Students and Student Learning" focuses on students as individuals, scholars, and members of various social and cultural groups. The articles highlight different aspects of students' lives and how they influence their academic behaviors and includes students' affective responses to their schooling and their beliefs about the value of education. The articles also address how schools socially construct student learning through the lenses of race, class, and gender. In addition, the articles show how students act as political agents to structure, direct, and often derail their academic progress. Arguing that multicultural education is necessary for everyone, the articles highlight specific racial and cultural groups as well as offer generalizations about the academic needs of all students.

Volume VI: Teachers and Teacher Education

The teacher education volume addresses issues of multicultural education for preservice and experienced teachers. The articles cover the racial and social demographics of the past and current teaching force in the United States and the impact of these demographics on the structure of multicultural teacher education programs. Several articles speak to the role(s) of the university concerning multicultural preservice and in-service education classes, field placements, and institutional support for veteran teachers. These articles explore the nature of teaching for social justice in higher education, the desire to attract teachers of color, and the juncture between theory and practice for newly licensed teachers.

ACKNOWLEDGEMENTS

There are many who deserve a public thank you for their support of and participation in this project. We would like to thank the many colleagues and graduate students who offered constructive criticism, suggested articles, read drafts of the introductions, and helped to conceptualize the placement of articles in the different volumes. These people include: Barbara Bales, Anthony Brown, Keffrelyn Brown, Nikola Hobbel, Etta Hollins, Gloria Ladson-Billings, Sonia Nieto, Carlos Ovando, Christine Sleeter, and Michael Zambon.

We would like to offer a special thank you to the journals that, because of the nature of the project, reduced or forgave their fees for re-printing.

Thanks to Director JoAnn Carr and the staff in the Center for Instructional Materials and Computing (CIMC) for putting up with our large piles of bound and unbound journals that we pulled from the shelves and made unavailable for others for days at a time. Thank you for re-shelving all the publications (sometimes over and over again) and never reprimanding us for the amount of work we created.

A super big thank you to Jennifer Austin for compiling, organizing, and maintaining our files of publishers' permission requests. Jennifer also contacted and reasonably harassed folks for us until they gave her the answers we needed. Brava!

Thank you to our families for their support and only occasionally asking "Aren't you finished yet?"

STATEMENT CONCERNING ARTICLE AVAILABILITY AND THE CONFLICT WITH REPRINT COST

During this insightful, extensive process, the goal was to share re-printings of all the articles with our readers. However, as we moved to the end of our journey, we discovered that it was financially unfeasible to secure permissions from the publishers of all the articles. We found most publishers more than willing to either donate articles or grant us significant breaks on their re-printing prices. Other publishers were more intractable with their fees. Even if the budget allowed for the purchasing of the 200-plus articles, the price of the books would have become prohibitive for most readers. Therefore, the printed articles found in the volumes do not represent all the articles that met the criteria outlined in the Preface and are discussed in each of the volumes' introductions.

At first we decided not to summarize these articles and use them solely as support for the rest of the volume(s). As we refined our introductions and re-read (and read again) the articles, we could not discount how these pieces continued to provide significant knowledge and historical reflections of the field that are unique and timely. Therefore, if the volumes are to represent the most often referenced examples and keenly situated representations of multicultural education and paint a historically conceptualized picture of the field, we had no choice but to include the works of these scholars in our introductions. Unfortunately, for the reasons explained here, some of these articles are not included in these volumes. In Appendix 2, we have provided a list of all the publishers and publishing houses so that individuals and organizations may access these articles from their local or university libraries or web services free of charge.

LIST OF JOURNALS REPRESENTED IN THE SIX-VOLUME SET

Action in Teacher Education
American Association of Colleges for Teacher Education
American Educational Research Association
American Journal of Education
American Sociological Association
Anthropology and Education
Association for Supervision and Curriculum Development
Comparative Education Review
Curriculum and Teaching
Education
Education and Urban Society
Educational Horizons
Educational Leadership
Educational Research Quarterly
Educators for Urban Minorities
English Journal
Exceptional Children
FOCUS
Harvard Educational Review
Interchange
Journal of Curriculum Studies
Journal of Curriculum and Supervision
Journal of Teacher Education
Journal of Research and Development in Education
Journal of Negro Education
Journal of Literacy Research (formerly *Journal of Reading Behavior*)
Journal of Educational Thought
Journal of Teacher Education
Language Arts
Momentum
Multicultural Education
National Catholic Educational Association
National Council for the Social Studies
National Educational Service
Negro Educational Review
Peabody Journal of Education

Phi Delta Kappan
Race, Class, and Gender in Education
Radical Teacher
Researching Today's Youth: The Community Circle of Caring Journal
Review of Educational Research
Southeastern Association of Educational Opportunity Program Personnel
  (SAEOPP)
Teacher Education and Special Education
Teachers College Record
The American Scholar
The Educational Forum
The High School Journal
The Journal of Educational Research
The New Advocate
The Social Studies
The Teacher Educator
The Urban Review
Theory into Practice
Viewpoints in Teaching and Learning
Young Children

INTRODUCTION TO VOLUME IV

As we compiled the articles for each of the six volumes, gaps and significant absences in the literature on multicultural education became quite apparent. Nowhere was the absence of multicultural education more profound than in our search for articles that specifically spoke to the creation and implementation of policy initiatives that used the language of multicultural education. By the language of multicultural education, we mean that very few authors proposed guidelines for discretionary action that could be adopted by specific agencies. Although the knowledge base on multicultural education overflows with conceptual models, practical templates, and content suggestions for multicultural education, there is a minimum of academic literature that focuses on targeted plans for districts and schools.

We, the editors, feel that the reasons for this lack of scholarship are three-fold.

1. Articulations of policy, particularly on multiculturalism, have not been given a wide venue in journal publications.
2. The language used by districts to address issues of equity and equality are framed in more benign phrases that would not cause the types of backlash experienced in states such as Michigan, California, and New York that used strong characteristics of racism, sexism, and heteronormativity to address changes in schools.
3. Researchers have not been able to document the affects of multicultural education policies on schools given the political struggles and resistance that weaken and alter the policy in the classroom.

Instead of documented empirical evidence of the effects of multicultural education policy on schools and districts, much of the publishing in this area focuses on conceptualizing policy and reacting to other policy initiatives that are aligned or in conflict with the goals of multicultural education.

For the purpose of this introduction, we define policy as "a course of action: a program of actions adopted by an individual, group, or government, or the set of principles on which they are based" (*Encarta*, 2004). The articles chosen for this volume speak to proposed programs of action that specify multicultural education as the goal and/or a set of principles defined by issues of equity and equality for all students, primarily those who have been most disenfranchised by the public education system in the United States. Given these parameters, the works in this volume fit into three categories: reactionary pieces, conceptualizations, and documented accounts of policy implementation. Each of these areas demonstrates how multicultural education policy is embedded within social and political contexts and historical events of the United States and the global arena. This volume is particularly important because readers will be able to better understand the contested nature of curriculum and instruction in public education and how policy is constructed through various social and political forces that seek to continuously shape what it means to be an educated citizen in the U.S.

Reactions to Policy

Education policy does not happen in a political or social vacuum. In fact, policies in education deeply reflect the greater political compass of the United States. These political swings and their subsequent policies have, at times, benefited multicultural education, and at other times, conflicted with the goals of multicultural education.

In the 1970s multicultural education policy paralleled the political push from the Civil Rights Movement to acknowledge the contributions of people of color and the struggle to gain equity in the workplace. Affirmative action, the mandate for ethnic studies courses and departments, the legislation of Title IX are examples of changes that were affecting the greater political arenas of schools, universities, and businesses. Multicultural education policy was able to ride the coattails of these changes. As universities were forced to create programs and course sequences that focused on the culture and accomplishments of racial and ethnic groups, public schools were being pressured to include more content by and about people of color and women.

The pressure to recognize the needs of diverse racial and ethnic groups and their languages manifested itself through public statements from national organizations. The American Association of Colleges for Teacher Education presented their statement on diversity in 1973 (No One Model America). This statement was then followed by several other national education organizations serving the education community (e.g. Association of Supervision of Curriculum Development) with similar statements on the need to embrace diversity, reform education, and guide policy to better reflect the demographics of American schools. As public sentiment for multicultural education grew, the number of states and districts that drafted policies to implement various aspects of multicultural education also increased (Baker, 1979). Baker cites those states and districts that wrote and implemented multicultural education policies during the 1960s and 1970s. Her article provides a historical overview of the early impact multicultural education had on schools. It is also during this time, at the end of the 1970s, that the achievement gap between White and Black students greatly decreased and was at its smallest increment (Orfield, 1987).

The gains made by multicultural educators were eroded in the 1980s when several research documents with explicit policy mandates were published. *A Nation at Risk* and the *Commission on Excellence* were two of the most powerful reports that documented the declining achievement of students in public schools. These reports, along with the Nation's shift to a more conservative political agenda, replaced the multicultural policy agenda that was being embraced in U.S. schools with an assessment and standards agenda that would play out in the next two decades. The marked shift in the political climate from the 1970s to the 1980s made it difficult for educators, administrators, and policymakers to align the liberal multicultural agenda that focused on diversity and equity with the conservative agenda of uniformity and standards.

Arguments for standardizing schools, creating greater accountability for districts, and increasing testing for teachers and students mark the 1980s as a period of active, public intellectual debate. These curriculum wars centered on questions of whose knowledge and experiences counted as American, what are the purposes of schools, and how do schools increase student achievement and accountability for all? These arguments often were framed by several government reports that constructed U.S. schools as crisis areas where few children were being served and White students who had previously been high achievers were now suffering from watered-down miscellaneous curricula.

Glazer's (1981) article is one example of the conservative response toward the significant policy changes of the 1960s and 1970s that created intellectual space in higher education and preK-12 education for racial groups and women. Glazer feared that the focus on racial and ethnic group identities would further prevent public schools from being what he considered to be successful schools. He defined the success of American schools as places where immigrants were able to learn English and begin to assimilate into the U.S. He pointed to recent federal and state policies on multicultural education and students' rights to their own language as divisive and harmful to fostering the goal of cultural pluralism. Glazer's comments on the declining state of public schools due to non-uniformity in the curriculum and a focus on the academic needs of specific groups are a preview to the curriculum wars fought in the 1980s between those who wished to diversify the curriculum and reform schools and those who wished to re-create a romanticized past of public schools with a standardized curriculum.

Education policy has a history of responding to the recommendations found in large-scale social science reports. The Commission on Excellence and the Committee of Eight both had national reports asserting that their approaches to high school curricula were better for public high schools. The Moynihan Report and The Coleman Report each presented deficit pictures of families of color and families in poverty that ironically were used to advocate for programs such as Head Start and Title 1 funding. Therefore, it is not surprising to see *A Nation at Risk* and a series of other reports, as catalogued by Shor (1986), have such a significant impact on school policy.

Shor also recounted smaller reports that presented information about the success and failures of public schools using different units of analysis that highlighted the gains of students of color and poor students during the late 1960s and 1970s, as well as demonstrated various ways to address public school challenges such as teacher shortages and resource allocations. Moreover, the 1980s broke from previous patterns of curriculum debate in that liberal educators had difficulty accessing public forums to dispute the picture of American education as painted by conservative educators; therefore the argument concerning issues of equity and equality in education did not receive equal attention in public.

Oakes (1986) responded to the issue of academic tracking that marginalizes students of color and poor students through institutional policy. In her article in this volume, Oakes first explains the history of tracking and how it has been preserved in schools. She then shows how school practices, based on the policy of tracking, keep students of color and poor students overly represented in the lower achieving tracks in schools. In her push towards greater equity and equality in public schools, Oakes puts forth other policy initiatives that could decrease the impact of tracking, if not abolish the policy at some point in the future of public schools.

Oakes's article exemplifies the ways in which education arguments were constructed in the 1980s. Interestingly, both sides of the debate focused on large, institutional reforms that affected every aspect of schools and schooling and called for administrators, teachers and students to make significant changes in the way the students experienced schools. Through the articles from the 1980s, the reader can see the disparate positions of conservative and liberal educators.

The seemingly polarized debates over teaching and learning in the 1980s were translated into a new language and set of reforms for educators who supported multicultural education. In the 1990s scholars on both sides of the debates attempted to reconcile the two seemingly binary positions. Asserting that multicultural education was not a pseudonym for watered-down curriculum that focused solely on the emotional responses of the students, multicultural scholars attempted to align a rigorous curriculum with the tenets of multicultural education through assessment reform.

Darling-Hammond (1996) proposed a broad set of policy initiatives for teacher education that included both sides of the debate. She contended that standards and academic rigor went hand in hand with culturally relevant practices and positive teacher dispositions. Darling-Hammond's article demonstrates the difficulties inherent in making and evaluating higher education policies that are supposed to eventually affect preK-12 public schools.

Bigelow (1999) was less optimistic than Darling-Hammond concerning ways that conservative and liberal education agendas could become aligned through education policy. He used the Oregon State tests to respond to the testing policies implemented in the 1990s. Bigelow showed how the state exam, in trying to please multiple stakeholders, over-simplified historical events and critical educational concepts. He posited that multicultural education could not be distilled into standardized test questions because it requires a level of critical thinking and dialogue that conflict with the very format of the tests.

Cherry A. Banks (1997) made a similar argument against the narrow framing of national and state standards. She contended that the goal to regulate and norm curricula and pedagogy conflicted with critical multiculturalism. She suggested that the diversity of experiences held by U.S. citizens could not be distilled into national standards that will serve all students.

As we move into the millennium, Valenzuela (2002) echoed Banks's position on standards and standardized testing. She asserts that policies are built upon research that does not adequately frame and encompass the many strengths and diverse needs of students. Valenzuela calls for research that poses students of color, their families, and communities as significant, valuable stakeholders in education, and does not commit these groups to deficit notions of students.

There is evidence of national, state, district, and institutional policies that attempted to blend the perspectives of multicultural educators into national and state standards. These inclusions mainly focused on teacher dispositions towards the cultural backgrounds of students and the inclusion of content by and about people of color and women, more so than an attempt to reform schools in multicultural ways (Hobbel, 2003). The 1990s and the millennium pushed the conversations around standards and normative assessments to include penalties and sanctions for those districts, schools, teachers, and students who were unable to meet the criteria. Scholars of multicultural education viewed policy initiatives that included more standardized testing as efforts to reinstantiate the status quo of the haves and have-nots in society by narrowing the foci of public school education.

Conceptualizations of MCE Policy

Within the debates over equity and equality in public schools, scholars have attempted to articulate multicultural education policies. Couched in arguments that espoused the need for multicultural education, these policy conceptualizations give pointed recommendations for districts, schools, and teacher education programs to institute. Much of the literature conceptualizing multicultural education policy for schools bound issues of pre-service teacher education and professional development opportunities as inter-connected with multicultural curricula.

This confluence between pedagogy, school practices, and curricula was explicated in the American Association of Colleges for Teacher Education (1973) statement on multicultural education. This statement provided both a definition, although limited to the celebration and recognition of cultures, for multicultural education and a series of recommendations for implementing multicultural education through policy. Emphasizing the connectedness of teachers, students, and classrooms, these policy suggestions were aimed at preK-12 schools and teacher education institutions. The AACTE statement was followed by several other professional education organizations that desired to show support for implementing multicultural programs in public schools and higher education institutions.

Policy statements on issues of race, gender, culture, and language were ratified by professional organizations such as the National Committee of Teachers of English (1972, 1974, 1978, 1980), the Association of Supervision and Curriculum Development (1962, 1978), and the National Committee on Social Studies (1976). These organizations developed sets of concepts, and proposed ways of thinking about students, teacher dispositions, pedagogy, and content, that were connected to the goals of the organization. They included some generalizations such as all students have a right to a good education, and specific recommendations such as content by and about people of color and women, that served as guidelines for practicing teachers and for teacher education programs to follow. It is unclear how influential these policy recommendations were for schools. Although the organizations provided professional development support and forums for discussion (mainly at annual conferences), their position statements detailing various courses of action did not carry incentives or sanctions for teachers or schools.

Many scholars in the 1980s continued to conceptualize multicultural education in more general policy reforms that could be embraced by federal, state, and district policy makers. Ovando (1983) shared specific recommendations for cross-cultural studies and a national policy on language. Although his argument was framed with bilingual/bicultural studies, his argument to include all language minorities and support home languages resonates with multicultural education practices. Moreover, multicultural education has a broad definition for language acceptance that includes formally recognized languages as well as ethnic dialects.

Payne (1984) supported the idea that multicultural education should be broadly defined and inclusive of all students. Before he applied his typology of MCE to policy recommendations, Payne framed his work with a brief history of separate-but-equal federal legislation that affects racial and ethnic groups beyond African Americans. His historical overview sets the stage for his conceptualization of and policy recommendations for MCE that go beyond the binary of White and Black students in public schools.

Cervantes (1984) contended that the growing racial and ethnic diversity in the U.S and the shrinking White population would necessitate changes to educational policy. He argued for diversified curricula based on past, present, and future racial demographics in the U.S. Cervantes maintained that policy must change to better reflect the demographic face of America's public schools and give all students the opportunity to succeed. His recommendations depart from those of other multicultural educators because he did not advocate for better teacher education programs or focused research. Instead he pushed for the "ethnocentric pedagogy," or Eurocentric focus and point of reference, entrenched in public school classrooms, to be dismantled through various policy reforms that would include an economically and socially contextualized look at public education.

Cuban (1989) affirmed the need for policy makers to consider the ways in which school problems are framed by different contexts inside and outside the school. He suggested that students who have stopped attending school can be viewed from a deficit lens of their families and behaviors or from school-related policies and practices that force students to leave before completion. He pointed to several policies and the system of beliefs behind them, that promote school dropout rates. He then provided a list of effective schooling strategies that have been proven successful with different populations of students.

Documented Policy Events

Unfortunately, the implementations of these various conceptualizations of policy have not been well documented in the professional literature. Because policy is contested and manipulated by various stakeholders at the state, local, and classroom level, there is very little empirical evidence as to how multicultural policy manifests itself in the classroom. The articles in this section of the volume document national, state, and district attempts to provide opportunities for equity and equality in public schools.

Shalala and Kelly (1973) gave a bleak picture of judicial mandates that were implemented with the goal to provide more equitable education to students of color and poor children, but were ignored, challenged, or manipulated by various stakeholders to maintain the status quo in public schools. They discussed the roles of teacher unions, school boards, tax base referendums, national and state entities, and the use of social science in blocking the progress of equitable education reforms. Although the article does not deal with multicultural education policy reform specifically, it paints a significant picture of how policy mandates following the *Brown* decision that focused on issues of equal education, were received or rejected in public spaces.

Baker was able to shine light on those states and districts that persevered with equal education proposals. Baker (1979) catalogued several of the states and districts that had multicultural education policies on their legal ledgers at the end of the 1970s. Her article provides a broad overview of federal, state, and local initiatives that were set in place to enact multicultural education. Baker insightfully predicted the difficulties involved with taking policy measures into classrooms and she suggested ways to support and enforce multicultural policy on the national, state, and local levels.

Baker's suggestions for enacting multicultural education policy are echoed by Bell (1983) who believed that parents of color must be part of the decision-making process in order to achieve significant reform. Bell stated that educational equality cannot be fashioned or maintained without significant input from those who have been marginalized by the policy-making process. He shares Shalala and Kelly's unflattering view of the educational policy process and suggested that the only way for parents of color to gain justice is to secure power at the local level and guide their own, homogenous schools.

Baker's predictions, Shalala and Kelly's reservations, and Bell's skepticism concerning the ability to promote equity and equality through multicultural education policy resonate in Fine's (1988), Cornbleth's (1995), and Smitherman's (1995) retrospective accounts of multicultural policy reforms. Fine's article takes a close look at sex education policy reforms in one urban high school. Fine focused on how pregnant teens and teen mothers negotiate their roles as parents and students through programs and relationships with teachers, administrators, and other students. Her look at the outcomes of specific programs that were outgrowths of policy reforms to better serve diverse student populations provides readers with one of the few studies in the literature to document how reforms translate to school practice. Fine catalogued those conservative discourses that remain unchanged in the school, even with such progressive programming, and prevent such reforms from being fully embraced by the faculty and staff in ways that would alter societal beliefs and outcomes for these students.

Cornbleth (1995) moved the focus to New York education policy to examine the upper echelons of stakeholders in the policy-making hierarchy. She provides a vivid account of the battles waged around the New York curriculum at the upper academic levels. She laid out the key stakeholders in the New York debates, their political and ideological positions on education, and how they chose to wield their power to shape the New York Board of Regents' policies. Her article shows how various groups were able to align themselves in order to block all or parts of the Rainbow Curriculum designed for the state of New York.

Smitherman (1995) recounted a different struggle to push multicultural policy to the forefront of educational conversations over equity and equality for all students. Unlike Cornbleth's study of actual policy creation and implementation at state and district levels, Smitherman discussed battles over multicultural policies in higher education. She recounted the story of how the Council on College Composition and Communication (CCCC, 1974) struggled to draft the policy resolution for Students' Right to their Own Language. Smitherman suggested that this resolution had far reaching implications for a number of professional organizations across the academic disciplines and political organizations founded by racial and ethnic groups in the U.S. She told how the policy was a response to the charged political climate in which racial and ethnic groups were gaining a stronger voice in the 1970s. She reflected on the process that academics underwent to produce the resolution, and shared her feelings towards the thirty year-old document. Whereas Cornbleth left her readers skeptical of the ability to move forward with multicultural education policy, Smitherman was more hopeful.

What's missing in these policy conversations

The documented policy reforms shared by Baker and other scholars provide the reader with a sense of what has been possible for multicultural policy reform. Unfortunately, what we, in the world of research, theory, and practice continue to miss from these conversations are the outcomes that resulted from the struggles over policy initiatives, the conceptualizations of multicultural policy, and the actual implementations of multicultural policy. Although veteran teachers around the country can point to professional development seminars and possible course work in the undergraduate and graduate teacher education programs, there are few descriptions or even paper trails that can be pieced together to illustrate the influence of past or present policy initiatives in multicultural education.

The reasons for the absence of data documenting educators' attempts to create, implement, and evaluate multicultural policy remain important to the current state of multicultural education. Few funding opportunities exist to conduct research on issues of race, class, and gender in ways that would produce meaningful data to further the implementation of multicultural education policy. Moreover, as the literature points out, the actual policy is rarely interpreted in uniform ways by schools in the same district or teachers in the same school. Thus it becomes difficult to tease out the viable connections between the policy and the practice.

One solution to decrease the disjuncture between policy and practice is to take a page from past education agendas and assign accountability to stakeholders for the implementation of multicultural policy. Although most major organizations in education have statements advocating for all aspects of the school to be sensitive to diversity through the curriculum and school policies, these policy statements carry no significant call for action. Federal and state sanctions were utilized to desegregate schools and are now being used to demonstrate national and state standards. These same forms of accountability as well as financial and resource incentives could be placed on districts and schools that are willing to address issues of equity and equality through multicultural education.

A second solution is to more closely follow patterns of reform and conduct longitudinal studies that document how schools implement new policies. This would help policy makers and reformers to better understand how and why policy is interpreted by administrators and teachers in particular ways. The demystification of policy implementation would benefit all educators, not just multicultural educators, as they go about the process of improving schools. A more rigorous approach to policy research serves everyone and may provide much needed answers to viable reform strategies and change. And in the end, what is important is not just to speak of change, but indeed, to make it happen.

References

American Association of Colleges for Teacher Education, C. o. M. E. (1973). No one model American: A statement on multicultural education. *Journal of Teacher Education, 24*(4), 264–265.

Baker, G. (1979). Policy issues in Multicultural Education in the United States. *Journal of Negro Education, 48*(3), 253–266.

Banks, C. A. (1997). The challenges of national standards in a multicultural society. *Educational Horizons, 75*(3), 126–132.

Bell, D. (1983). Learning from our losses: Is school desegregation still feasible in the 1980s? *Phi Delta Kappan, 64*(8), 572–575.

Bigelow, B. (1999). Why standardized tests threaten multiculturalism. *Educational Leadership, 56*(7), 37–40.

Cervantes, R. (1984). Ethnocentric pedagogy and minority student growth: Implications for the common school. *Education and Urban Society, 16*(3), 274–293.

Cornbleth, C. (1995). Controlling curriculum knowledge: multicultural politics and policymaking. *Journal of Curriculum Studies, 27*(2), 165–185.

Cuban, L. (1989). The at-risk label and the problem of urban school-reform. *Phi Delta Kappan, 70*(10), 780–784, 799–801.

Darling-Hammond, L. (1996). The right to learn and the advancement of teaching: Research, policy, and practice for democratic education. *Educational Researcher, 25*(6), 5–17.

Encarta (2004). Retrieved November 4, 2004, from http://encarta.msn.com/dictionary_/policy.html

Fine, M. (1988). Sexuality, schooling, and adolescent females: The missing discourse of desire. *Harvard Educational Review, 58*(1), 29–53.

Glazer, N. (1981). Ethnicity and education: Some hard questions. *Phi Delta Kappan, 62*(5), 386–389.

Oakes, J. (1986). Keeping track, Part 1: The policy and practice of curriculum inequality. *Phi Delta Kappan, 68*(1), 12–17.

Orfield, G. (1987). School desegregation needed now. *FOCUS, 15*(7), 5–7.

Ovando, C. (1983). Bilingual/bicultural education: Its legacy and its future. *Phi Delta Kappan, 64*(8), 564–568.

Payne, C. (1984). Multicultural education and racism in American schools. *Theory Into Practice, 23*(2), 124–131.

Shalala, D. E., & Kelly, J. A. (1973). Politics, the courts, and educational policy. *Teachers College Record, 75*(2), 223–237.

Shor, I. (1986). Equality is excellence: Transforming teacher education and the learning process. *Harvard Educational Review, 56*(4), 406–426.

Smitherman, G. (1995). "Students' right to their own language": A retrospective. *English Journal, 84*(1), 21–27.

Valenzuela, A. (2002). Reflections on the subtractive underpinnings of educational research and policy. *Journal of Teacher Education, 53*(3), 235–241.

PART 1

REACTIONS TO POLICY

CHAPTER 1

SCHOOL DESEGREGATION NEEDED NOW (1987)

Gary Orfield

School desegregation has been the dormant issue in educational policy discussions in the 1980s. It is no longer front-page news, nor can it claim the progress it achieved from the mid-1960s to the early 1970s, particularly throughout the South. In our view, however, it is a vital, effective policy that has proven surprisingly resilient to the political hostility or indifference of the past four presidential administrations.

In the first term of the Reagan administration, a period of federal hostility to urban desegregation, there was no major trend toward greater or lesser school desegregation. (See Figure 1.1, which shows national and regional trends from 1968 to 1984.) Even more significant, however, are the data we have collected which show that desegregation plans have been successful for a generation in many cities that adopted such plans. Conversely, as our data also show, schools in areas without desegregation plans became increasingly segregated along racial lines. Our data also identify a relatively unnoticed trend: high and increasing segregation among Hispanics.

High integration, low black enrollment

The states with the most integrated schools tend to have few black students. Of the 11 states in which more than half of the black students attend predominantly white schools, only 3 have high levels of black student enrollment—Delaware (25.8 percent), Florida (23.1 percent), and North Carolina (30.0 percent). The other most integrated states are Oklahoma, Kansas, Washington, Colorado, Nevada, and Rhode Island, all of which have black student populations of less than 10 percent, and Indiana and Kentucky, where black students are almost 11 percent of the population.

A number of these states with highly integrated schools were subject to court-ordered metropolitan desegregation plans. In Delaware and Kentucky, for instance, court orders virtually eliminated segregated education in the largest cities, Wilmington and Louisville; as a result, by 1984, 91 percent of black students in Kentucky and 94 percent of black students in Delaware attended predominantly white schools. Similarly, in North Carolina, the 1971 Charlotte city-suburban desegregation plan (the first in the nation) achieved a high level of integration. Shortly after the Charlotte plan was adopted, Florida began to desegregate most of the schools in its large metropolitan areas, with lasting success.

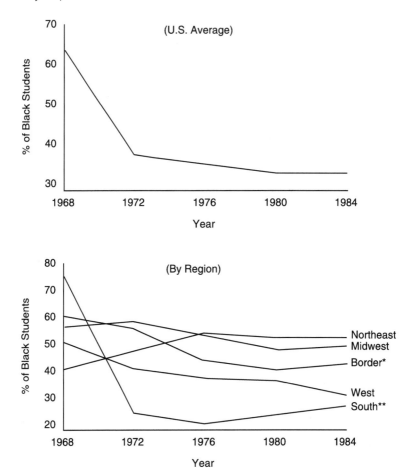

Figure 1.1 Percentage of black students in 90–100% minority schools, 1968–1984

Northern segregation

As Figure 1.2 shows, the states with the most segregated schools are in the North. The three states with the highest levels of school segregation include two of the old hotbeds of abolitionism, Illinois and Michigan, and a pioneer in modern civil rights law, New York.

Each of these three states is characterized by segregated residential areas, fragmented school districts within large metropolitan areas, and the absence of any city-suburban desegregation plans in their largest metropolitan areas. For instance, New York, Detroit, and Chicago have neither a comprehensive plan within their overwhelmingly minority central city school systems nor a voluntary program for the exchange of students with suburban school districts.

The other states with the most segregated schools are New Jersey, California, Pennsylvania, Missouri, Maryland, and Mississippi, which is the only state from

**Percentage of Black Students in Schools
With 10% or Fewer White Students**

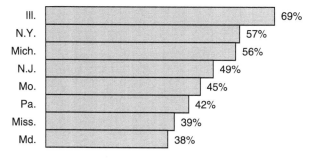

Ill.	69%
N.Y.	57%
Mich.	56%
N.J.	49%
Mo.	45%
Pa.	42%
Miss.	39%
Md.	38%

**Percentage of White Students in School
of "Typical Black Student"**

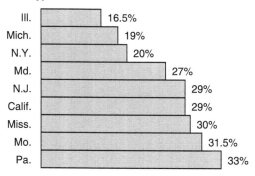

Ill.	16.5%
Mich.	19%
N.Y.	20%
Md.	27%
N.J.	29%
Calif.	29%
Miss.	30%
Mo.	31.5%
Pa.	33%

* For details on the method of deriving this index, see Gary Orfield,
Public School Desegregation in the United States, 1968–1980
(Joint Center for Political Studies, 1983).

Figure 1.2 States with the highest levels of school segregation for blacks

the Deep South in this group. Mississippi, it is worth noting, has a greater proportion of black students (50.4 percent) and is more integrated than all the northern
states listed here, except Maryland.

Hispanic segregation trends

Though school segregation has been widely understood as a problem for blacks,
it is now an issue that should concern Hispanics as well. Today, black students
are less likely than Hispanic students to attend a class where less than half the
students are white; in addition, the level of segregated schooling for blacks is
much less than it was in 1968, but for Hispanics it is higher.

Segregation is high in the states where most Hispanic children are enrolled in
schools, as shown in Table 1.1.

Not only is Hispanic segregation high, but it has been growing rapidly in
California, Florida, and Illinois and has remained at very high levels in New York
and Texas.

The most integrated state with a substantial Hispanic enrollment was Colorado,
where 53 percent of the Hispanic students attended predominantly white schools.

Table 1.1 Percentage of Hispanics in schools where enrollment is . . .

	Less than 50% white	*Less than 10% white*
New York	85	59
Illinois	80	41
Texas	78	40
California	74	27
Florida	68	26

Not surprisingly, the largest city in the state, Denver, has been under a mandatory desegregation court order since 1973, when the U.S. Supreme Court ruled that Hispanics were legally entitled to desegregation remedies.

In summary, Hispanic segregation levels continued to increase for the entire period for which data are available and for almost all regions of the country. Unlike segregation for blacks, which is subject to court orders, the isolation of Hispanics looks much more like a product of long-established and deeply rooted patterns. There has been very little organized effort to reverse this trend.

Variation among cities

As Table 1.2 shows, there are vast differences in the levels of desegregation in urban areas. What explains these differences? The answer is that the cities with the most integrated schools were under large-scale, mandatory, city-suburban desegregation plans while the others, with exceptions to be explained later, have never had a major, mandatory, city-wide or metropolitan busing plan.

Among the cities with the least school integration, Miami and Houston have had limited busing plans—but they were of a very strange nature. In both cases, Hispanics were counted as whites; low-income blacks were bused to low-income Hispanic schools, and vice-versa; and white middle-class schools were substantially untouched. In Memphis, too, there was a busing plan, but it proved to be ineffective when local leaders created a very large, parallel, private school system.

In Detroit and Philadelphia, the desegregation plans are limited to the central city school districts and do not include busing to the suburbs. The Philadelphia plan is completely voluntary. In St. Louis, a combined mandatory and magnet plan is in effect and, since 1984, has showed some positive effects, which are not reported in the table.

Policy issues

There are at least three reasons to think that the time has come to again place school desegregation in the forefront of national politics. First, there is very broad support in American public opinion for the general ideal of integrated education. Second, national surveys have revealed major shifts in public opinion in favor of school busing, particularly among those who have been bussed and among the young. (See box below.) Third, a growing body of research shows that integrated education has positive effects on college-going and college-completion, on obtaining jobs in growth sectors of the economy, and on the likelihood of living in integrated communities as adults.

Table 1.2 Levels of school integration in cities

City	% of Whites in school of typical black student*	Mandatory busing plan
Most Integrated		
Tampa-St. Petersburg, Fla.	66.3	Yes
Wilmington, Del.	65.7	Yes
Louisville, Ky.	65.4	Yes
Minneapolis, Minn.	63.2	Yes
Greenville, S.C.	61.1	Yes
Greensboro, N.C.	57.6	Yes
Indianapolis, Ind.	56.2	Yes
Columbus, Ohio	53.0	Yes
Orlando, Fla.	51.1	Yes
Milwaukee, Wis.	34.5	No
Boston, Mass.	31.9	Yes
Cincinnati, Ohio	31.5	No
Least Integrated		
Chicago, Ill.	8.6	No
Newark, N.J.	8.7	No
Detroit, Mich.	9.2	Yes
New York, N.Y.	11.4	No
Baltimore, Md.	15.8	No
St. Louis, Mo.	16.0	Yes
Miami, Fla.	16.1	No
Philadelphia, Pa.	16.6	No
Atlanta, Ga.	17.2	No
New Orleans, La.	18.0	No
Memphis, Tenn.	18.4	Yes
Houston, Tex.	19.0	No

* For details on the method of deriving this index, see Gary Orfield, *Public School Desegregation in the United States, 1968–1980* (Joint Center for Political Studies, 1983).

Those Who Were Bussed Liked It

Perhaps the most surprising aspect of school desegregation policy has been the development, in the 1980s, of a major public opinion trend in favor of school busing.

The Harris Survey, showing a shift of opinion between 1981 and 1986, reports that 71 percent of all families whose children were bussed said the experience was "very satisfactory." The survey also found that 66 percent of blacks, 58 percent of Hispanics, and 36 percent of whites now support busing; among those under 30, a majority of Americans support busing.

Among recent college freshmen—those most likely to have been bussed throughout their schooling—support for busing has risen in the last several years, from 45.8 percent in 1980 to 54.4 percent in 1985 to 56.1 percent in 1986, according to an annual survey by the American Council of Education.

The 1987 American Chicklet Youth Poll, conducted by the Roper Organization, found that students aged 8–17 favored busing by a margin of 64 percent to 23 percent, with 13 percent expressing no opinion. In other words, almost three-fourths of those who expressed an opinion favored busing.

A more urgent reason, however, is the deepening isolation of children growing up in inner city ghettos and barrios, who attend schools that are almost totally segregated by race and class. The children from these schools usually have almost no real connection to any paths of mobility in education and employment; it may well be that they are even more totally isolated from the mainstream middle-class society and economy than were southern black children during Jim Crow segregation.

The time is ripe for a national effort to halt the trend towards segregated urban schools for large numbers of blacks and Hispanics. If separate and unequal schools aroused this nation to act against Jim Crow in the fifties and sixties, we should be doing no less today to help the most needy in the urban ghettos and barrios that are growing more and more segregated with each passing school year. School desegregation is far from a panacea for unequal education, but no urban community has yet been able to produce segregated schools that are equal.

CHAPTER 2

ETHNICITY AND EDUCATION (1981)
Some hard questions
Nathan Glazer

Twenty years ago, had the *Kappan* been celebrating an earlier anniversary, there would have been no need for an article on ethnicity and education. Blacks and education, certainly: Six years after the Supreme Court decision in *Brown*, we still had the resistance of the Deep South. But the rapid acquiescence of the Middle States and the District of Columbia still permitted us to believe, in our innocence, that all that remained was for the states of the old Confederacy to follow the example of Missouri, Kentucky, Maryland, and Delaware in eliminating state requirements for segregation and all would be well.

Immigration was still controlled by quota requirements favoring Northern and Western Europe. The quotas had been instituted in the early 1920s and were only symbolically modified by the McCarran-Walter Act in the 1950s. We could still believe—even if liberals resisted the immigration restrictions—that ours was to be an overwhelmingly European nation, with only one large minority, the blacks, and with scattered communities from Asia and Latin America.

The problems of education, if we could recapture that moment, were problems of academic substance. In the wake of Sputnik, the issue was how we could teach our youngsters mathematics, science, and foreign languages while preventing those from lower socioeconomic groups, black and white, from dropping out prematurely and thus cutting off their access to a higher education we were then rapidly expanding. (We still called it higher, not postsecondary, education.)

The transformation has been startling. The civil rights movement, after its great successes in the middle 1960s, rapidly moved from a demand that blacks should get just what everyone else got in education to a demand—resisted by many black leaders—that blacks needed, and by rights should have, something different: education suited to their needs; education aimed not only at bringing them to the same place in educational achievement as others but education that would seek out, nurture, and develop something distinctive and different.

That this remained essentially an ideology, expressed in action only tangentially, did not reduce the significance of a startling transformation. We have seen scattered examples of a new segregation, now imposed by blacks (with the acquiescence of school authorities) on blacks for purposes of learning more effectively about their distinctive heritage. We now have a principle of uncertain reach put forth by a federal judge in the case of the children of the Martin Luther King, Jr., School against the Ann Arbor (Michigan) School District. The judge declared that "a language barrier existed between the plaintiff children and the teachers . . . because of the failure of the teachers to take into account the home language or dialect of the children in trying to teach them to read standard English," and the Ann Arbor schools were ordered to take "appropriate action." This is the language of a federal statute of 1972, prohibiting the denial of equal opportunity on account of race, color, sex, or national origin, and specifying that one form of this was the failure to take "appropriate action to overcome language barriers." The National Institute of Education has already conducted a conference on the implications of this decision, and we may well see the spread at the elementary and secondary school levels of the teaching of teachers (and if of teachers, can students be far behind?) of "black English."[1] The impact of the demand for a distinctive education for blacks has probably had its greatest institutional influence at the college and university level, where black studies departments or programs are now regularly established in most leading institutions and in many lesser ones.

European ethnic groups were not far behind in demanding something different, too. Perhaps the most remarkable success has been the establishment and spread of studies of the Holocaust. Since Jews are the merest fragment of American public school children—far fewer than their 3% of the American population, owing to the very low Jewish birthrate and the rising impact of private education for Jewish children—the demand for Holocaust studies at the primary and secondary levels did not rival the demand for black studies. But its impact has been felt, and it has affected the high school curriculum.

Far more significant in bringing ethnic issues in education to the fore than developments among blacks and the descendants of European immigrants has been the great increase in Hispanic populations. The increase is apparent in the Latin American dominance of immigration statistics, and there is substantial undocumented immigration. Europeans have become a small minority of immigrants. They have been replaced by Latin Americans and Asians—Chinese, Filipinos, Koreans, Vietnamese, and Indians—and each group raises separate and different issues for education.[2]

Immigration became an ever more significant issue during the decade of the Seventies, and the easy optimism of the assertion that the U.S. could well absorb 400,000 immigrants a year was shaken by the sharp increase at the end of the decade to perhaps 700,000 a year. Much of that increase was determined not by individual choice and by our own immigration policy but by cynical political actions of hostile countries that pushed out the people they did not want. And the U.S. had to take them in, for it had a political position to maintain in the world as the country of refuge and its own principles to maintain as a country of opportunity.

The new waves of immigration are now principally Hispanic and Asian, but there is no reason to believe that streams from other Third World countries (the Middle East? Africa?) will not follow them. They raise the gravest questions for the American polity and economy. These questions are peculiarly agonizing when it comes to the issue of education. For three other things have happened in this country since the last great waves of immigrant children and children of immigrants were being educated in the Twenties, Thirties, and Forties.

The first has been a general decline of self-confidence in the distinctive virtues of American society, government, and culture. The American economy no longer dominates the world. It has been a strange experience for those of us who went to school in the Thirties and Forties and recall the age of American dominance in the 20 years after World War II to get used to the fact that the U.S. is no longer the richest country in the world, its inhabitants not the most fortunate in the posses- sion of automobiles, telephones, and the other paraphernalia of modern civiliza- tion. Or to get used to the fact that we are no longer considered—in the world at large or among a substantial part of our own educated populace—a country of distinctive virtue. It is hard to get used to being called "the Great Satan," and one hears little demurral from this assessment in the developing world, or indeed the free world of those who share with us a common commitment to a democratic polity and an open society. Must not a change in perception of the role of one's country and culture affect the educational system?

It must, and it has. Laws that once self-confidently insisted—admittedly as a result of a good deal of ignorance and prejudice—that English must be the language of the schools have fallen left and right, to new state legislation, to interpretations of federal legislation, and to judicial orders.

And yet a second important change transforms the discussion of ethnicity and education from what it was during the last great wave of immigration: the grow- ing role of the federal government as a shaper of educational policy for the entire nation. It has always been a matter for wonder and analysis that, despite the paramount role of the states in public education and the weight of the tradition of local control, American education has not been more diverse than it is. But the option of diversity has always existed—and was indeed exercised. There was great variation from district to district in how many immigrant children there were and of what kinds; there was substantial diversity as to how districts responded to the presence of immigrant children. San Francisco tried to segre- gate Japanese children and created an international crisis. New York had, it would appear, no policy at all except to take them as they came and hope for the best. It was surprising under these circumstances that a permanent class of uneducated, undereducated, and unemployable young people did not develop in the New York City of the 1920s and 1930s, when it was overwhelmingly a city of immigrants and their children. Indeed, those are seen as halcyon years in the history of New York City education by those of us who can still remember them—our memories undoubtedly distorted by the passage of time. Malice or indifference are now featured in accounts of the experience of immigrant chil- dren of the Twenties and Thirties. Yet there were many positive experiences; sympathetic teachers and administrators helped children into a new language and a new culture. We are told these were the fortunate and successful few. And yet there must have been more than a few, for the income and occupations of immigrant Europeans and their children equals or surpasses persons of American parentage.

Undoubtedly this diversity will persist even in the face of federal regulation. Thousands of school districts, and millions of administrators and teachers, are not so easily homogenized. Yet there are consequences of federal regulation that change the relationship between ethnicity and education. In the absence of such regulation, the issue in each school district or school is, What account should be taken of diversity? Black history? Chanukah as well as Christmas programs, or neither? Teaching in Spanish? Or intensive teaching in English? The decisions are endless, and they are the outcome of conflict and argument among administrators, school boards, legislators, the mass media, ethnic representatives, teachers and their organizations, and parents. But federal regulation introduces an interesting shift in the relative power of the disputants: The issue now is who has access to the regulators—indeed, who are the regulators? Clearly they will be different under a President Carter, committed to the appointment of minorities and women (which generally means the appointment of young women lawyers who have come out of an activist tradition), than under a President Reagan.

The federal role in shaping a national policy will not go away, even if President Reagan's appointees are committed to withdrawing the federal government from establishing national standards in bilingual education and other areas. Federal courts, pushed into the fight by skillful advocates educated in the techniques of using constitutional and statutory language to force administrators to undertake the actions the advocates and their constituencies feel desirable, will not let the federal authorities remove themselves from the fray. The federal government must, alas, play a role. Legislation has turned the modest support it gives local school districts into a club to impose national requirements affecting the education of the handicapped, the segregation of the sexes, the employment and distribution of teachers and administrators, the assignment of children by race and ethnic group—and if government refuses to use the club it may well be forced to by successful litigants and powerful judges.

And a final change: In the inner cities, where the impact of the new wave of immigrants is greatest, the public schools have lost much of the prestige they possessed when they dealt with the last great wave of immigrant schoolchildren speaking foreign languages in the 1920s. They are challenged today, far more than they were then, by private schools and by arguments and ideologies supporting them. Catholic parochial school systems, despite some decline in numbers, are still strong competitors to public schools in the inner cities, and they are now joined by Jewish schools, Christian schools, fundamentalist schools, segregationist schools, black schools. Undoubtedly the decline in respect for the public schools is itself the product of a failure—the failure to effectively educate the low-income black populations of the schools, which exploded in the years after blacks replaced European immigrants in great migrations to the Northeast, Midwest, and the West in the Forties, Fifties, and Sixties.

These are the circumstances in which another great wave of immigrant children is coming into American schools, and particularly into inner-city schools, for the central cities are still the main port of entry for immigrants. How will the schools respond? Three quite different models present themselves: positive hostility, official disinterest, and positive reinforcement. The model of positive hostility could be found when laws forbade the use of any language but English in the schools, when children were punished for not speaking English, when their language and background were ridiculed. Officially, this is outlawed. Among the thousands of school districts, tens of thousands of schools, millions of administrators and teachers, some such practices undoubtedly survive. But I doubt that practices of crude Americanization are widespread; whether or not they are, no one speaks in favor of them.

On the other hand, the model of official disinterest has a great deal of support. (I use "disinterest" both in its original sense and in its common contemporary sense, as meaning "indifference.") Despite the fact that tens of millions of people speaking other tongues emigrated here, the United States remained an English-speaking nation. The establishment of newspapers, schools, churches, and organizations using foreign languages flourished. On the whole, little official notice was taken of this, either to encourage or hamper it. But it turned out that it was hard to maintain this pattern into the second and third generations. The newspapers and schools disappeared; the churches and organizations shifted to English. Was this for the best? Should official policy today try to emulate this earlier policy of disinterest? Children of various backgrounds found that the schools for the most part ignored their backgrounds; whether they came from Russia, Italy, Germany, Ireland, or any of the other countries that made up the American population, the schools taught them that the fathers and heroes of their country were George Washington, Thomas Jefferson, Abraham Lincoln—men very far from these children's own background and roots. It was an odd experience, as anyone who went through these schools can testify, and each of us undoubtedly asked, Should we really take seriously those other fathers and heroes we hear about at home and in ethnic schools, when they seem to be banned from the official and grander American school?

The model of positive reinforcement is probably now the dominant one among educators—not among teachers and administrators and school boards but among those who write and think about the schools and education. How are we to view this new model? As part of a positive development from prejudice to indifference to tolerance to understanding and a true commitment to cultural pluralism? Or should we find in the earlier policies some element of wisdom that we should not abandon? The arguments for the new policy of positive encouragement are clear enough. There are first the simple educational arguments—these children will learn better if they are taught for some period of time in their native tongues, and if the school shows recognition and respect for their heritage. Added to this are political arguments, at least for the large Spanish-speaking groups: This is a demand of at least major segments of the Mexican-American and Puerto Rican communities; they, too, are part of the American polity, and on what basis can this demand *not* be granted? Finally, there are practical arguments: These are ways of bringing teachers and administrators from these communities into the schools, where they are now underrepresented.

The arguments on the other side are at the moment less well formulated. They are in fact scarcely arguments but outbursts, as in the case of the vote in Dade County, Florida, apparently against any use of Spanish that involves expending public funds. Yet the fact that we have a good deal of unthinking resentment and resistance of this kind to bilingual and bicultural education should not blind us to some real problems.

Whatever their other failures, the big-city public schools of the age of immigration taught their charges English. Any child who had spent a few years in these schools could speak English. The circumstances were in many ways similar to those of the Mexican-American and Puerto Rican children for whom we are now told a different approach is necessary. They lived in dense ethnic communities, spoke their mother tongue at home, and played on the street with children of the community who used the same language. If they were to learn English, some forceful intervention from outside was necessary.

By contrast, in one major bilingual and bicultural program currently conducted under court order for Spanish-speaking children in New York, the children get only one double class in English daily and may participate in art, physical education, and shop classes taught in English. They spend almost the entire school day learning in Spanish. Visiting some of the model schools in this program—a high school, a junior high, and an elementary school—I wondered when they were transferred into English-language classes. It did not seem urgent to the teachers in the elementary school; the children would only be there a maximum of six years, they explained, and it put them under strain to move them away from their playmates: Let the junior high school make the transition. But the change hardly seemed urgent in the junior high school either: They would be there for only three years. Or in the high school—they would be there for only three years.

What troubled me was the fact that these children will nevertheless have to make their way in an English-speaking environment. One could count on television, the streets, the learning experiences of jobs in which they would have to work with others—but the double class in English seemed paltry indeed as an influence. Nor was I impressed by the argument that many middle-class children are sent by their parents to private schools conducted in a foreign language so as to gain the cultural advantage of two languages. These middle-class children, in contrast to the majority of the Spanish-speaking children in the public schools, already speak English at home. The experience of immersion in French or Spanish does them good. But the Puerto Rican and Mexican-American children are already immersed in Spanish. If we are to use the lessons of successful experiments in language teaching to young children, their need is to be immersed in English. Yet a combination of federal requirements, court orders, and local political pressures often prevent them from getting this immersion.

Despite the diversity of present-day immigration, I speak of Mexican-American and Puerto Rican children, for the pressure for bilingualism and biculturalism comes from these communities. I do not see the same pressure from the varied groups of Asian immigrants or from immigrants from other Latin American countries, all of whom seem willing to follow the path of earlier European immigrants. They see the school as an assimilating agency, and on the whole they approve. For Koreans, Filipinos, Vietnamese, Chinese, and Asian Indians, I suspect bilingual and bicultural programs are a matter of indifference; among some one finds a positive hostility.

It is impossible to deal adequately with this issue in a brief article. It will be settled in elections, in fights over legislation, in the courts. I suspect that educational arguments will have precious little to do with what happens. Critics of the new course of positive reinforcement see a departure from the experience of the past, which created a great nation speaking a single language. They see in particular the political dangers of a public polity that maintains language competence and pride in a growing ethnic group stemming from a rapidly growing nation—one with grievances against the U.S.—next door. After one of the studies of immigration that have been completed during the troubled Seventies, a congressman said to me, "We have heard testimony that by the end of the century there will be 140 million Mexicans—and half of them will be living north of the Rio Grande." It is the fate of the polity that will most strongly motivate resistance to the firm establishment of rights to public education in a non-English language.

On the other side, too, I suspect educational arguments are pretexts. A different vision of the United States drives the proponents of the new approach, but it is one whose outlines can scarcely yet be discerned. A key element of course is cultural pluralism. Another is a vision of a future world in which it is no longer necessary for a great nation to worry about its strength and the elements that enhance it. The U.S. in this vision remains the gathering place of the nations, but the nation itself is a cumulative product of the distinctive streams that make it up, each maintaining language and culture. Could such a nation, one wonders, have fought World War II? The new vision insists that war is no longer a relevant test. Perhaps it is not. But the fear that the new responsiveness to ethnicity is undermining what has been on the whole a success will not go away.

Notes

1   See Nathan Glazer, "Black English and Reluctant Judges," *The Public Interest*, forthcoming.
2   For 1971–77, only 20% of documented immigrants were from Europe. Some 32% came from Asia and 45% from Latin America. *Statistical Abstract*, 1978, p. 88.

CHAPTER 3

KEEPING TRACK, PART 1 (1986)
The policy and practice of curriculum inequality
Jeannie Oakes

The idea of educational equality has fallen from favor. In the 1980s policy makers, school practitioners, and the public have turned their attention instead to what many consider a competing goal: excellence. Attempts to "equalize" schooling in the Sixties and Seventies have been judged extravagant and naive. Worse, critics imply that those well-meant efforts to correct inequality may have compromised the central mission of the schools: teaching academics well. And current critics warn that, given the precarious position of the United States in the global competition for economic, technological, and military superiority, we can no longer sacrifice the quality of our schools to social goals. This view promotes the judicious spending of limited educational resources in ways that will produce the greatest return on "human capital." Phrased in these economic terms, special provisions for underachieving poor and minority students become a bad investment. In short, equality is out; academic excellence is in.

On the other hand, many people still argue vociferously that the distinction between promoting excellence and providing equality is false, that one cannot be achieved without the other. Unfortunately, whether "tight-fisted" conservatives or "fuzzy-headed" liberals are in the ascendancy, the heat of the rhetoric surrounding the argument largely obscures a more serious problem: the possibility that the unquestioned *assumptions* that drive school practice and the *basic features of schools* may themselves lock schools into patterns that make it difficult to achieve *either* excellence *or* equality.

The practice of tracking in secondary schools illustrates this possibility and provides evidence of how schools, even as they voice commitment to equality and excellence, organize and deliver curriculum in ways that advance neither. Nearly all schools track students. Because tracking enables schools to provide educational treatments matched to particular groups of students, it is believed to promote higher achievement for all students under conditions of equal educational opportunity. However, rather than promoting higher achievement, tracking contributes to mediocre schooling for *most* secondary students. And because it places the greatest obstacles to achievement in the path of those children least advantaged in American society—poor and minority children—tracking forces schools to play an active role in perpetuating social and economic inequalities as well. Evidence about the influence of tracking on student outcomes and analyses of how tracking affects the day-to-day school experiences of young people support the argument that such basic elements of schooling can *prevent* rather than *promote* educational goals.

What is tracking?

Tracking is the practice of dividing students into separate classes for high-, average-, and low-achievers; it lays out different curriculum paths for students headed for college and for the those who are bound directly for the workplace. In most senior high schools, students are assigned to one or another *curriculum track* that lays out sequences of courses for college-preparatory, vocational, or general track students. Junior and senior high schools also make use of *ability grouping*—that is, they divide academic subjects (typically English, mathematics, science, and social studies) into classes geared to different "levels" for students of different abilities. In many high schools these two systems overlap, as schools provide college-preparatory, general, and vocational sequences of courses and also practice ability grouping in academic subjects. More likely than not, the student in the vocational curriculum track will be in one of the lower ability groups. Because similar overlapping exists for college-bound students, the distinction between the two types of tracking is sometimes difficult to assess.

But tracking does not proceed as neatly as the description above implies. Both curriculum tracking and ability grouping vary from school to school in the number of subjects that are tracked, in the number of levels provided, and in the ways in which students are placed. Moreover, tracking is confounded by the inflexibilities and idiosyncrasies of "master schedules," which can create unplanned tracking, generate further variations among tracking systems, and affect the courses taken by individual students as well. Elective subjects, such as art and home economics, sometimes become low-track classes because college-preparatory students rarely have time in their schedules to take them; required classes, such as drivers' training, health, or physical education, though they are intended to be heterogeneous, become tracked when the requirements of other courses that *are* tracked keep students together for large portions of the day.

Despite these variations, tracking has common and predictable characteristics:

- The intellectual performance of students is judged, and these judgments determine placement with particular groups.
- Classes and tracks are labeled according to the performance levels of the students in them (e.g., advanced, average, remedial) or according to students' postsecondary destinations (e.g., college-preparatory, vocational).
- The curriculum and instruction in various tracks are tailored to the perceived needs and abilities of the students assigned to them.
- The groups that are formed are not merely a collection of different but equally-valued instructional groups. They form a hierarchy, with the most advanced tracks (and the students in them) seen as being on top.
- Students in various tracks and ability levels experience school in very different ways.

Underlying assumptions

First, and clearly most important, teachers and administrators generally assume that tracking promotes overall student achievement—that is, that the academic needs of all students will be better met when they learn in groups with similar capabilities or prior levels of achievement. Given the inevitable diversity of student populations, tracking is seen as the best way to address individual needs and to cope with individual differences. This assumption stems from a view of human capabilities that includes the belief that students' capacities to master schoolwork are so disparate that they require different and separate schooling experiences. The extreme position contends that some students cannot learn at all.

A second assumption that underlies tracking is that less-capable students will suffer emotional as well as educational damage from daily classroom contact and competition with their brighter peers. Lowered self-concepts and negative attitudes toward learning are widely considered to be consequences of mixed-ability grouping for slower learners. It is also widely assumed that students can be placed in tracks and groups both accurately and fairly. And finally, most teachers and administrators contend that tracking greatly eases the teaching task and is, perhaps, the *only* way to manage student differences.

The record of tracking

Students clearly differ when they enter secondary schools, and these differences just as clearly influence learning. But separating students to better accommodate these differences appears to be neither necessary, effective, nor appropriate.

Does tracking work?

At the risk of oversimplifying a complex body of research literature, it is safe to conclude that *there is little evidence to support any of the assumptions about tracking*. The effects of tracking on student outcomes have been widely investigated, and the bulk of this work *does not* support commonly-held beliefs that tracking increases student learning. Nor does the evidence support tracking as a way to improve students' attitudes about themselves or about schooling.[1] Although existing tracking systems *appear* to provide advantages for students who are placed in the top tracks, the literature suggests that students at all ability levels can achieve at least as well in heterogeneous classrooms.

Students who are *not* in top tracks—a group that includes about 60% of senior high school students—suffer clear and consistent disadvantages from tracking. Among students identified as average or slow, tracking often appears to retard academic progress. Indeed, one study documented the fact that the lowered I.Q. scores of senior high school students followed their placement in low tracks.[2] Students who are placed in vocational tracks do not even seem to reap any benefits in the job market. Indeed, graduates of vocational programs may be less employable and, when they do find jobs, may earn lower wages than other high school graduates.[3]

Most tracking research does not support the assumption that slow students suffer emotional strains when enrolled in mixed-ability classes. Often the opposite result has been found. Rather than helping students feel more comfortable about themselves, tracking can reduce self-esteem, lower aspirations, and foster negative attitudes toward school. Some studies have also concluded that tracking leads low-track students to misbehave and eventually to drop out altogether.[4]

The net effect of tracking is to exaggerate the initial differences among students rather than to provide the means to better accommodate them. For example, studies show that senior high school students who are initially similar in background and prior achievement become *increasingly* different in achievement and future aspirations when they are placed in different tracks.[5] Moreover, this effect is likely to be cumulative over most of the students' school careers, since track placements tend to remain fixed. Students placed in low-ability groups in elementary school are likely to continue in these groups in middle school or junior high school; in senior high school these students are typically placed in non-college-preparatory tracks. Studies that have documented increased gaps between initially comparable high school students placed in different tracks probably capture only a fraction of this effect.

Is tracking fair?

Compounding the lack of empirical evidence to support tracking as a way to enhance student outcomes are compelling arguments that favor exposing all students to a common curriculum, *even if differences among them prevent all students from benefiting equally*. These arguments counter both the assumption that tracking can be carried out "fairly" and the view that tracking is a legitimate means to ease the task of teaching.

Central to the issue of fairness is the well-established link between track placements and student background characteristics. Poor and minority youngsters (principally black and Hispanic) are disproportionately placed in tracks for low-ability or non-college-bound students. By the same token, minority students are consistently underrepresented in programs for the gifted and talented. In addition, differentiation by race and class occurs within vocational tracks, with blacks and Hispanics more frequently enrolled in programs that train students for the lowest-level occupations (e.g., building maintenance, commercial sewing, and institutional care). These differences in placement by race and social class appear regardless of whether test scores, counselor and teacher recommendations, or student and parent choices are used as the basis for placement.[6]

Even if these track placements are ostensibly based on merit—that is, determined by prior school achievement rather than by race, class, or student choice—they usually come to signify judgments about supposedly fixed abilities. We might find appropriate the disproportionate placements of poor and minority students in low-track classes if these youngsters were, in fact, known to be innately less capable of learning than middle- and upper-middle-class whites. But that is not the case. Or we might think of these track placements as appropriate *if* they served to remediate the obvious educational deficiencies that many poor and minority students exhibit. If being in a low track prepared disadvantaged students for success in higher tracks and opened future educational opportunities to them, we would not question the need for tracking. However, this rarely happens.

The assumption that tracking makes teaching easier pales in importance when held up against the abundant evidence of the general ineffectiveness of tracking and the disproportionate harm it works on poor and minority students. But even if this were not the case, the assumption that tracking makes teaching easier would stand up *only if* the tracks were made up of truly homogeneous groups. In fact, they are not. Even within tracks, the variability of students' learning speed, cognitive style, interest, effort, and aptitude for various tasks is often considerable. Tracking simply masks the fact that instruction for any group of 20 to 35 people requires considerable variety in instructional strategies, tasks, materials, feedback, and guidance. It also requires multiple criteria for success and a variety of rewards. Unfortunately, for many schools and teachers, tracking deflects attention from these instructional realities. When instruction fails, the problem is too often attributed to the child or perhaps to a "wrong placement." The fact that tracking *may* make teaching easier for some teachers should not cloud our judgment about whether that teaching is best for any group of students—whatever their abilities.

Finally, a profound ethical concern emerges from all the above. In the words of educational philosopher Gary Fenstermacher, "[U]sing individual differences in aptitude, ability, or interest as the basis for curricular variation denies students equal access to the knowledge and understanding available to humankind." He continues, "[I]t is possible that some students may not benefit equally from unrestricted access to knowledge, but this fact does not entitle us to control access in ways that effectively prohibit all students from encountering what Dewey called 'the funded capital of civilization.' "[7] Surely educators do not intend any such unfairness when by tracking they seek to accommodate differences among students.

Why such disappointing effects?

As those of us who were working with John Goodlad on A Study of Schooling began to analyze the extensive set of data we had gathered about 38 schools across the U.S., we wanted to find out more about tracking.[8] We wanted to gather specific information about the knowledge and skills that students were taught in tracked classes, about the learning activities they experienced, about the ways in which teachers managed instruction, about the classroom relationships, and about how involved students were in their learning. By studying tracked classes directly and asking over and over whether such classes differed, we hoped to begin to understand why the effects of tracking have been so disappointing for so many students. We wanted to be able to raise some reasonable hypotheses about the ways in which the good intentions of practitioners seem to go wrong.

We selected a representative group of 300 English and mathematics classes. We chose these subjects because they are most often tracked and because nearly all secondary students take them. Our sample included relatively equal numbers of high-, average-, low-, and mixed-ability groups. We had a great deal of information about these classes because teachers and students had completed extensive questionnaires, teachers had been interviewed, and teachers had put together packages of materials about their classes, including lists of the topics and skills they taught, the textbooks they used, and the ways in which they evaluated student learning. Many teachers also gave us sample lesson plans, worksheets, and tests. Trained observers recorded what students and teachers were doing and documented their interactions.

The data gathered on these classes provided some clear and consistent insights. In the three areas we studied—curriculum content, instructional quality, and classroom climate—we found remarkable and disturbing differences between classes in different tracks. These included important discrepancies in student access to knowledge, in their classroom instructional opportunities, and in their classroom learning environments.

Access to knowledge

In both English and math classes, we found that students had access to considerably different types of knowledge and had opportunities to develop quite different intellectual skills. For example, students in high-track English classes were exposed to content that can be called "high-status knowledge." This included topics and skills that are required for college. High-track students studied both classic and modern fiction. They learned the characteristics of literary genres and analyzed the elements of good narrative writing. These students were expected to write thematic essays and reports of library research, and they learned vocabulary that would boost their scores on college entrance exams. It was the high-track students in our sample who had the most opportunities to think critically or to solve interesting problems.

Low-track English classes, on the other hand, rarely, if ever, encountered similar types of knowledge. Nor were they expected to learn the same skills. Instruction in basic reading skills held a prominent place in low-track classes, and these skills were taught mostly through workbooks, kits, and "young adult" fiction. Students wrote simple paragraphs, completed worksheets on English usage, and practiced filling out applications for jobs and other kinds of forms. Their learning tasks were largely restricted to memorization or low-level comprehension.

The differences in mathematics content followed much the same pattern. High-track classes focused primarily on mathematical concepts; low-track classes stressed basic computational skills and math facts.

These differences are not merely curricular adaptations to individual needs, though they are certainly thought of as such. Differences in access to knowledge have important long-term social and educational consequences as well. For example, low-track students are probably prevented from *ever* encountering at school the knowledge our society values most. Much of the curriculum of low-track classes was likely to lock students into a continuing series of such bottom-level placements because important concepts and skills were neglected. Thus these students were denied the knowledge that would enable them to move successfully into higher-track classes.

Opportunities to learn

We also looked at two classroom conditions known to influence how much students will learn: instructional time and teaching quality. The marked differences we found in our data consistently showed that students in higher tracks had better classroom opportunities. For example, all our data on classroom time pointed to the same conclusion: students in high tracks get more; students in low tracks get less. Teachers of high-track classes set aside more class time for learning, and our observers found that more actual class time was spent on learning activities. High-track students were also expected to spend more time doing homework, fewer high-track students were observed to be off-task during class activities, and more of them told us that learning took up most of their class time, rather than discipline problems, socializing, or class routines.

Instruction in high-track classes more often included a whole range of teacher behaviors likely to enhance learning. High-track teachers were more enthusiastic, and their instruction was clearer. They used strong criticism or ridicule less frequently than did teachers of low-track classes. Classroom tasks were more various and more highly organized in high-track classes, and grades were more relevant to student learning.

These differences in learning opportunities portray a fundamental irony of schooling: those students who need more time to learn appear to be getting less; those students who have the most difficulty learning are being exposed least to the sort of teaching that best facilitates learning.

Classroom climate

We were interested in studying classroom climates in various tracks because we were convinced that supportive relationships and positive feelings in class are more than just nice accompaniments to learning. When teachers and students trust one another, classroom time and energy are freed for teaching and learning. Without this trust, students spend a great deal of time and energy establishing less productive relationships with others and interfering with the teacher's instructional agenda; teachers spend their time and energy trying to maintain control. In such classes, less learning is likely to occur.

The data from A Study of Schooling permitted us to investigate three important aspects of classroom environments: relationships between teachers and students, relationships among the students themselves, and the intensity of student involvement in learning. Once again, we discovered a distressing pattern of advantages for high-track classes and disadvantages for low-track classes. In high-track classes students thought that their teachers were more concerned about them and less punitive. Teachers in high-track classes spent less time on student behavior, and they more often encouraged their students to become independent, questioning, critical thinkers. In low-track classes teachers were seen as less concerned and more punitive. Teachers in low-track classes emphasized matters of discipline and behavior, and they often listed such things as "following directions," "respecting my position," "punctuality," and "learning to take a direct order" as among the five most important things they wanted their class to learn during the year.

We found similar differences in the relationships that students established with one another in class. Students in low-track classes agreed far more often that "students in this class are unfriendly to me" or that "I often feel left out of class activities." They said that their classes were interrupted by problems and by arguing in class. Generally, they seemed to like each other less. Not surprisingly, given these differences in relationships, students in high-track classes appeared to be much more involved in their classwork. Students in low-track classes were more apathetic and indicated more often that they didn't care about what went on or that failing didn't bother most of their classmates.

In these data, we found once again a pattern of classroom experience that seems to enhance the possibilities of learning for those students already disposed to do well—that is, those in high-track classes. We saw even more clearly a pattern of classroom experience likely to inhibit the learning of those in the bottom tracks. As with access to knowledge and opportunities to learn, we found that those who most needed support from a positive, nurturing environment got the least.

Although these data do show clear instructional advantages for high-achieving students and clear disadvantages for their low-achieving peers, other data from our work suggest that the quality of the experience of *average* students falls somewhere between these two extremes. Average students, too, were deprived of the best circumstances schools have to offer, though their classes were typically more like those of high-track students. Taken together, these findings begin to suggest *why* students who are not in the top tracks are likely to suffer because of their placements: their education is of considerably lower quality.

It would be a serious mistake to interpret these data as the "inevitable" outcome of the differences in the students who populate the various tracks. Many of the mixed-ability classes in our study showed that high-quality experiences are very possible in classes that include all types of students. But neither should we attribute these differences to consciously mean-spirited or blatantly discriminatory actions by schoolpeople. Obviously, the content teachers decide to teach and the ways in which they teach it are greatly influenced by the students with whom they interact. And it is unlikely that students are passive participants in tracking processes. It seems more likely that students' achievements, attitudes, interests, perceptions of themselves, and behaviors (growing increasingly disparate over time) help produce some of the effects of tracking. Thus groups of students who, by conventional wisdom, seem less able and less eager to learn are very likely to affect a teacher's ability or even willingness to provide the best possible learning opportunities. The obvious conclusion about the effects of these track-specific differences on the ability of the schools to achieve academic excellence is that students who are exposed to less content and lower-quality teaching are unlikely to get the full benefit out of their schooling. Yet this less-fruitful experience seems to be the norm when average- and low-achieving students are grouped together for instruction.

I believe that these data reveal frightening patterns of curricular inequality. Although these patterns would be disturbing under any circumstances (and though many white, suburban schools consign a good number of their students to mediocre experiences in low-ability and general-track classes), they become particularly distressing in light of the prevailing pattern of placing disproportionate numbers of poor and minority students in the lowest-track classes. A self-fulfilling prophecy can be seen to work at the institutional level to prevent schools from providing equal educational opportunity. Tracking appears to teach and reinforce the notion that those not defined as the best are *expected* to do less well. Few students and teachers can defy those expectations.

Tracking, equality, and excellence

Tracking is assumed to promote educational excellence because it enables schools to provide students with the curriculum and instruction they need to maximize their potential and achieve excellence on their own terms. But the evidence about tracking suggests the contrary. Certainly students bring differences with them to school, but, by tracking, schools help to widen rather than narrow these differences. Students who are judged to be different from one another are separated into different classes and then provided knowledge, opportunities to learn, and classroom environments that are vastly different. Many of the students in top tracks (only about 40% of high-schoolers) do benefit from the advantages they receive in their classes. But, in their quest for higher standards and superior academic performance, schools seem to have locked themselves into a structure that may *unnecessarily* buy the achievement of a few at the expense of many. Such a structure provides but a shaky foundation for excellence.

At the same time, the evidence about tracking calls into question the widely held view that schools provide students who have the "right stuff" with a neutral environment in which they can rise to the top (with "special" classes providing an extra boost to those who might need it). Everywhere we turn we find that the differentiated structure of schools throws up barriers to achievement for poor and minority students. Measures of talent clearly seem to work against them, which leads to their disproportionate placement in groups identified as slow. Once there, their achievement seems to be further inhibited by the type of knowledge they are taught and by the quality of the learning opportunities they are afforded. Moreover, the social and psychological dimensions of classes at the bottom of the hierarchy of schooling seem to restrict their chances for school success even further.

Good intentions, including those of advocates of "excellence" and of "equity," characterize the rhetoric of schooling. Tracking, because it is usually taken to be a neutral practice and a part of the mechanics of schooling, has escaped the attention of those who mean well. But by failing to scrutinize the effects of tracking, schools unwittingly subvert their well-meant efforts to promote academic excellence and to provide conditions that will enable all students to achieve it.

Notes

1   Some recent reviews of studies on the effects of tracking include: Robert C. Calfee and Roger Brown, "Grouping Students for Instruction," in *Classroom Management* (Chicago: 78th Yearbook of the National Society for the Study of Education, University of Chicago Press, 1979); Dominick Esposito, "Homogeneous and Heterogeneous Ability Grouping: Principal Findings and Implications for Evaluating and Designing More Effective Educational Environments," *Review of Educational Research*, vol. 43, 1973, pp. 163–79; Jeannie Oakes, "Tracking: A Contextual Perspective on How Schools Structure Differences," *Educational Psychologist*, in press; Caroline J. Persell, *Education and Inequality: The Roots and Results of Stratification in America's Schools* (New York: Free Press, 1977); and James E. Rosenbaum, "The Social Implications of Educational Grouping," in David C. Berliner, ed., *Review of Research in Education, Vol. 8* (Washington, D.C.: American Educational Research Association, 1980), pp. 361–401.

2   James E. Rosenbaum, *Making Inequality: The Hidden Curriculum of High School Tracking* (New York: Wiley, 1976).

3   See, for example, David Stern et al., *One Million Hours a Day: Vocational Education in California Public Secondary Schools* (Berkeley: Report to the California Policy Seminar, University of California School of Education, 1985).

4   Rosenbaum, "The Social Implications . . ."; and William E. Shafer and Carol Olexa, *Tracking and Opportunity* (Scranton, Pa.: Chandler, 1971).

5   Karl A. Alexander and Edward L. McDill, "Selection and Allocation Within Schools: Some Causes and Consequences of Curriculum Placement," *American Sociological Review*, vol. 41, 1976, pp. 969–80; Karl A. Alexander, Martha Cook, and Edward L. McDill, "Curriculum Tracking and Educational Stratification: Some Further Evidence," *American Sociological Review*, vol. 43, 1978, pp. 47–66; and Donald A. Rock et al., *Study of Excellence in High School Education: Longitudinal Study, 1980–82* (Princeton, N.J.: Educational Testing Service, Final Report, 1985).

6   Persell, *Education and Inequality . . .*; and Jeannie Oakes, *Keeping Track: How Schools Structure Inequality* (New Haven, Conn.: Yale University Press, 1985).

7   Gary D. Fenstermacher, "Introduction," in Gary D. Fenstermacher and John I. Goodlad, eds., *Individual Differences and the Common Curriculum* (Chicago: 82nd Yearbook of the National Society for the Study of Education, University of Chicago Press, 1983), p. 3.

8   John I. Goodlad, *A Place Called School* (New York: McGraw-Hill, 1984).

CHAPTER 4

THE CHALLENGES OF NATIONAL STANDARDS IN A MULTICULTURAL SOCIETY (1997)

Cherry A. McGee Banks

Since the late 1980s, national standards have been part of the discourse on school reform. An examination of that discourse reveals the extent to which the development and implementation of national standards have been shaped by forces that minimize the importance of diversity in U.S. society. Diversity is a salient characteristic of U.S. society. It is manifested in the racial and ethnic diversity of its citizens, their multiple identities, and the social-class positions they occupy. Developing and implementing national standards in a multicultural society should incorporate and give voice to diversity. When diversity is recognized as an important component of national standards questions such as "Whose Standards?" "Who benefits from the standards?" and "Whom will the standards harm?" will be raised by people outside the standards movement, but rarely by those within it.

When questions related to equity are raised by people inside the standards movement, they are addressed with a promise of high standards for all students. However, this promise will go unfulfilled if it is not accompanied by essential resources. In this article, I discuss the development of national standards and examine three types of standards: content, performance, and opportunity to learn. I then discuss multicultural literacy, a standard that is missing from the discourse on national standards.

The development of national standards

The development of national standards can be viewed as a case study in the way to develop educational policy without recognition of the complex characteristics of U.S. schools and students. The developers of national standards, who used a "top down" approach, did not realize the extent to which state governments and local school districts would oppose attempts to direct school reform from the federal level. Nor were they prepared to provide funding to address the tremendous inequalities in the facilities, resources, curricula, and teachers in schools.[1] Most important, the purpose of schooling has not been a significant topic in the discourse on national standards. The assumption that schooling was essentially preparation for the world of work was such a fundamental part of the thinking of those framing national standards that it was rarely questioned. The idea that schooling should also be a means for developing democratic values and commitments to social justice and equity was rarely considered or discussed.[2]

The standards movement was officially launched in 1989 when President George Bush held an education summit for the nation's governors in Charlottesville, Virginia. The summit took place at a time when the manufactured reality that our schools were in a dire condition and that drastic action was required was widely accepted without question.[3] The lack of discourse about the multiple interpretations of student performance and the realities of U.S. schools resulted in a national obsession about fixing the nation's schools. There was increasing concern about the ability of U.S. students to compete in a global economy. Business leaders pointed out that the U.S. economy had undergone significant changes, but the nation's schools had remained essentially the same as they had been for most of the twentieth century. The perceived mismatch between schools and the needs of the economy was the focus of media attention. Books describing how bad U.S. schools had become and listing what every educated person needed to know became best-sellers.[4] Proposed solutions for fixing the schools included returning to the basics, developing a national curriculum, and using standardized tests to assess student knowledge.

Within this atmosphere, President Bush and the state governors proposed six goals to guide educational reform and to raise the achievement levels of all students by the year 2000. The goals, known as America 2000, moved national standards to the center of school reform discourse. To support America 2000, Congress created the National Council on Education Standards and Testing (NCEST) in 1991 to advise it on matters related to standards and testing. "Raising Standards for American Education," a report issued by NCEST in 1992, defined and affirmed the importance of content standards, performance standards, assessment, and opportunity to learn.

President Clinton, who attended Bush's education summit, began work on his own education program after he became president in 1993. His education program, which proposed voluntary goals for the states, was signed into law in 1994 as the Goals 2000: Educate America Act. Communities throughout the United States began using Goals 2000 to facilitate their own standards-based education improvements. In 1996, state governors joined with business leaders to issue a policy statement endorsing academic and performance standards. The policy statement, along with an appropriation bill that amended the Goals 2000: Educate America Act, was designed to strengthen the role of the states in the standards movement and to make standards more palatable to the conservatives who saw national standards as an expansion of the federal government's role in education. Language related to opportunity-to-learn and the National Education Standards and Improvement Council were eliminated from Goals 2000. Little, however, was done to assuage the concerns of educators who believe that standards can increase race and class stratification in U.S. society.

The meaning and possible consequences of national standards

National standards is a multifaceted idea. Three types of standards comprise national standards: content, performance, and opportunity to learn. Each type of standard provides different insights into the meaning and possible consequences of national standards. Some aspects of national standards focus on course content and teaching methods. Others focus on student performance; still others focus on factors that influence student achievement.

Content standards

Content standards provide a structure to guide curriculum and instruction by framing core academic content areas in terms of what and how teachers should teach and what students should know and be able to do. Emphasis is put on students' developing an understanding of the key concepts and issues in the content area and being able to reason and communicate in ways that are characteristic of the discipline. Content standards have been developed in a number of disciplines, including history, science, and mathematics.

The National History Standards (NHS) are an example of content standards. The NHS, frequently misrepresented in the media as a school text, was a series of guidelines for teaching U.S. and world history. The first version of the history standards was published in November 1994. Those standards were revised in the spring of 1996 and reduced from three volumes to one. Both versions were directed by Charlotte Crabtree and Gary B. Nash at the National Center for History in the Schools at the University of California, Los Angeles, and funded by the National Endowment for the Humanities and the U.S. Department of Education. The development of the history standards purported to be an objective approach for reforming schools. However, the response they received upon their publication, which included political intervention and the privileging of conservative ideological perspectives, suggested otherwise.

The response to the NHS was immediate, bitter, and widespread. The NHS were perceived by conservatives as not focusing on what was most worth knowing in history.[5] Conservatives believed the NHS devoted too much space to women and people of color. Critics of the standards—many of whom are not historians—counted the number of times historical figures they admired were included in the standards. They concluded that major historical figures had been omitted or slighted in the NHS.[6] Conservatives called for the repeal of the NHS and the development of what they termed "true reliable national standards."

Even though the NHS were strongly supported by the two leading history professional associations, the American Historical Association and the Organization of American Historians, the attacks continued and eventually culminated in an official repudiation of the standards by the U.S. Congress. Sen. Slade Gordon of Washington state led the attack on the history standards on the floor of the U.S. Senate. He argued that the standards were not balanced or objective because they emphasized what was negative in America's past and celebrated "politically correct" culture and causes.

The attack on the original version of the history standards and their forced revision raises the specter of political power coupled with intimidation, public attack, and humiliation as a means to create "official" history.[7] The original history standards were neither as radical nor as irresponsible as they were described by their critics. They did, however, provide a framework for teachers and students to uncover unlearned lessons from the past and to study U.S. history from the perspective of the vanquished as well as the victors. The attacks on the history standards helped to maintain the established history curriculum and to halt efforts to legitimize the histories, voices, and experiences of groups who traditionally have been excluded from school history.[8]

Democracy requires citizens who understand that the development of the United States has not been a straight path to freedom, liberty, and justice.[9] Many groups of Americans have been victimized in the past and are still being victimized today. If we are to build a just society, we must give students opportunities to learn from our mistakes as well as to celebrate our victories. An authentic history of the U.S. must not only include the stories of people who are at the center of U.S. society; also it must include the historic struggles of people on the margins. Students need to understand how these struggles are reflected in quests for equality today. The discourse on the national history standards was shaped by forces that muted the importance of diversity in U.S. society. In arguing against the history standards, conservatives failed to recognize that U.S. history is the story of all its peoples, not just the powerful few who want school history to tell only their stories.

Opportunity to learn standards

Opportunity-to-learn (OTL) is a concept that was introduced in the 1960s by researchers who were trying to validate cross-national comparisons of mathematics achievement. These researchers recognized that achievement is complex and influenced by many factors. They identified three different levels of curricula that influence achievement: the intended curriculum, the implemented curriculum, and the attained curriculum. The intended curriculum is articulated by officials at the national level. The implemented curriculum is enacted by teachers in their classrooms. Student achievement on standardized tests provides evidence of the attained curriculum. Disaggregating the curriculum into three components reveals the extent to which education is a highly contextualized system and highlights the relationship between educational experiences and student achievement.

Opportunity to learn (OTL) is used by advocates of disenfranchised students to acknowledge the political and economic link between schools and society and to identify and demonstrate how factors such as income and access to knowledge, influence academic achievement. OTL is also used to identify how variables such as quality of school facilities, availability of teaching materials, and teacher expertise influence achievement. Language related to opportunity to learn was included in both America 2000 and Goals 2000. However, it was deleted from the 1996 budget bill for Goals 2000 and from the 1996 National Education Summit policy statement. Conservatives were able to argue successfully that OTL standards would take attention away from achievement and put the focus on resources or input variables. They took the position that OTL issues should be addressed at the state level, not directed by the federal government. As a result, addressing OTL factors will likely have a low priority as states and local school districts respond to the national standards. The money saved by deleting OTL standards from the national standards agenda will be paid for by sacrificing the futures of disenfranchised students.

OTL factors highlight the inequalities that exist in the educational experiences of many low-income students and students of color. For example, students who are placed in general or vocational tracks have limited access to college preparatory courses.[10] Students of color and low-income students are disproportionately represented in general and vocational tracks. In 1985, 51.5 percent of white students and only 28.1 percent of black and Hispanic students were enrolled in academic math classes.[11] Students who are tracked into college-preparatory courses have greater access to more challenging and rewarding curricula than students in lower tracks. Students in college-preparation tracks are disproportionately from advantaged socioeconomic groups. Moreover, important gate-keeping courses such as calculus are not available in many schools with large numbers of low-income students and students of color.

OTL factors also call attention to the differences in the quality and credentials of teachers of students who teach in central city schools and those who teach in middle-class suburban schools. Students in the central city are more likely to be taught by teachers who have less experience and who are less qualified than suburban teachers. In 1983, more than 14 percent of the new teachers in central cities were uncertified in their primary fields of instruction. This was almost double the percentage of such teachers in suburban districts.[12]

Schools in central-city schools have fewer resources and less funding than suburban schools. In Savage Inequalities, Jonathan Kozol describes a school that offered a computer course but did not have computers for students.[13] Disparity in funding among districts is especially evident when school districts that are primarily populated by upper-middle-class students are compared to school districts in which most of the students are from low-income families. For example, in the 1990–91 school year New York City, which has a large percentage of low-income students and students of color, spent $7,300 per student, while Great Neck, a nearby suburban school district, spent $15,000 per student.[14]

Given the tremendous disparity in educational resources and opportunities of U.S. students, it is understandable why OTL factors are embraced by advocates of disenfranchised students. OTL standards are very meaningful for low-income students, students of color, students who do not speak English as their first language, and other disenfranchised students. Disparity in the educational resources affects the course offerings, facilities, books, computers, labs, the quality of teachers, and the quality of teaching in the schools they attend. School reform efforts that do not acknowledge these disparities will fail.

Performance standards

Performance standards provide concrete examples and explicit definitions of what students need to know and be able to do in order to demonstrate proficiency in the skills and knowledge specified by content standards. Most advocates of national standards believe that performance standards are a logical consequence of content standards and that content standards would be meaningless without performance standards. Therefore, as new curriculum frameworks are being developed, new assessments are also being developed. The New Standards Project developed and piloted performance tasks that are designed to provide information on what students know and can do. These tasks, sometimes referred to as authentic assessment, are also intended to improve teaching and curriculum. They include videotapes of performances, debates, exhibitions, teacher observations and inventories of student work, as well as other examples of student behavior in real-world situations. Although these new approaches to assessment will be more closely aligned to the curriculum than in the past, they do not provide a means for educators and policymakers to differentiate levels of achievement in terms of OTL factors.

Proponents of performance standards claim that differentiating levels of achievement in terms of OTL factors is not necessary. They argue that performance standards are the best hope for low-income students and students of color because performance standards promote "high standards for all students." Without resources, that slogan will be an empty promise. Low-income students and students of color will be left to suffer the consequences of low performance on their own. Consequences such as grade retention, placement in remedial programs, and denial of diplomas can have a devastating impact on students.

Moreover, these kinds of consequences are not only ineffective, they may serve as justifications for further exclusion.

Parents who are concerned about consequences that will likely be viewed as a confirmation of their students' low ability will have very few options available to them. They can talk to their children's teachers; have their children transferred to new schools; put their children in private or parochial schools; complain to the principal, superintendent, or school board; implement a tutorial program at home; or engage in some other form of action. All of these options assume that all students have informed, active, and academically capable parents. Students whose parents face language, financial, or other barriers to active school involvement will not likely benefit from performance standards.

The lack of recognition and response to the connection between assessment and performance, perhaps more than any other aspect of the standards movement, raises historic and troubling concerns related to fairness, justice, and educational equality. Even though we know that unequal resources can affect quality of teachers, availability of advanced courses, the safety of the school environment, and other factors that can contribute to what students know and can do, performance assessments do not account for these factors. Without information on the factors that contribute to high and low performance, students from low-income families as well as many students of color may fall victim to historic beliefs about their genetic inferiority that are accepted by many educators. The success of The Bell Curve attests to the continuing saliency of beliefs about inherited ability and academic achievement.[15]

Highly motivated students who have high potential should not be penalized for factors in the school or community environment that are beyond their control. To be effective, assessments must consider the adequacy of resources when identifying what a student knows and can do. In that way assessment will not simply be a way to identify what students know and can do. They will identify what students know and can do as a result of their educational experiences.

National standards will not substitute for needed resources and programs such as bilingual education. The number of students who do not speak English is increasing as the funding for bilingual programs is decreasing. In 1990, 14 percent of school-age youths lived in homes in which English was not their first language.[16] Parents whose children speak English poorly will be more interested in what the school is doing to teach their children English than their children's scores on tests that they had trouble reading.

The missing standard: multicultural literacy

In a society that continues to be deeply divided along race, gender, and social-class lines, students need to recognize and understand the historic and contemporary role of diversity in U.S. society. Multicultural literacy will provide a framework for teachers to develop course content that will challenge students to recognize the multifaceted and complex ways in which structural inequality continues to exist in U.S. society.[17] For example, even though many African-Americans have historically viewed education as a means to upward mobility, many inner-city African-American students know that an education will not necessarily result in a better life.[18] They see many people in their communities who have a very difficult time securing gainful employment even when they have a high school diploma. In 1992, more than half of African-American high school graduates, compared to almost three-fourths of high school dropouts were unemployed. While less than twenty percent of white high school graduates, compared to more than one third of high school dropouts were unemployed.[19] White males and females are more likely to hire a white female over either an African-American male or female.[20] These data suggest that blacks have fewer economic incentives to stay in school than whites.

Racial incidents and gender discrimination are increasing in U.S. society and in the nation's schools. Prejudice and discrimination not only indicate the level of injustice in our society, they are also barriers to learning.[21] Multicultural literacy helps schools to resolve intergroup tensions in the schools and society and students to develop the knowledge, skills, and commitment needed to participate in personal, social, and civic action to make our society more democratic and just.[22] Teachers need support and further education to work effectively with students to reduce sexism, racism, and class inequality.

Multicultural literacy would provide a vehicle for schools to recognize the importance of educating the hearts as well as the minds of students. It would also provide a basis for students to think deeply about citizenship in a pluralistic democratic society and encourage students to engage in citizen action to extend the principles of freedom, equality, and justice. Multicultural literacy is needed to develop creative and reflective citizens who are prepared to compete in a global workforce, but who also have the skills, knowledge, and confidence to question the status quo and to work for social justice.[23]

Conclusion

The standards movement is our latest magic bullet in a long line of school-reform strategies. Standards provide a false sense of security by suggesting that we have found a way to cure our educational ills. However, the cure may prove to be more deleterious than the problems. The active involvement of politicians, commentators, and political appointees in what should have been a professional and academic endeavor raises questions about who constructs school knowledge and for what purposes. The almost exclusive focus on the relationship between schooling and the world of work potentially marginalizes subjects such as art, music, and foreign languages and raises the question of what knowledge will be privileged in the school curriculum. Most important, even though diversity is increasing in U.S. society, content that can help students become effective citizens in a pluralistic democratic society has been jeopardized by the standards movement. Many of the responses to the history standards questioned whether the roles of women and people of color should be integral parts of U.S. history.

National standards obscure more than they reveal. They divert attention from the realities of schools in low-income, rural, and urban communities. Those realities include schools with leaky roofs, limited access to advanced curricula offerings, and teachers who are overworked and underpaid. In the next few decades, the nation's schools will enroll increasing numbers of low-income students, students of color, and students who do not speak English as their first language. These students will need more than content and performance standards to increase their academic achievement and social success in school. Many of the advocates of national standards seem prepared to abandon these students if they are not able to succeed against great odds. If educators ignore how opportunities to learn influence student performance, these students are likely to be blamed for their academic failure and doomed to second-class citizenship.

Notes

1 Michael W. Apple, "The Dangers of a National Curriculum," *In These Times* 17 (November 15, 1993): 26–27.

2 James A. Banks, *Educating Citizens in a Multicultural Society* (New York: Teachers College Press, 1997).

3 David C. Berliner, Bruce J. Biddle, and James Bell, *The Manufactured Crisis: Myths, Fraud, and the Attack on America's Public Schools* (Reading, Mass.: Addison Wesley, Longman, 1996).

4 Diane Ravitch and Chester E. Finn, Jr., *What Do Our 17-Year-Olds Know?* (New York: Harper & Row, 1987) and E.D. Hirsch, Jr., *Cultural Literacy: What Every American Needs to Know* (Boston: Houghton Mifflin, 1987).

5 Lynne V. Cheney, "The End of History," *Wall Street Journal*, 20 October 1994, 26, and David W. Sax, "The National History Standards: Time for Common Sense," *Social Education* 60 (January 1995): 44–48.

6 Robert Cohen, "Moving Beyond Name Games: The Conservative Attack on the U.S. History," *Social Education* 60 (January 1995): 49–54.

7 Gary B. Nash and Ross E. Dunn, "National History Standards: Controversy and Commentary," *Social Studies Review* 34 (Winter 1995): 4–12.

8 Joyce Appleby, "Controversy Over the National History Standards," *OAH Magazine of History* 9 (Spring 1995), 4.

9 Arthur M. Schlesinger, Jr., *The Cycles of American History* (Boston: Houghton Mifflin, 1986).

10 Gretchen Guiton and Jeannie Oakes, "Opportunity to Learn and Conceptions of Educational Equality," *Educational Evaluation and Policy Analysis* 17 (Fall 1995): 323–336.

11 National Center for Education Statistics, *The Condition of Education* (Washington, D.C.: U.S. Department of Education, 1985).

12 Linda Darling-Hammond, "Inequality and Access to Knowledge," in *Handbook of Research on Multicultural Education*, ed. James A. Banks and Cherry A. McGee Banks (New York: Macmillan, 1995).

13 Jonathan Kozol, *Savage Inequalities* (New York: Crown Publishing, 1991).

14 Ibid.

15 Richard Hernstein and Charles Murray, *The Bell Curve* (New York: Free Press, 1994).

16 Committee on Developing a Research Agenda on the Education of Limited-English-Proficient and Bilingual Students Board on Children, Youth, and Families, *Improving Schooling for Language-Minority Children* (New York: National Academy Press, 1997).

17 James A. Banks and Cherry A. McGee Banks, *Handbook of Research on Multicultural Education* (New York: Macmillan, 1995).

18 William Julius Wilson, *When Work Disappears: The World of the Urban Poor* (New York: Knopf, 1996).

19 Antoine M. Garibaldi, "African-American Students as Dropouts," in *Encyclopedia of African-American Culture and History*, ed. Jack Salzman, David Lionel Smith, and Cornel West (New York: Macmillan, 1996), 181–184.

20 Luethel Tate Green, "Gender Differences and African-American Education" in *Encyclopedia of African-American Culture and History*, ed. Jack Salzman, David Lionel Smith, and Cornel West (New York: Macmillan, 1996), 181–184.

21 Claude M. Steele and Joshua Aronson, "Stereotype Threat and the Intellectual Test Performance of African Americans," *Journal of Personality and Social Psychology* 69, No. 5: 797–811.

22 Cherry A. McGee Banks and James A. Banks, "Teaching for Multicultural Literacy," *Louisiana Social Studies Journal* 16 (Fall 1989): 5–9.

23 Ibid.

CHAPTER 5

REFLECTIONS ON THE SUBTRACTIVE UNDERPINNINGS OF EDUCATIONAL RESEARCH AND POLICY (2002)

Angela Valenzuela

The study of teacher education generally, including that conducted by Wilson, Floden, and Ferrini-Mundy (2002 [this issue]), begs for analyses from a minority perspective. Specifically, their analysis fails to incorporate in a substantive manner the problem of unequal power relations between a dominant Anglo research and policy establishment and the diverse and often disempowered communities about whom they frequently write. Taken together, advances in minority scholarship alongside the fact of changing demographics in a prevailing context of culturally chauvinist schooling suggest, as I propose here, a need for scholarship on teacher education that is increasingly centered on these developments and issues. My goal here is to suggest, therefore, the utility of key constructs like additive schooling and culturally relevant pedagogy to guide a refashioning of schools, teacher preparation programs, evaluation research of teacher quality, and ultimately, education policy itself.

Cloaked in the language of "objective" social science, Florio-Ruane (2002 [this issue]) aptly critiques the nomological approach as privileging the method and language of social policy while portraying teaching as causally related to student learning. A complex view of teaching and learning is not only desirable but necessary given the conditions created by a predominantly Anglo teaching force in increasingly poor and minority inner-city schools throughout our nation. This complex perspective needs to be grounded in an understanding of majority-minority relations, where issues of race, class, gender, culture, and language are viewed as central to the mission of teacher education. Although a lack of attention to diversity issues is probably in some measure due to its lack of centrality in most teacher preparation programs, researchers are no less responsible to the communities served by the schools that they study. Not to address majority-minority relations is to participate in the reproduction of social inequality.

The contributions of minority scholarship

Much scholarship on minority youth points to the central role of culturally relevant, politically aware teaching in urban, minority education (Delgado-Gaitan, 1991, 1996; Delpit, 1995; Foster, 1995; Henry, 1998; Ladson-Billings, 1994; Stanton-Salazar, 2001; Valenzuela, 1999; Vasquez, Pease-Alvarez, and Shannon, 1994). For this to occur, teacher education and teaching need to be evaluated in terms of their commitment to social justice. The research framework for evaluating teacher education programs and outcomes needs to be expanded beyond "objective" data like students' test scores (regressed on a multiplicity of teacher preparation variables) to include the extent to which schools promote success in terms valued by the communities that they serve.[1]

To move in this direction, every single practitioner needs to possess the intellectual capital that enables him or her to distinguish between teaching that is culturally relevant and politically aware and that which is culturally subtractive and politically unaware (Bartolomé, 1994; Valenzuela, 1999). The central paradigm war in teacher education evaluation research is therefore not between quantitative and interpretive methods but rather between their ideological underpinnings, regardless of method.

In *Subtractive Schooling: U.S.-Mexican Youth and the Politics of Caring* (Valenzuela, 1999), I make the case that schools and teaching are fraught with cultural and political content even if unbeknownst to the teachers themselves. Specifically, I argue that in Texas, a culturally neutral perspective on teaching is untenable because the existing educational framework inscribed in Texas education policy is "culturally subtractive." That is, if schools are in compliance with state law, their function is not to promote bilingualism, biliteracy, and biculturalism in an additive fashion but rather to subtract Mexican American children's culture, language, and community-based identities. In my analysis, I demonstrate that this substraction is consequential to students' academic achievement measured in terms of grades.[2]

When applying these findings to teacher education research, the central question that emerges is not whether "good" teacher preparation, based on a clinical definition of teaching, produces higher test scores and other measurable outcomes in children. Indeed, a "good teacher," according to this definition, will likely be just as culturally invasive, patronizing, and chauvinistic as any other. Rather, the central question is whether teacher education and schooling for Mexican-origin as well as other minority youth is culturally additive or subtractive.

The concept of culturally subtractive schooling is illustrated by an evaluation conducted several years ago of a Houston K-8 charter school where the children were predominantly of Mexican origin and the staff was predominantly Anglo. The principal and several other members of the staff were formerly Teach for America teachers who were now running a school that boasted a 100% passing rate on the Texas Assessment of Academic Skills (TAAS).[3] As they showcased their school to a group of community stakeholders that included me, I found their condescending commentary on the community they served quite appalling. When we asked questions about parent involvement, they responded that because the parents did not speak English, they were not yet involved. Indeed, there was only one parent represented on the day of the evaluation. To "remedy" the situation, the school offered English as a second language classes to parents on Saturdays so that they could learn English well enough to participate eventually in the school.

To explain their high TAAS scores, teachers and administrators at the school spoke as if their expectations of the children were extraordinary. When I spoke to the single parent in Spanish about the school's expectations, she said that they were normal. In Spanish, she told me that she had gone to school in Mexico City and that by the fourth grade, she knew the anatomy of the human body. She also spoke of children having higher mathematics skills and abilities than children in the United States seem to have at the same grade level. She herself had received a secondary-level education, making her an exceptional resource to her child. In Mexico, only 16.9% of all middle school age children attend middle school (Gutek, 1993). Therefore, for any parent or immigrant child to possess such an advanced level of human capital translates into a uniquely competent experience within a U.S. context (Valenzuela, 1999)—capital that a school can draw on to support children's education.

I inquired about the education levels of other parents of the children in the school, but no one knew. They focused instead on the children's prowess and attributed it to their labor-intensive form of caring. For instance, the teachers all had cell phones and students had carte blanche access to them at all times. They also worked beyond the call of duty, providing after-hours tutoring and personal support.

I was impressed with the staff in terms of their energy and commitment but was troubled, nevertheless, by their condescending, deficit-oriented ideology. Their school song, sung to us by a classroom of students, contained the following words: "Knowledge is power. Power is money. No shortcuts." These are not Mexican cultural values, though they may be for drug dealers or Enron executives. Nor was this ideological stance consistent: If the staff truly believed in their own rhetoric, they would have embraced biliteracy as a goal because of its remunerative potential. On hearing the song, I grew especially concerned about the language and assumptions of the curriculum on one hand and the parents' lack of access to it on the other.

When I later saw several of the children and their principal on national television standing behind George W. Bush during the Republican National Convention, the implicit capitalist and conservative agenda became exceedingly apparent. I felt concerned once again about the undue influence this school was exerting on the children. I have since pondered how alienated these children must be from their communities. Will they look down on their communities as places to shun? Will they acquire an out-of-the-barrio ethos that renders them indistinguishable from many Anglos whose middle-class definition of success leads them to disparage the collectivist values shared by many Mexican Americans? Will they become unrecognizable to their parents who in good faith entrusted the school with not only their children's intellectual development but also their moral and social development?

This experience was highly instructive. It taught me that a 100% passing rate on the TAAS does not necessarily a good school make. Personally, I would never have allowed either of my two children to attend this school and would have discouraged any other parent from doing so. It has forever reminded me to avoid the simplistic equation of efficiency with virtue. Although technically speaking, the children appeared to be learning the three Rs, their harsh persuasion into a materialistic, status-seeking value system was profound. Much of the scholarship in teacher education and teacher preparation vis-à-vis culturally diverse students concurs that sound educational practice includes teachers who manifest a strong, politically aware connectedness to students (Darder, 1991; Nieto, 1999; Noddings, 1992; Valenzuela, 1999). As this case suggests, however, there are instances when conservative politics and connectedness trouble this equation. As Lubeck (1995) suggests, unless practice is truly situated in a community's struggle to define language and policy in its own terms, the children's educational experience is shortchanged, and the community's well-being is compromised.

What will it take for schools to be culturally additive?

Besides leadership at school, district, and state levels, a change in teachers' instructional practices is necessary but not sufficient to make schools culturally additive. There must also be a change in education policy at state and local levels. For this change to occur, the language and content of education policy must be analyzed, critiqued, and refashioned through the lens of key constructs located within minority scholarship. Ladson-Billings (1994) calls for culturally relevant pedagogy. Delpit (1995) calls for teaching children about codes of power. Bartolomé (1994) calls for abandoning the extant project of cultural eradication. I similarly have called for an additive, power conscious, and politically aware education (Valenzuela, 1999). Nieto (1999) further reminds us that both teacher education research and teacher education are most culturally relevant when they incorporate a civil rights agenda of moving beyond psychological explanations of school failure and success to address the sociocultural and sociopolitical context of unequal power relations between Anglos and communities of color.

I turn now to "test" the extent to which Texas' model of accountability is culturally additive. Texas' accountability system—with high-stakes testing as its centerpiece for reform—was devised to address historically low academic expectations held toward minority populations. Key slogans such as "all children count" or "all children can learn" are capable of seducing the casual media consumer into thinking that the twin "problems" of changing demographics and minority achievement have been addressed. Yet when one reads through the pages of the state's framework on accountability (www.capitol.state.tx.us/statutes/ed), race, class, and culture do not inform the reform in any substantive way. Instead, race and ethnicity are control variables rather than analytical categories with historic, social, and cultural substance.

Specifically, the Accountability section calls for students' standardized test scores to be disaggregated by ethnicity and socioeconomic status. This precise information, broken down into school and district ratings, appears occasionally in newspapers across the state creating an illusion of accountability to all children, regardless of race or class. With respect to class or socioeconomic status, this section also fails to address class in a substantive manner. The concentration of poor and minority children in inferior schools (not all children of color) is not addressed even though according to the Texas Education Agency (1997), approximately 48% of Texas students are considered economically disadvantaged. Nor are differences in opportunities to learn the state curriculum because of these historic differences in human and material resources within and across districts mentioned as aspects of accountability. Although in another section, the law does address school finance proper, an absence of such language within the Accountability section suggests falsely that these are unrelated.

Next to students' TAAS scores in the newspapers, there are never any disclaimers to suggest that scores in given schools were attained despite a lack of access to books, lab equipment, or other resources. The public therefore gets an ostensibly objective rating system that erroneously suggests a level playing field. At the 10th grade exit level, where the TAAS test is offered in English only, neither the presence nor the concentration of English-language learners in particular schools and districts are highlighted, despite their predictable negative impact on the school as a whole.[4] Also not mentioned are the numbers of students exempted from testing due to their designation as either special education or limited English proficient students.[5]

Not surprisingly, because higher exemption rates correlate to higher scores, perverse incentives exist to game the system by exempting these children from testing to the greatest degree possible (McNeil & Valenzuela, 2001; Valenzuela, 2001). Recent analyses of Department of Education data conducted by Haney (2001) show that the Houston Independent School District ranks 89th of the 100 largest U.S. cities in the percentage of the students it graduates (46.7%). These dynamics render explicable a situation of rising test scores proclaimed by politicians along-side one of the highest dropout rates in the country. State policies themselves therefore mask the dysfunctionality of schools while lowering the public's sense of an urgent need for substantive reform.

In its present form, bilingual education is a subset of the accountability system. For example, in the press for ever-greater accountability, English-language learn-ers are now required by law to be tested annually in Grades 3 through 8 (on yet another exam) in English to assess their readiness to take the TAAS test in English. Once children test well in English, however, they no longer qualify for bilingual education. Bilingual educators and administrators throughout the state tell me that this new procedure will further erode their bilingual education programs. Hence, layered over a subtractive curriculum framework, the current system of testing exacerbates, through excessive testing in English, the prior subtractive policy framework.

To rectify this problem, accountability could be reconceptualized as a subset of bilingual education, and the latter would have to be reframed in additive terms because most programs, except for dual language and late exit models, are tran-sitional in nature. Conflict with either Anglo or African American children and their parents need not occur if the target language is made equally available to them through dual language programs. Because, at a minimum, a dual language curriculum offers instruction in the second language at least 50% of the time, biliteracy is ensured. In states like Texas where large concentrations of people speak Spanish and where human resources can be made to exist in abundance, additive schooling is a realizable goal.

Conclusion

The objective measures that exist to date fail to capture those aspects of effective teaching among minority youth that extend beyond the embedded ideology of technical expertise that is apparent in the Wilson et al. analysis. A more robust perspective considers Nieto's (1999) injunction from her research in the area of teacher preparation: "The way students are thought about and treated by society and consequently by the schools they attend and the educators who teach them is fundamental in creating academic success or failure" (p. 167).

Inferring teacher quality from students' test scores in any subject and other objective measures is a potentially dangerous enterprise. With respect to test scores, the reader knows not whether the teacher, at the behest of the principal or the state, did little more than prepare the children for the test. Nor is the reader privy to institutional decision making that may result in exempting some students from testing whose anticipated scores are potentially hazardous to school ratings. Moreover, as the charter school example above suggests, more culturally, if not politically, relevant measures of school and teacher quality are necessary.

To the degree that the Wilson et al. study involves an a priori judgment about methods utilized to study the quality of teacher preparation research, the research process may be characterized as having been taken out of its cultural, social, and historical context. To the degree that these individual studies are in turn similarly decontextualized, the problem of representation is compounded. This differs little from the use of students' test scores to judge school, teacher, and district quality.

Indeed, if we are to command any moral and intellectual authority on the misuses of tests and other forms of data on students, we must similarly avoid reductionist measures of teacher quality and student achievement.

I am not suggesting that numerical data should not play a role in evaluation research in teacher education. I am cautioning instead against an overreliance on these measures and thus their reification as the driving force behind a quality education. As scholars, it is our responsibility to ground our assessments in the social and political realities of the communities that schools serve. Dual language programs, for example, have been shown to promote both equity and achievement for all groups (e.g., Lindholm & Zierlein, 1991). I myself am observing this in the study of a dual language school in Houston as part of an evaluation study for the Annenberg Foundation. The "at promise" Mexican immigrant and Mexican American children in the segregated school (Grades 3 through 5) compete solidly with other children in the Houston Independent School District on literally all available measures of achievement. Leadership, resources, and a clear, culturally relevant vision have turned the school around.

To counter these reductionist tendencies, studies need to be meta-analyzed in terms of how social circumstances dictate the types of data that are gathered, including the types of questions that get asked as well as how researchers view and analyze such data. One possibility for future meta-analyses of teacher preparation research is to cluster analyze the studies according to time periods, permitting comparative analyses during a particular period. For example, the national accountability agenda may encourage input-output conceptualizations as opposed to models that consider through-puts or mediating processes. Research may be thus considered a cultural icon that is itself subject to a changing—or little-changing, hegemonic—research program.

As a policy researcher, I fully understand and appreciate how our voices and credibility are based to some degree on the soundness of our research, writing, and argumentation, allowing us to be players in public policy circles. As an advocate of minority youth, however, I strive never to compromise their futures to a narrow, power-evasive political agenda. Our children and their teachers deserve no less.

Notes

1   Although I object to summarizing school and teacher quality in terms of students' test scores, I understand that at this point in our history they are difficult to circumvent.

2   Throughout the United States, the central mission of bilingual education is to transfer children into the all-English curriculum. This framework fails to build on the strengths of the children and compromises the very prospects for achievement sought by state officials and practitioners (Cummins, 1981, 1986).

3   The Texas Assessment of Academic Skills is offered in Grades 3 through 8 and in the 10th grade to all students in the state except for those exempted because of either a special education or a limited English proficiency designation. Although for the child, the test functions as a high-stakes examination at the 10th-grade exit level, a system of rewards and sanctions makes it a high-stakes instrument for teachers and administrators at every level at which it is offered (McNeil & Valenzuela, 2001).

4   Valenzuela (1999) and McNeil and Valenzuela (2001) made the case that test scores misrepresent limited English proficient (LEP), immigrant youth's true potential because of the language-dependent nature of the exit exam.

5   Technically, whereas all LEP students are English-language learners, not all English-language learners are LEP students. Students who have successfully transitioned out of the bilingual education programs, for example, are no longer classified as LEP. Also,

many LED students in the state do not receive either bilingual or English as a second language (ESL) instruction.

Acknowledgement

The author would like to thank Olga Vasquez for providing critical feedback on this article.

References

Bartolomé, L. (1994). Beyond the methods fetish: Toward a humanizing pedagogy. *Harvard Educational Review, 64*, 173–194.

Cummins, J. (1981). The role of primary language development in promoting educational success for language minority students. In *Schooling and language minority students* (pp. 3–49). Sacramento: California Department of Education.

Cummins, J. (1986). Empowering minority students: A framework for intervention. *Harvard Educational Review, 56*, 18–36.

Darder, A. (1991). *Culture and power in the classroom: A critical foundation for bicultural education.* New York: Bergin & Garvey.

Delgado-Gaitan, C. (1991). Involving parents in the schools: A process of empowerment. *American Journal of Education, 100*(1), 20–47.

Delgado-Gaitan, C. (1996). *Protean literacy: Extending discourse on empowerment.* London: Falmer.

Delpit, L. (1995). *Other people's children: Cultural conflict in the classroom.* New York: New Press.

Florio-Ruane, S. (2002). More light: An argument for complexity in studies of teaching and teacher education. *Journal of Teacher Education, 53*, 206–217.

Foster, M. (1995). Talkin that talk: The language of control, curriculum and critique. *Linguistics and Education, 7*, 120–150.

Gutek, G. L. (1993). *American education in a global society: Internationalizing teacher education.* White Plains, NY: Longman.

Haney, W.M. (2001, January). *Revisiting the myth of the Texas miracle in education: Lessons about dropout research and dropout prevention.* Paper presented at the Dropout Research: Accurate Counts and Positive Interventions Conference, Harvard Civil Rights Project, Cambridge, MA.

Henry, A. (1998). *African American teachers.* New York: State University of New York Press.

Ladson-Billings, G. (1994). *Dreamkeepers: Successful teachers of African American children.* San Francisco: Jossey-Bass.

Lindholm, K.J., & Zierlein, A. (1991). Bilingual proficiency as a bridge to academic achievement: Results from bilingual/immersion programs. *Journal of Education, 173*, 99–113.

Lubeck, S. (1995). *Children and families "at promise": Deconstructing the discourse of risk.* Albany: State University of New York Press.

McNeil, L., & Valenzuela, A. (2001). The harmful impact of the TAAS system of testing in Texas: Beneath the accountability rhetoric. In M. Kornhaber & G. Orfield (Eds.), *Raising standards or raising barriers? Inequality and high stakes testing in public education* (pp. 127–150). New York: Century Foundation.

Nieto, S. (1999). *The light in their eyes: Creating multicultural learning communities.* New York: Teachers College Press.

Noddings, N. (1992). *The challenge to care in schools: An alternative approach to education.* New York: Teachers College Press.

Stanton-Salazar, R. (2001). *Manufacturing hope and despair: The school and kin support networks of U.S.-Mexican youth.* New York: Teachers College Press.

Texas Education Agency. 1997. *Pocket edition: 1996–97 Texas public school statistics.* Austin: Texas Education Agency.

Valenzuela, A. (1999). *Subtractive schooling: U.S.-Mexican youth and the politics of caring.* New York: State University of New York Press.

Valenzuela, A. (2001). *High-stakes testing and Mexican American students.* Unpublished monograph.

Vasquez, O., Pease-Alvarez, L., & Shannon, S. (1994). *Pushing boundaries: Language and culture in a Mexicano community.* Boston: Cambridge University Press.

Wilson, S. M., Floden, R. E., & Ferrini-Mundy, J. (2002). Teacher preparation research: An insider's view from the outside. *Journal of Teacher Education, 53,* 191–205.

CHAPTER 6

THE RIGHT TO LEARN AND THE ADVANCEMENT OF TEACHING (1996)
Research, policy, and practice for democratic education
Linda Darling-Hammond

In the darkening days of the early McCarthy era, W. E. B. DuBois (1949/1970) wrote these words:

> Of all the civil rights for which the world has struggled and fought for 5,000 years, the right to learn is undoubtedly the most fundamental. . . . The freedom to learn . . . has been bought by bitter sacrifice. And whatever we may think of the curtailment of other civil rights, we should fight to the last ditch to keep open the right to learn, the right to have examined in our schools not only what we believe, but what we do not believe; not only what our leaders say, but what the leaders of other groups and nations, and the leaders of other centuries have said. We must insist upon this to give our children the fairness of a start which will equip them with such an array of facts and such an attitude toward truth that they can have a real chance to judge what the world is and what its greater minds have thought it might be. (pp. 230–231)

DuBois knew, as did Thomas Jefferson when he conceived our public education system, that America's capacity to survive as a democracy relies not only on the provision of free public education, although that is a crucial foundation; it rests on the kind of education that arms people with an intelligence capable of free and independent thought. In addition, it rests on an education that helps people to build common ground across diverse experiences and ideas. As Maxine Greene (1982) reminds us, if we are to create a public space for democracy, schools must consciously create community from the sharing of multiple perspectives and develop "the kinds of conditions in which people can be themselves" (Greene, 1984, p. 4). This is an education that seeks competence as well as community, that enables all people to find and act on who they are, what their passions, gifts, and talents may be, what they care about, and how they want to make a contribution to each other and the world.

These days, it is not fashionable to talk about education that is humane as well as rigorous, about the importance of caring for students and honoring each one's potential. These days the talk is tough: standards must be higher and more exacting, outcomes must be measurable and comparable, accountability must be hard-edged and punitive, and sanctions must be applied almost everywhere—to students and teachers, especially—although not to those whose decisions determine the possibilities for learning in schools. Yet, if we are to educate for democratic life, I believe we must be concerned about education that nurtures the spirit as well as the mind, so that each student finds and develops something of value on which to build a life while learning to value what others offer as well. It is the education each of us wants for our own children, but it is an education available to very few. Here, as always, John Dewey (1900/1968) offers a central touchstone to guide our work:

> What the best and wisest parent wants for his own child, that must the community want for all of its children. Any other ideal for our schools is narrow and unlovely; acted upon, it destroys our democracy. (p. 3)

The struggle for democratic education

Providing most Americans with such an education has always been a struggle, and it remains one today. From the time southern states made it a crime to teach an enslaved person to read through decades of separate and unequal schooling that continue to the present, the right to learn in ways that develop both competence and community has been a myth rather than a reality for many Americans. The struggle was articulated in the great debates between DuBois and Booker T. Washington about whether black children must be trained as laborers or might be educated in ways that could allow them to think for a living (DuBois, 1930/1970); it was also enacted in the ideological battles that shaped urban schools for the children of immigrants at the turn of the century (Tyack, 1974).

Factory model schools with highly developed tracking systems that stressed rote learning and unwavering compliance for the children of the poor were counterposed against small elite schools—and carefully insulated special tracks within comprehensive schools—that offered a stimulating curriculum, personalized attention, high-quality teaching, and a wealth of intellectual resources for an advantaged few. Some of these have been democratic schools that have worked to create an "equity pedagogy" (Banks, 1993), seeking to construct a thinking curriculum for diverse students who learn to live and work together. However, most "good" schools have secured their advantages by excluding—by economics, neighborhood, achievement scores, or racial codes—those who represent the other half (or more) of children.

That unhappy resolution remains in force today. International assessments reveal that America's schools are among the most unequal in the industrialized world in terms of spending, curriculum offerings, and teaching quality (McKnight et al., 1987; ETS, 1989b) and are only slightly less disparate today than when Arthur Wise wrote *Rich Schools, Poor Schools* a quarter century ago (Wise, 1972). Differential spending ratios of more than 10 to 1 show up most vividly in the quality of teaching children experience (ETS, 1989a, 1991). Recent research illustrates that money makes a difference in the quality of education, especially as it is used to pay for more expert teachers, whose levels of preparation and skill prove to be the single most important determinant of student achievement (Armour-Thomas, 1989; Ferguson, 1991). Students' right to learn is directly tied to their teachers' opportunities to learn what they need to know to teach well.

Surprisingly, in the United States of America, children who are required by law to attend school are not guaranteed the right to a knowledgeable teacher. Underprepared teachers constitute more than 25% of those hired each year (National Commission on Teaching and America's Future, in press; NDRC, 1993), and they are assigned disproportionately to schools and classrooms serving the most educationally vulnerable children (Darling-Hammond, 1990a, 1992a; Oakes, 1990).

Studies have consistently found that, with little knowledge of learning or child development to guide them, teachers who lack preparation are more reliant on rote methods of learning, more autocratic in the ways they manage their class-rooms, less skilled at managing complex forms of instruction aimed at deeper levels of understanding, less capable of identifying children's learning styles and needs, and less likely to see it as their job to do so, blaming students when their teaching is not successful. (For a review, see Darling-Hammond, 1992a.) Because of the capacities of their teachers, most classrooms serving poor and minority children continue to provide students with significantly less engaging and effective learning experiences (Darling-Hammond, 1995; Dreeben, 1987; Oakes, 1985).

The challenges we face

These are especially critical times for democratic education. The pace of economic, technological, and social change is breathtaking. Peter Drucker (1994) calls the rise and fall of the blue collar class between 1950 and the year 2000 the most rapid of any class in the history of the world. From half of all jobs at mid-century, blue collar employment will comprise only 10% of the U.S. total by the end of this decade. People trained for these routine forms of work are often unable to move into the more intellectually and interpersonally demanding jobs the new economy has to offer, which require more capacity to take initiative, to organize work with others, and to deal with novel problems.

With knowledge-work jobs now comprising nearly half of the total, those with low levels of education can rarely find jobs at all. High school dropouts, for example, now have less than one chance in three of finding work, and, if they can find any job, they earn less than half as much as high school dropouts did 15 years ago (W. T. Grant Foundation, Commission on Work, Family, and Citizenship, 1988). They increasingly become part of a growing underclass cut off from pro-ductive engagement in society. These changes are provoking fiscal limitations, growing tensions between races and classes, and fears about the future.

Meanwhile, the growth in the U.S. population and its potential for social renewal is largely among immigrants and people of color who have long struggled for voice and educational opportunity in this country. As we incorporate the largest wave of immigration ever in our history, our success in embracing and enhancing the talents of all of our new and previously unincluded members will determine much of our future. Repairing the torn social fabric that increasingly arrays one group against another will require creating an inclusive social dialogue in which individuals can converse from a public space that brings together diverse experiences and points of view. This suggests not only education *for* democracy, in the sense that we think of students needing to learn trades and good citizenship, but education *as* democracy (Glickman, 1995)—education that gives students access to social understanding developed by actually participating in a pluralistic community by talking and making decisions with one another and coming to understand multiple perspectives.

Most schools, however, are poor places in which to learn democracy: They often illustrate authoritarian and coercive forms of social control, as well as social stratification both across schools and among tracks within schools. Two thirds of minority students, for example, still attend predominantly minority schools (Orfield, Monfort, & Aaron, 1989), and of the remainder, another two thirds are isolated in lower tracks that provide a separate and unequal educational experi-ence that is qualitatively different in form, function, and content from that offered to "high track students" (Oakes, 1985, 1990). This experience too often fails to prepare them to participate fully as democratic citizens or to meet the requirements of contemporary economic life.

For all of these reasons, schools are under enormous pressure to change. All around the world, demands for higher levels of education for much larger numbers of citizens are being imposed upon educational institutions designed a century ago for different purposes. The enormous complexity of today's world and the even greater complications of tomorrow's signal a new mission for education, one that requires schools not merely to deliver instruction but to ensure that students learn—and to do so in more powerful ways than ever before. If schools are to meet this new challenge, they must dramatically increase the intellectual opportunities they offer while meeting the diverse needs of students who bring with them varying experiences, talents, and beliefs about what school means for them.

This is the first time in history that the success, perhaps even the survival, of nations and people has been so tightly tied to their ability to learn. Because of this, our future depends now, as never before, on our ability to teach. Two years ago, in her presidential address titled "The Advancement of Learning," Ann Brown (1994) described our progress over the last century in understanding human learning. In tandem with these advances, I will argue that the problem of the next century will be "the advancement of teaching," and its resolution will depend on our ability to develop knowledge for a very different kind of teaching than what has been the norm for most of this century. If we want all students to actually learn in the way that new standards suggest and today's complex society demands, we will need to develop teaching that goes far beyond dispensing information, giving a test, and giving a grade. We will need to understand how to teach in ways that respond to students diverse approaches to learning, that are structured to take advantage of students' unique starting points, and that carefully scaffold work aimed at more proficient performances. We will also need to understand what schools must do to organize themselves to support such teaching and learning.

Robert Glaser (1990) has argued that 21st-century schools must shift from a selective mode—"characterized by minimal variation in the conditions for learning" in which "a narrow range of instructional options and a limited number of ways to succeed are available"—to an adaptive mode in which "the educational environment can provide for a range of opportunities for success. Modes of teaching are adjusted to individuals—their backgrounds, talents, interests, and the nature of past performance" (pp. 16–17). Adaptive education focuses on developing the potential of each individual to a high extent, a critical mission for a pluralistic society with increasing needs for talent development. Such powerful teaching and learning require schools that value and evaluate serious intellectual performances, that support responsive teaching, and that allow teachers to build strong, long-term relationships with students and their parents. If we cannot build such schools at this moment in history, I believe that a deeply stratified society—one divided by access to knowledge and the opportunity to learn—could undo our chances for democratic life and government.

The contributions of research

I have some confidence that our efforts can contribute in important ways to this work. Throughout my own life, I have profited from the work of researchers and educators who sought to enact the ideals of democratic education. During the 1960s, in the days when school systems were expanding and reforming, my parents moved and sacrificed many times to ensure that my siblings and I secured the right to learn. They managed to find schools where we profited from programs stimulated by educational research and funded by a government eager to catch up with the Russians. I was the beneficiary of curriculum informed by Jerome Bruner, Joseph Schwab, and Jean Piaget as well as the efforts of folks like Kenneth Clark. I studied and loved the "new math," "hands-on science," and new approaches to foreign language instruction. I was enchanted by experiments with open education that gave students choices and opportunities to tackle rich, interesting projects. I had great teachers who were the products of Teacher Corps programs and National Science Foundation investments in teacher preparation. Under another federal program, I had a chance to serve as a teacher's aide, an opportunity that triggered my zeal for teaching and, as it turned out later, sealed my fate. I was enabled to attend an Ivy League college because of financial aid policies aimed at equal access, and I entered teaching myself on a National Defense Student Loan.

I knew enough to be grateful for these opportunities because I had seen something of the alternative in schools we passed through—a teacher who, on her good days, used erasers rather than the books she usually employed to hit children on the head; several who counted as teaching reading directly from the teacher's manual and assigning workbook pages by the hundreds; an occasional encounter with behaviorist curriculum innovations of the times (those that evolved from the studies of rats and pigeons Ann Brown (1994) described so vividly). I remember being dumbfounded by programmed instructional texts that were intended to teach English grammar in endless series of one-sentence skill bites with mini tests after each. And I could not imagine why someone would make students stop reading books to march their way through color-coded SRA reading kits. (I remember putting Dostoyevsky aside to demonstrate that I could make my way from green to purple cards featuring short, decontextualized passages followed by multiple-choice questions.) I also saw how my brother, who had a number of disabilities, had a much less supportive experience in these same highly tracked schools than I did.

But I had not seen the full extent of American inequality in education—or the backwardness of curriculum policy for the poor—until I began student teaching in Camden, New Jersey, many years later. In this grossly underfunded district that has been a subject of school finance lawsuits for more than 25 years, I found a crumbling warehouse high school managed by dehumanizing and sometimes cruel procedures, staffed by underprepared and often downright unqualified teachers, an empty book room, and a curriculum so rigid and narrow that teachers could barely stay awake to teach it.

Although all of my 12th-grade students had flunked English the year before and many had barely learned to read or write, the curriculum instructed me to spend several weeks teaching them to memorize the Dewey decimal system. When I instead engaged them in reading and writing about material they cared about, I was warned about the penalties for failing to "follow the curriculum." I began to understand what it was my parents were escaping as they moved in search of good schools. Not incidentally, I found some brilliant students in that classroom and many others who were thoughtful, serious, and willing to work hard. When given a chance to do so, virtually all of them learned to read and write. Having been regularly denied the right to learn did not render them incapable of learning.

However, I have since seen the same confluence of underfunding, underqualified teachers, and rigid, thoughtless curriculum mandates in my later teaching and research in many other cities. Today as then, the education offered the children of the poor is one equally uninformed by educational research and democratic principles.

An agenda for research, practice, and policy

The challenges of today's society pose difficult questions for us as researchers, teachers, and agents of democratic schooling. What would it actually mean to teach all children to the high standards politicians talk about and educators are trying to fashion? What are the real educational implications of the school reform mantra "all children can learn"? What kinds of teaching practices support learning that enables higher levels of performance and understanding for different kinds of learners? What kinds of knowledge and skills would teachers need to have to develop such practice? What kinds of school organizations would need to be developed to allow this kind of teaching to occur? How can this be done in ways that also build greater cross-cultural understanding and cooperative possibilities across individuals and groups? What would our policy system and our schools of education have to do to make this possible?

These are central research questions for the contemporary reinvention of democratic education. Their answers rest in part, I believe, on our growing ability to produce knowledge *for* and *with* educators and policymakers in ways that provide a foundation for a more complex form of teaching practice, one that attends simultaneously to students and their diverse needs on one hand and to the demands of more challenging subject matter standards on the other. This kind of practice must manage the devilishly difficult dialectic between a set of high common expectations for learning and a constructivist learning process through which students take different pathways to achieve these understandings. If well tended, this process should also enable students to go beyond these common expectations to develop their unique talents in ways that allow for "individually configured excellence" (Gardner, 1991).

Building this kind of democratic education is extremely knowledge intensive for all actors in the educational system. It cannot be accomplished by top-down mandates or teacher-proof curricula of the sort most policies have relied upon throughout this century. To build the kind of schools I have described, educators must know a great deal about learning and teaching, school organizations, and educational change. These schools will need to be supported by policies that are grounded in similar kinds of understandings. Thus, when I talk about increasing "our" understanding of teaching, I am not referring only to the community of researchers who work with and write for one another, but also to the community of educators and policymakers who are trying to improve teaching and learning. If research is to be meaningful to them, it must address their concerns and "mind-frames" (Shavelson, 1988), acknowledging the realities they face and creating knowledge from the inside out as well as the outside in (Lieberman, 1992).

We need to worry more intensely and more productively about how research connects to policy and practice, how productive change occurs, and what must happen to move schools from where they are to where research suggests they could be. We know a great deal more than we once did about the problems and dilemmas of change, and we know more about the ways that people develop and use knowledge in support of their actions as practitioners and policymakers. The days of assuming that research knowledge will be put into practice by disseminating findings through journal articles, report mailings, or even bulleted synopses of study findings are long gone.

We will need to continue to build forms of scholarly activity that span boundaries (Lieberman, 1992) so that practitioners' concerns and dilemmas can influence our work and, consequently, our work can influence work in schools. We need what David Cohen and Carol Barnes (1993) have called not only a new "policy for pedagogy"—that is, policies that support improved teaching— but also a "new pedagogy for policy"—that is, more productive ways of informing and shaping the policies that inform and shape schools. Creating a broader community of knowledge producers and users among teachers, teacher educators, administrators, policymakers, and researchers—a community that makes knowledge itself more democratic—is an important agenda that AERA has begun to assume by expanding its audiences and its participants.

While this is a tall order, we have a great deal of prior experience to learn from—experience that illuminates the possibilities for democratic education and the fundamental dilemmas of knowledge and change. Over the course of the last century, there have been recurring efforts to create schools that can offer an empowering education for all students. At the turn of the last century, in the 1930s, and in the 1960s, progressives banded together to invent schools that enabled all of their students to develop high levels of competence within democratically run communities. Many similar reforms were pursued in each of these eras: a "thinking" curriculum aimed at deep understanding; cooperative learning within communities of learners; interdisciplinary and multicultural curricula; projects, portfolios, and other "alternative assessments" that challenged students to integrate ideas and demonstrate their capabilities. Indeed, with the addition of a few computers, current scenarios for 21st-century schools are virtually identical to the 20th-century ideal offered by John Dewey in 1900.

Many of these schools were extraordinarily successful. Dewey, Ella Flagg, and many others created and studied hundreds of schools at the turn of the century that stood in glorious contrast to the factory-model alternatives that one study found were viewed by dropouts as more horrible than the sweatshops they worked in. In the 1930s, the famous Eight-Year Study, led by Ralph Tyler, documented painstakingly through a variety of creative measures how students from experimental progressive schools were more academically successful, practically resourceful, and socially responsible than matched samples of peers from traditional schools (Smith & Tyler, 1942; Chamberlin & Chamberlin, 1942). Research from some of the experiments of the 1960s found similar successes where reforms had permeated deeply but much unevenness because most schools and teachers called upon to enact new ideas did not understand them and did not know how to bring them to life. (For reviews, see Dunkin & Biddle, 1974; Glass et al., 1977; Horwitz, 1979; Peterson, 1979.)

To the astonishment and chagrin of educational researchers, the fact that research pronounced such efforts successful was not enough to ensure their continuation. In all of these periods, thousands of highly successful schools were created, yet they failed to replicate their successes and most vanished in the succeeding decades. Lawrence Cremin's (1961) analysis was that the successes of progressive education reforms never spread widely because such practice required "infinitely skilled teachers" who were never prepared in sufficient numbers to sustain these complex forms of teaching and schooling. The lack of investment in professional education that would allow teachers to acquire the knowledge they would need to undertake this kind of practice was one problem. Another was the lack of investment in policy development that could encourage the growth of such schools rather than maintaining them—as they exist today—as exceptions, on waiver, and at the margins.

Today a growing number of schools are once again reinventing teaching and learning, roles and responsibilities, and relationships with parents and communities so that they can help a greater range of students learn more powerfully and productively. They are focusing on more challenging and exciting kinds of learning and helping students to actively construct, use, and generate their own knowledge. They are creating communities of learners engaged in research and reciprocal teaching that empower students to seek their own answers and to pose their own questions. And they are finding new ways to reach diverse learners more effectively and developing personalized structures and more adaptive teaching strategies to support their success.

Research from the Center on Organizational Restructuring of Schools, the Center for Research on Teaching in School Contexts, the National Center for Restructuring Education, Schools, and Teaching, and elsewhere is beginning to produce findings like those of earlier eras: that more performance-oriented pedagogies and more communal school organizations support higher levels of student success (Newmann & Wehlage, 1995; Darling-Hammond, Ancess, & Falk, 1995; Lieberman, 1995; Cohen, McLaughlin, & Talbert, 1993).

However, as we enter the second decade of a school reform movement that will undoubtedly continue well into the next century, I am persuaded that, if these initiatives are to survive and spread, we need to give serious research attention to understanding the professional knowledge needed as well as the practical and political requirements of building a system full of such schools. As in earlier eras of reform, many schools and classrooms are beginning to display the inevitable dilution and misapplication of ideas that are poorly understood by those asked to enact them.

In particular, teachers and administrators often find it difficult to develop settings that are both learning-centered—that is, focused on challenging curriculum goals for all students—and learner-centered—that is, attentive to the needs and interests of individual learners. They often tend to lose one in the course of pursuing the other, trying to be more child-centered by letting go of teacher influence and core curriculum goals or trying to be more subject-centered by ignoring students while the curriculum marches on ahead. In the 1960s, educators' inability to manage these complex goals led to the perception and, often, the reality that schools had lost any sense of academic rigor in their eagerness to be relevant and attend to students' needs.

Successful democratic practice maintains both sets of concerns, allowing neither to overwhelm the other. It sets up a dialectic that requires enormously thoughtful and flexible teaching grounded in deep knowledge of both subjects and students. Teachers must maintain two intertwining strands of thought at all times: How am I doing at moving the students toward high levels of understanding and proficient performance, and how am I doing at taking into account what students know and care about in the process of moving them toward these curriculum goals *and* developing their individual talents? They must continuously evaluate what students are thinking and understanding and reshape their plans to take account of what they've discovered as they build curriculum to meet their goals. They need to do this in a school context where challenging curriculum goals are widely shared and support systems that allow attention to student needs are widely available.

Transmission teaching, on the other hand, offers a simpler way of moving through the curriculum. Teachers can go through texts and workbooks. Classroom routines are straightforward, and controls are easier to enforce. There is a sense of certainty and accomplishment when a lecture has been given, a list of facts has been covered, or a chapter has been finished, even if the result is relatively little effective learning for students. When a teacher is lecturing, it is easy to say, "I taught that," even if students did not learn it. Structuring active learning situations for students infuses more uncertainty in the learning process from the teacher's point of view. When a student is constructing his or her own understanding through a research project or experiment, a teacher does not know what he or she is learning without well-designed strategies for eliciting the student's thinking and probing for understanding. Many teachers' preparation has not taught them to evaluate how and what kids are learning or how to create situations in which learners can have real breakthroughs in understanding. Especially in settings that are not structured for or supportive of this kind of endeavor, it seems a very risky business indeed.

Even today, most curriculum reforms do not consider what teachers and schools need to learn to put them into effect (Cohen & Barnes, 1993). They fail to consider that teachers teach from what they understand and believe about learning, what they know how to do, and what their environments will allow. Investments in professional development for teachers are extremely small, and inside-the-school supports for collegial experimentation and learning are rare.

Research findings on the fate of the 1960s reforms are already being reiterated in studies of the implementation of California's new mathematics curriculum framework aimed at promoting deeper understanding. This kind of curriculum requires sophisticated knowledge of subject matter and pedagogy and well-developed abilities to make complex judgments about what students are learning that most teachers have not had the opportunity to develop. As a set of case studies conducted by researchers from Michigan State University found, teachers striving to use the new framework struggled to figure out how to teach in new ways (Cohen et al., 1990). One teacher commented to a researcher, "My biggest hurdle to doing all these new methods . . . is my knowledge of what I've done all these years." Another asked plaintively, "Still, how do you teach problem solving? I do not know" (Darling-Hammond, 1990b, p. 239).

It is possible that, as in the past, the inability of schools to enact a complex set of reforms will cause progressive practices to give way to a backlash of standardizing influences such as those that occurred in the efficiency movement of the 1920s, the teacher-proof curriculum reforms of the 1950s, and the "back to the basics" movement of the 1970s and 1980s. The capacity of teachers and other educators to deeply understand teaching and learning, to produce and use knowledge on behalf of their practice, I would argue, is central to the realization of a genuine right to learn. And our capacity as researchers to develop knowledge that empowers teachers in these ways is equally central to democratic education.

Building knowledge for teaching

How do we build knowledge for powerful teaching? I have come to believe that our chances for helping teachers develop a wide repertoire of teaching strategies that responds to the demands of subject matter as well as to the needs of students depend on putting more usefully framed and contextualized knowledge directly into the hands of teachers—contributing to their education as teachers and researchers rather than trying to derive broad-gauged generalizations to control their actions. This suggests some major shifts in how knowledge is disseminated as well as how it is produced.

Knowledge in support of adaptive teaching

Ellen Lageman once observed that the history of American education in the 20th century is best understood if one knows that E. L. Thorndike won and John Dewey lost. She was contrasting the focus of behavioral psychology on developing laws for teachers to follow with what John Dewey (1929) had in mind in *The Sources of a Science of Education*, where he described knowledge of methods, students, and subjects that would empower teachers to make more intelligent, flexible, and adaptive decisions—knowledge that would make teaching *less* routine rather than more so.

Thorndike's work—and that of other psychologists who have illuminated much about learning and teaching—cannot be faulted for the misguided scientism that gripped schools. But, as Lageman noted, Dewey's interest in empowering teachers with knowledge for thoughtful, adaptive teaching did not win out with policymakers. The confluence of behavioral learning theory and bureaucratic-organizational theory led to simultaneous efforts to deskill and control teaching by limiting both teachers' autonomy and their levels of education. Throughout this century, the thin and greatly uneven preparation of educators—and the systematic distribution of the least well-prepared teachers to the children of the poor—has meant that educators who are not themselves deeply knowledgeable about teaching and learning or about research have been unable either to use research well or to engage in the powerful kinds of thinking and problem-solving needed to transform schools.

For most of this century, policymakers sought knowledge that could become the basis for control of curriculum and teaching rather than for the support of sophisticated teaching decisions. Researchers typically produced knowledge for administrators and outside experts who used it to create the design specifications for teaching: texts, curriculum packages, and teaching formulas. This trickle-down theory of knowledge envisioned that teachers could get what they needed to know from these tools and by following the teachers' manuals and procedures that had been designed: five rules for a foolproof classroom management system or seven steps to a perfect lesson. When these proved inadequate to the real complexities of teaching, teachers were left to their own knowledge base, largely composed of how they themselves were taught.

Early research on teaching was more helpful to researchers than to teachers trying to understand their practice. Correlational studies that found modest associations between certain generic teaching behaviors and multiple-choice achievement test scores mostly reified already established prescriptions—fairly straightforward routines moving students through texts, workbooks, homework reviews, and the like. These studies were useful in establishing signposts that suggested what researchers should look at more closely. As David Berliner (1986) explained, later studies of teaching expertise were able to build on measures—such as the fact that homework reviews are important—to find out what expert teachers actually do to make them so.

However, lists of "teachers should" statements that derived from this research were not directly helpful to teachers in helping them build a sophisticated, learner-responsive kind of practice. Furthermore, simplistic applications of such research have proved to be positively dangerous as a guide for policy. "Research-based" teacher evaluation instruments and teacher education requirements in many states have enforced a set of uniform teaching behaviors (often trivial but easy to measure, such as "keeps a brisk pace of instruction," "manages routines," and "writes behavioral objectives") with no regard to subject matter, curriculum, or student learning (Darling-Hammond, 1992b). These policy tools, which continue to shape teacher education and evaluation in a large number of states, largely ignore the guts of teaching and learning. This has often had the bizarre effect of promoting teaching that is insensitive to learning while undermining good teaching.

A school board member in Arizona once proudly confided to me that the board had just adopted a new "research-based" teacher evaluation scheme that had led them to fire one of the district's most popular teachers—widely requested by parents and esteemed by colleagues—because he did not use the seven-step lesson plan required by the instrument. In another part of the country, Florida's 1986 Teacher of the Year (also a runner-up in NASA's Teacher in Space program) found that he could not pass review for a merit pay award according to Florida's Performance Measurement System (FPMS), another "research-based" checklist, because his principal could not find enough of the required teaching behaviors to check off during the laboratory lesson he observed. Furthermore, the form required that the teacher be marked down for answering a question with a question, a practice forbidden by FPMS, though popular with Socrates and some other popular teachers. Like that favored by many other such instruments, the approach to teaching is distinctly ill-suited to the development of students' critical thinking abilities and out of sync with most recent research on student cognition.

The implications of teaching for understanding

Since the time this early research on teaching was incorporated into many policies, we have learned that teaching routines that impart information and enforce highly structured drill and practice may produce good scores on multiple-choice standardized achievement tests, but they do not generally enable students to transform and apply what they know in new circumstances or to develop competence in complex performance tasks. So while many states are urging teachers to teach to new, high standards that seek greater understanding, the kind of teaching needed to do this is actively discouraged by many state and local policies governing curriculum and testing, teacher evaluation and supervision, and teacher education. These policies, in turn, restrict teachers' capacity to build and use knowledge about teaching as they discourage teachers from inquiring into their practice or from adapting their instruction to their students and subjects (Darling-Hammond, 1992b).

There is a great deal of work to do to develop measures of teaching effectiveness that evaluate learning for understanding rather than for the superficial mastery of algorithms or recall of information. The disputes during the 1960s and 1970s between the relative effectiveness of direct instruction and indirect instruction illustrate how important it is to be clear about the kind of learning that is being sought and evaluated. These two streams of research looked at very different kinds of teaching and evaluated them against very different measures of learning. As it turned out, the kinds of teaching behaviors that produce high scores on tests of recall and recognition were decidedly different from those that produced high scores on assessments of writing, problem solving, student independence in learning, and critical thinking (Darling-Hammond, Wise, & Pease, 1983; Glass et al., 1977; Horwitz, 1979; Peterson, 1979).

What's more, teaching for understanding cannot be packaged for teacher-proof implementation. This kind of teaching is more complex and uncertain that the rote forms it aims to replace. It requires deeper knowledge of subjects and more flexible forms of pedagogy, as well as tools that access student thinking so that teachers can understand it and build upon it. The kinds of knowledge useful for this task—knowledge about cognition and development, assessment and curriculum building, and the structures of the disciplines—have been available to only a relatively few teachers in a relatively small number of teacher education programs (Goodlad, 1990).

There has been such a large divide between research and practice in education that knowledge that exists in one part of the school of education has often been unable to jump the great wall that separates teacher education from the rest of the enterprise. This has been a function of the low status of teaching and teacher education, the divide in the professorate between those who do research and those who educate practitioners, and the belief that teachers do not need sophisticated knowledge for their work: they need only to be able to follow the texts, packaged curriculum, and simple recipes distilled for them by others. So while many researchers were producing systematic knowledge about teaching and learning, many teachers—and teacher educators—were wholly unaware of it.

Thankfully, this has begun to change as schools of education are beginning to pay more attention to the preparation of teachers, as research and teacher education are increasingly conducted in collaborative ways—sometimes by the same people—and as research on teacher learning and teacher education are becoming major lines of study in more universities and schools.

The implications of diversity among learners and contexts

Careful work over the past two decades on teacher thinking and decision making (Clark, 1983), comparisons of expert and novice teachers (Berliner, 1986), studies of the nature of pedagogical content knowledge (Shulman, 1986), and teachers' practical knowledge (Clandinin, 1986; Grimmett & Mackinnon, 1992) are beginning to build a rich case knowledge of teaching that examines teaching actions and decisions in different contexts and for diverse kinds of learners. As these studies cumulate, they are beginning to allow for generalization not by ignoring context but by building a body of case knowledge that can be read and interpreted across contexts.

In his most recent work, Lee Shulman and his students are investigating pedagogical reasoning through the development of teaching cases that derive from serious conceptual problems that arise in subject-matter teaching—the concept of geological time, for example, or the teaching of ratio and proportion. In analogous work at Teachers College, some colleagues and I have developed similar cases that derive from challenges that arise in teaching diverse learners (Darling-Hammond, Ancess, & Falk, 1995; Macdonald, 1995; Joseph, 1995). We are examining how expert teachers consciously build forms of practice that seek to draw upon students' experiences, interests, and approaches to learning as they also aim to teach for understanding and highly developed performances. We are studying such teachers in urban schools that include a wide range of language, cultural, economic, and family diversity and in classrooms that are heterogeneously grouped in terms of previous academic achievement.

Across these cases, we are finding that teachers who seem to succeed at developing real understanding of challenging subjects—and who seem able to do so for an array of students who include those traditionally thought to be at risk—have developed a practice with some common features:

- They develop engaging tasks that give students meaningful work to do, projects and performances that use the methods of a field of study and represent a whole piece of work within that field: doing historical research, writing and "publishing" a short book, developing a computer simulation or scale model.

- They design these to allow students choices and different entry points into the work. This helps motivate effort and allows students to build on their strengths and interests as they reach for new and more difficult performances.

- They develop what I call "two-way pedagogies" to find out what students are thinking, puzzling over, feeling, and struggling with. The tools of these pedagogies include student presentations, skillful discussions, journals and learning logs, debriefings, interviews, and conferences. Teachers consciously develop pedagogical knowledge about the specific learners in their classroom while relying on knowledge about learning generally.

- They constantly assess students to identify their strengths and learning approaches as well as their needs and to examine the effects of different instructional efforts. They understand assessment as a measure of their teaching as well as a measure of student learning. They publicly point to students' different strengths and accomplishments, creating a platform for legitimation and growth for each student in the classroom.

- They painstakingly scaffold a process of successive conversations, steps, and learning experiences that take students from their very different starting points to a proficient performance—including a great many opportunities for approximation and practice, debriefing and conversing, sharing work in progress, and continual revision.

- They pay attention to developing student confidence, motivation, and effort and to making students feel connected and capable in school. They teach from the heart as well as from the head. Strong relationships with students and with parents become especially important because the work is harder and riskier. Successful teachers' strategies for supporting learning extend beyond technical teaching techniques. They practice what John Dewey called "manner" as method: Their voiced and enacted commitment to student learning and success supports students in the risky quest for knowledge.

Our work is not unique. Many other researchers in Canada and the United States are looking closely at the contexts and textures of teaching. In combination, these kinds of inquiry are beginning to illustrate how teachers use knowledge about learners and learning, subject matter, curriculum, and teaching; how they construct pedagogical content knowledge and pedagogical learner knowledge in ways that ultimately meet at the intersection of subjects and students; and how they vary their practice in different contexts depending on their instructional goals, the demands of challenging content, and the needs of particular students and classes.

Building knowledge with teachers

Much of this research has been constructed *with* preservice and in-service teachers who are involved in developing cases of practice, who help to develop and interpret data in detailed studies of their classroom work, or who think aloud about their reasoning and decision making. This engagement of teachers in research is, in fact, a powerful way of learning about both teaching and research. It can improve the responsiveness of research to the realities of teaching while also developing the kind of thinking good teachers must engage in as they continually evaluate information about their students, their practice, and its effects.

In another set of studies, some colleagues and I are looking at teacher education programs that prepare teachers so distinctively that their practice is identifiable and highly developed from their very first years in teaching. In this work, we are finding that such programs carefully and explicitly prepare teachers to be observers and documenters of children and researchers of learning rather than consumers of dicta for practice. They are learning to use research by becoming researchers rather than by reading synopses of research results translated into "teacher should" statements. Teacher engagement in research helps create a clientele for profession-wide knowledge while it also builds teachers' personal knowledge of students and learning in ways that are often transformatory for teaching.

This training in inquiry also helps teachers learn how to look at the world from multiple perspectives, including those of students whose experiences are quite different from the teacher's, and to use this knowledge in developing pedagogies that can reach diverse learners. Learning to reach out to students—those who are difficult to know as well as those who are easy to know—requires boundary crossing, the ability to elicit knowledge of others and to understand it when it is offered. This takes social and intellectual work.

Embracing perspectives

Lisa Delpit (1995) reminds us that "we all interpret behaviors, information, and situations through our own cultural lenses; these lenses operate involuntarily, below the level of conscious awareness, making it seem that our own view is simply 'the way it is' " (p. 151). As both teachers and researchers concerned with democratic education, we must develop an ever keener awareness of the perspectives we bring and how these can be enlarged to avoid "communicentric bias" (Gordon, 1990), which limits our understanding of what we study and of those we teach.

This capacity for expanded perspective is also critical for building a democratic profession—one that creates alliances with students, parents and communities rather than achieving professional status by sequestering knowledge and insulating practitioners from those they serve. More inclusive kinds of knowledge-building are also central to the development of schools that are successful in preparing a wide range of students for success.

Crossing boundaries is essential to social learning. This is true for learning across disciplines and methodologies, for learning across communities and cultures, for learning across ideas and ideologies, and for learning across the many groups of individuals—parents and teachers, staff and students—who make up a school. Educative institutions actively strive to construct and manage diversity rather than trying to suppress it.

The basic idea of the common school was to create a public space within which diverse people could communicate and forge a joint experience that would allow them to build a broader community. The early university was designed to bring people together from around the world who could build knowledge by sharing different cultural experiences and areas of study. There is no doubt that this is uncomfortable and problematic: It is always easier to talk with those who think as we do, who have had common experiences, and who agree with us. That is one appeal of homogeneous neighborhoods, private schools, and tracking systems. However, it is essential to try to expand our associations and experiences beyond the boundaries that initially define them if we are to create new and larger common ground, which is the foundation for democratic life. Democratic schools seek out diversity in people, perspectives, and ideas and construct educative means to learn from those multifaceted experiences and expertise.

Building democratic schools

Modern schools were developed to limit diversity, to create as much homogeneity as possible in the ideas under study, the methods of instruction, and the students convened to study together. Like manufacturing industries, they were designed as highly specialized organizations—divided into grade levels and subject-matter departments, separate tracks and programs—to facilitate the use of routines and procedures.

The school structures created to implement this conception of teaching and learning are explicitly impersonal. Students move along a conveyer belt from one teacher to the next, grade to grade, and class period to class period to be stamped with a lesson before they pass on to the next. They have little opportunity to become well known over a sustained period of time by any adults who can consider them as whole people or as developing intellects. Secondary school teachers may see 150 students or more each day in schools that house 2,000 or more, precluded by this structure from coming to know any individual student well. Elementary teachers have only about seven or eight good months with their students, between start-ups and wind-downs, before they have to pass them off to another teacher who will start all over trying to get to know them. This is an important difference from many European and Asian schools, where teachers stay with their students for more than one year and teach them multiple subjects as well as serving as counselors (Darling-Hammond, in press). These strategies help them to know their students well enough to teach them effectively.

Teachers work in isolation from one another with little time to plan together or share their knowledge. Students, too, work alone and passively, listening to lectures and memorizing facts and algorithms at separate desks in independent seat work. Rarely do teachers have the opportunity to work with any group of students for longer than that daily 45-minute period or for more than a year of their school careers. Rarely do students have the chance to learn to work together.

Growing research evidence illustrates the success of alternative organizational arrangements—smaller, more communitarian structures fostering more cooperative modes of learning, less departmentalization and tracking, a more common curriculum for students, stronger relationships between teachers and students that extend over multiple years, greater use of team teaching, and participation of parents, teachers, and students in making decisions about schooling (Braddock & McPartland, 1993; Darling-Hammond, 1996; Fine, 1994; Lee, Bryk, & Smith, 1993; Wehlage et al., 1990). This participation appears to be most productive when schools create many opportunities for developing shared knowledge among teachers, administrators, parents, and community members and when they create joint work in which this knowledge can be used and deepened.

In our work at the National Center for Restructuring Education, Schools, and Teaching (NCREST), we have been studying how these features are sustained in city schools that produce dramatically unexpected outcomes for low-income and minority students and for others typically labelled at risk. Many of these schools are affiliated with the Coalition of Essential Schools. (Case studies of these schools are included in Darling-Hammond, Ancess, & Falk, 1995, and Darling-Hammond et al., 1993.) If these students attended the comprehensive high schools in their neighborhoods, over half would drop out, and very few would go on to college. Instead, in the high schools we are studying, over 90% of students graduate and go on to post-secondary education, and the vast majority of them succeed at college. Following an untracked common core curriculum, students are challenged to meet high standards embodied in graduation requirements requiring research papers, scientific experiments, mathematical models, essays and literary critiques, and oral defenses of their work—the kind of work these same students in most schools would be presumed unable to attempt, much less master.

Our research has tried to understand what enables them to meet these standards and what enables their teachers to help them do so—in other words, how their schools support powerful teaching and learning. We are trying to document and co-dissect practice (seeking to understand it from the outside in and the inside out) and to understand how people handle its many problems and dilemmas.

Rather than asking "what are the correlates of marginally greater success within the parameters of traditional schools?" we are asking "what entirely different parameters for schooling appear to enable far greater numbers of students of all kinds to succeed in ways that are not found within traditional schools?"

We have identified several factors that seem to be important:

(a) *Structures for caring* and *structures for serious learning*—that is, structures that enable teachers to know students well and to work with them intensely. In addition to the personalization made possible by smaller school size, all of these schools cluster students and teachers together in ways that allow teachers to work for longer periods of time over the day, week, and years with a smaller number of the same students. These structures range from interdisciplinary clusters to multi-year advisories, but they all allow teachers to know more about how their students think and learn, to undertake more ambitious chunks of curriculum work, and to have the time to develop difficult performances that require intense work and sustained effort. These structures are especially important for more challenging and indeterminate forms of learning that ask students to construct knowledge rather than having it fed to them. Our analysis suggests that to manage the risks of teaching for understanding, teachers need school structures that provide them with more extended time with individual students enabling deeper knowledge of students' learning, as well as stronger relationships that can leverage motivation and commitment.

(b) *Shared exhibitions of student work* that make it clear what the school values and how students are doing. Symbolically, the walls of these schools are literally plastered with student work. Student writing, designs, models, and artwork cover hallways, classrooms, and offices. Teachers work collectively to create assessments and set standards and to document and evaluate student learning within and across classrooms. This serves to decentralize information about student learning and about teaching in other classrooms. As teachers look at the work of their own students, they learn what is working as they had hoped and what is not. As they look at the work of other teachers' students, they have a window into the curriculum and teaching strategies used in other classrooms.

(c) *Structures that support teacher collaboration* focused on student learning. The higher levels of skill and expertise required by teachers to do this work must be continually developed. A very strong organizational feature of many of these schools is that faculty work in two kinds of teams: one that focuses on curriculum planning within subject areas and another that focuses on a shared group of students and their needs. In houses, teams, or divisions, groups of teachers assume common responsibility for a number of students, working with them across multiple subjects and counseling them over multiple years. These structures allow teachers to become more accountable for student success. They also motivate teachers by increasing their expectancies of success: As team structures increase teachers' reach over students' lives and their control over the total learning process, they reduce uncertainty and thus increase teacher willingness to invest even more effort (Darling-Hammond, 1996).

The schools have also constructed shared curriculum and assessment work that cuts across teams. This work includes collective assessments of student learning and analyses of student progress that require teachers to focus together on academic issues across the entire school. All of these strategies help to develop knowledge about students as well as about subjects and help to develop shared standards of practice as well as incentives for ongoing change. As one teacher explained

> With my colleagues, we've had to work together on curriculum and look at each other's work. We're forced to be more collaborative. So there's a loss of freedom to some extent, but I think it's compensated for by the lack of isolation and by the feedback you get. With feedback, there's growth. It's kind of hard at first, but it's good for you.

(d) *Structures for shared decision making*, and shared discourse about teaching and learning among teachers, often with students and parents as well. Teachers are engaged in hiring their colleagues, developing evaluation systems, conducting peer reviews, making curriculum decisions, setting standards for assessing student and teacher work, and deciding on professional development. Students and parents are frequently included in these activities. Each school has articulated its own set of educational ideals that is a touchstone for organizational decisions. This provides the coherence that enables decentralization to operate responsibly. Because the schools are deliberately small, governance engages every teacher and many parents and students; this enables the collective decision making that provides a sense of empowerment and access for more voices. These in turn create a greater sense of shared purpose, commitment, and effort and allow education to function as a democracy.

There are challenges in conducting this kind of inquiry: Researchers must have deep knowledge of teaching and schooling to be able to ferret out what's important among the many variables that can be examined. Emerging hypotheses must ultimately be tested in more formal ways to find out if and where they hold up. Co-constructing meaning with those whose work is being studied raises issues about how to attend honestly to unpleasant realities or contradictory evidence, while honoring the importance of multiple perspectives and the fragility of practice.

Perhaps the most important challenge is to try to understand how such practice is built, what obstacles and conundrums it encounters, what context-specific solutions and compromises are made, what features of school and classroom life, of teachers' and parents' learning opportunities, and of community circumstances provide the supports that allow it to be built and sustained. For at the end of any process of understanding successful practice, we cannot reduce our findings to a set of dicta to be imposed on other schools that must confront difficult obstacles and that may lack the conditions that are prerequisites for success. If we succumb to the urge to boil our findings down to formulas that are passed on through policy mandate, we will undoubtedly feed another generation of failure and cynicism characterized by practitioners' views that "Yes, we tried that and it doesn't work." It is as important to understand what can be done to create the conditions that enable good practice to grow and take root as it is to understand what the practices themselves are.

Building new partnerships between research, policy, and practice

It is clear that ordinary schools can succeed in extraordinary ways when they refocus their work on the needs of students rather than on the demands of bureaucracies. The work of restructuring is difficult but not impossible. However, much of this work is being done on waivers from existing policies; schools like those we study exist in constant tension with the central offices and state agencies that oversee a regulatory system invented for a different time and a different set of educational purposes. Creating widespread change will require an infrastructure for adaptive, learning-centered education: policies that develop more intelligent professional preparation; that support appropriate teaching, learning, and assessment practices; and that provide educators with continuous opportunities to learn and with the resources to enable them.

It seems to me that building knowledge and capacity in schools will require constructivist relationships between research, policy, and practice that allow reciprocal learning to occur. We cannot hand knowledge to policymakers to enact in new mandates. We must work with policymakers to develop strategies for professional development that will infuse greater knowledge in schools and with schools of education to strengthen their ability to transmit and develop knowledge for practice.

In our search for what works, we must also be prepared to deal with the dilemmas of change, to acknowledge that getting there is extremely hard work that requires massive learning from us all. "Schools should" statements will not get us from research to practice. As Milbrey McLaughlin observed, "you cannot mandate what matters most," and trying to do so, without building capacity for new practice, leads to certain failure.

For example, while substantial research suggests that tracking tends to harm low-tracked students without greatly benefiting high-tracked students (Oakes, 1985, 1990; Hoffer, 1992; Kulik & Kulik, 1982), there are profound problems of pedagogy, organization, and community politics to be solved by schools that would like to invent alternatives to tracking. We cannot take these lightly. Otherwise, we will, once again, have "tried reform" and found that "it doesn't work." Similarly, while a large body of research indicates that retaining students in grades actually slows down their learning and dramatically increases dropout rates (Holmes & Matthews, 1984; Shepard & Smith, 1986; Wehlage et al., 1990), we need to help schools think and work productively on the question of what are the alternatives. How can schools develop powerful pedagogies and school organizational forms that will allow productive attention to the needs of students who are not succeeding? The same issues arise with new teaching strategies and forms of assessment, and they are as troublesome at the state and district levels as at the school level. If we have learned anything about change, it is that all of the actors in the system need to develop firsthand deep understanding of new ideas and of the complex kinds of practice needed to carry them off.

Partnerships for what we might call dilemma-ridden research are being formed in many places across the country to address these concerns. These often feature hyphenated roles for researchers, teachers, and policymakers who are *doing* policy, school reform, and teaching as well as looking at it: I think of the rolled-up-sleeves work of folks like Tony Bryk, James Comer, Ted Sizer, Michael Fullan, Michelle Fine, Maggie Lampert and Debra Ball, Gloria Ladson-Billings, Lee Shulman, Ann Brown, Jeannie Oakes, Lauren Resnick, Ann Lieberman, and my colleagues at NCREST. These efforts are part of building a profession that is less balkanized and school organizations that are less "Taylorized." Many activists are moving beyond a world in which those who think and plan are separated from those who teach and do the work; they are working to understand schooling, teaching, and change by engaging in the work as well as by studying it and by creating collaboratives for democratic work and action.

For all of us who are doing the inside-out and outside-in work of research, teaching, teacher education, standards building, assessment development, and policy development, the struggles often seem endless and insurmountable, and the insights and epiphanies are always accompanied by difficulties and setbacks. I want to close with the words of another great democrat, Langston Hughes, who talked about the work of building democracy in a poem called "Freedom's Plow":

> When a man starts out with nothing,
> When a man starts out with his hands
> Empty, but clean,
> When a man starts out to build a world,
> He starts first with himself
> And the faith that is in his heart—
> The strength there,
> The will there to build.
>
> First in the heart is the dream.
> Then the mind starts seeking a way.
> His eyes look out on the world.
> On the great wooded world,
> On the rich soil of the world,
> On the rivers of the world.
>
> The eyes see there materials for building,
> See the difficulties, too, and the obstacles.
> The hand seeks tools to cut the wood,
> To till the soil, and harness the power of the waters.
> Then the hand seeks other hands to help,
> A community of hands to help—
> Thus the dream becomes not one man's dream alone,
> But a community dream.

Not my dream alone, but *our* dream.
Not my world alone,
But *your world and my world*,
Belonging to all the hands who build.

———————

America is a dream.
The poet says it was promises.
The people say it *is* promises—that will come true.
The people do not always say things out loud,
Nor write them down on paper.
The people often hold
Great thoughts in their deepest hearts
And sometimes only blunderingly express them,
Haltingly and stumbling say them,
And faultily put them into practice.
The people do not always understand each other.
But there is, somewhere there,
Always the *trying* to understand,
And the *trying* to say,
"You are a man. You are a woman. Together we are building our land."

America!
Land created in common,
Dream nourished in common,
Keep your hand on the plow! Hold on!
If the house is not yet finished,
Don't be discouraged, builder!
If the fight is not yet won,
Don't be weary, soldier!
The plan and the pattern is here,
Woven from the beginning
Into the warp and woof of America:

>   ALL MEN ARE CREATED EQUAL.

>   NO MAN IS GOOD ENOUGH
>   TO GOVERN ANOTHER MAN WITHOUT
>   THAT OTHER'S CONSENT.

>   BETTER DIE FREE, THAN LIVE SLAVES.

Who owns those words? America!

>   FREEDOM!
>   BROTHERHOOD!
>   DEMOCRACY!

A long time ago,
An enslaved people heading toward freedom
Made up a song:
    Keep Your Hand On The Plow! Hold On!
That plow plowed a new furrow
Across the field of history.
Into that furrow the freedom seed was dropped.

From that seed a tree grew, is growing, will ever grow.
That tree is for everybody,
For all America, for all the world.
May its branches spread and its shelter grow
Until all races and all peoples know its shade.

KEEP YOUR HAND ON THE PLOW!
HOLD ON!

References

Armour-Thomas, E., Clay, C., Domanico, R., Bruno, K., & Allen, B. (1989). *An outlier study of elementary and middle schools in New York City: Final report*. New York: New York City Board of Education.

Banks, J. (1993). Multicultural education: Historical development, dimensions, and practices. In L. Darling-Hammond (Ed.), *Review of research in education* (Vol. 19, pp. 3–49). Washington, DC: American Education Research Association.

Berliner, D. C. (1986). In pursuit of the expert pedagogue. *Educational Researcher, 15*(6), 5–13.

Braddock, J., & McPartland, J. (1993). Education of early adolescents. In L. Darling-Hammond (Ed.), *Review of research in education* (Vol. 19, pp. 135–170). Washington, DC: American Educational Research Association.

Brown, A. L. (1994). The advancement of learning. *Educational Researcher, 23*(8), 4–12.

Chamberlin, D., & Chamberlin, E. (1942). *Adventure in American education: Vol. 4. Did they succeed in college?* New York: Harper & Brothers.

Clandinin, J. (1986). *Classroom practice: Teacher images in action*. London: Falmer Press.

Clark, C. M. (1983). Research on teacher planning: An inventory of the knowledge base. In D. Smith (Ed.), *Essential knowledge for beginning educators*. Washington, DC: American Association for Colleges of Teacher Education.

Cohen, D. K., & Barnes, C. A. (1993). Conclusion: A new pedagogy for policy? In D. K. Cohen, M. W. McLaughlin, & J. E. Talbert (Eds.), *Teaching for understanding: Challenges for policy and practice* (pp. 240–276). San Francisco: Jossey-Bass.

Cohen, D. K., McLaughlin, M. W., & Talbert, J. E. (Eds.). (1993). *Teaching for understanding: Challenges for policy and practice*. San Francisco: Jossey-Bass.

Cohen, D. K., Ball, D. L., Peterson, P., Wiemers, N. J., Wilson, S. M., Darling-Hammond, L., & Sykes, G. (1990). *Educational Evaluation and Policy Analysis, 12*(3).

Cremin, L. (1961). *The transformation of the school: Progressivism in American education, 1876–1957*. New York: Vintage Books.

Darling-Hammond, L. (1990a). Teacher quality and equality. In J. Goodlad, & P. Keating (Eds.), *Access to knowledge: An agenda for our nation's schools* (pp. 237–258). New York: College Entrance Examination Board.

Darling-Hammond, L. (1990b). Instructional policy into practice: "The power of the bottom over the top." *Educational Evaluation and Policy Analysis, 12*(3), 233–242.

Darling-Hammond, L. (1992a). Teaching and knowledge: Policy issues posed by alternate certification for teachers. *Peabody Journal of Education, 67*(3), 123–154.

Darling-Hammond, L. (with Sclan, E.). (1992b). Policy for supervision. In C. Glickman (Ed.), *Supervision in transition* (pp. 7–29). Alexandria, VA: Association for Supervision and Curriculum Development.

Darling-Hammond, L. (1995). Inequality and access to knowledge. In J. Banks (Ed.), *Handbook of research on multicultural education*. New York: Macmillan.

Darling-Hammond, L. (1996). Beyond bureaucracy: Restructuring schools for "high performance." In J. O'Day & S. Fuhrman (Eds.), *Rewards and reform* (pp. 144–192). San Francisco: Jossey-Bass.

Darling-Hammond, L. (in press). *The right to learn: Beyond bureaucracy in American schools*. San Francisco: Jossey-Bass.

Darling-Hammond, L., Ancess, J., & Falk, B. (1995). *Authentic assessment in action: Studies of schools and students at work*. New York: Teachers College Press.

Darling-Hammond, L., Snyder, J., Ancess, J., Einbender, L., Goodwin, A. L., & Macdonald,

M. B. (1993). *Creating learner-centered accountability.* New York: National Center for Restructuring Education, Schools, and Teaching, Teachers College, Columbia University.

Darling-Hammond, L., Wise, A. E., & Pease, S. (1983). Teacher evaluation in the organizational context: A review of the literature. *Review of Educational Research, 53*(3), 285–328.

Delpit, L. (1995). *Other people's children: Cultural conflicts in the classrooms.* New York: The New Press.

Dewey, J. (1929). *The sources of a science of education.* New York: Horace Liveright.

Dewey, J. (1968). *The school and society.* Chicago: University of Chicago Press. (Original work published 1900)

Dreeben, R. (1987). Closing the divide: What teachers and administrators can do to help black students reach their reading potential. *American Educator, 11*(4), 28–35.

Drucker, P. F. (1994, November). The age of social transformation. *Atlantic Monthly,* 53–80.

DuBois, W. E. B. (1970). Education and work. In P. S. Foner (Ed.), *W. E. B. DuBois speaks* (pp. 55–76). New York: Pathfinder. (Original work published 1930)

DuBois, W. E. B. (1970). The freedom to learn. In P. S. Foner (Ed.), *W. E. B. DuBois speaks* (pp. 228–231). New York: Pathfinder. (Original work published 1949)

Dunkin, M., & Biddle, B. (1974). *The study of teaching.* New York: Holt, Rinehart, and Winston.

Educational Testing Service (ETS). (1989a). *Crossroads in American education.* Princeton, NJ: Author.

Educational Testing Service (ETS). (1989b). *A world of differences: An international assessment of mathematics and science.* Princeton, NJ: Author.

Educational Testing Service (ETS). (1991). *The state of inequality.* Princeton, NJ: Author.

Ferguson, R. F. (1991). Paying for public education: New evidence on how and why money matters. *Harvard Journal on Legislation, 28*(2), 465–498.

Fine, M. (1994). *Chartering urban school reform.* New York: National Center for Restructuring Education, Schools, and Teaching, Teachers College, Columbia University.

Gardner, H. (1991). *The unschooled mind.* New York: Basic Books.

Glaser, R. (1990). *Testing and assessment: O tempora! O mores!* Pittsburgh, PA: University of Pittsburgh, Learning Research and Development Center.

Glass, G. V., Coulter, D., Hartley, S., Hearold, S., Kahl, S., Kalk, J., & Sherretz, L. (1977). *Teacher "indirectness" and pupil achievement: An integration of findings.* Boulder, CO: Laboratory of Educational Research, University of Colorado.

Glickman, C. (1995). Super-vision for democratic education: Returning to our core. *Educational Horizons, 73*(2), 81–88.

Goodlad, J. (1990). *Teachers for our nation's schools.* San Francisco: Jossey-Bass.

Gordon, E. W., Miller, F., & Rollock, D. (1990). Coping with communicentric bias in knowledge production in the social sciences. *Educational Researcher, 19*(3), 14–19.

Greene, M. (1982). Public education and the public space. *Educational Researcher 11*(6), 4–9.

Greene, M. (1984). *Education, freedom, and possibility.* Inaugural lecture as William F. Russell Professor in the Foundations of Education, Teachers College, Columbia University, New York.

Grimmett, P., & Mackinnon, A. (1992). Craft knowledge and the education of teachers. In G. Grant (Ed.), *Review of research in education* (Vol. 18, pp. 385–456). Washington, DC: American Educational Research Association.

Hoffer, T. B. (1992). Middle school ability grouping and student achievement in science and mathematics. *Educational Evaluation and Policy Analysis, 14*(3), 205–227.

Holmes, C. T., & Matthews, K. M. (1984). The effects of nonpromotion on elementary and junior high school pupils: A meta-analysis. *Review of Educational Research, 54,* 225–236.

Horwitz, R. A. (1979). Effects of the "open" classroom. In H. J. Walberg (Ed.), *Educational environments and effects: Evaluation, policy and productivity.* Berkeley, CA: McCutchan.

Joseph, E. (1995). *An exemplary urban elementary school teacher: Her knowledge, thoughts, and actions.* Unpublished doctoral dissertation, Teachers College, Columbia University, New York.

Kulik, C. C., & Kulik, J. A. (1982). Effects of ability grouping on secondary school students: A meta-analysis of evaluation findings. *American Education Research Journal, 19,* 415–428.

Lee, V. E., Bryk, A. S., & Smith, J. B. (1993). The organization of effective secondary schools. In L. Darling-Hammond (Ed.), *Review of research in education* (Vol. 19, pp. 171–267). Washington, DC: American Educational Research Association.

Lieberman, A. (1992). The meaning of scholarly activity and the building of community. *Educational Researcher, 21*(6), 5–12.

Lieberman, A. (1995). *The work of restructuring schools: Building from the ground up.* New York: Teachers College Press.

Macdonald, M. (1995). *Teaching to learn: An expert teacher's quest for an equity pedagogy.* Unpublished doctoral dissertation, Teachers College, Columbia University, New York.

McKnight, C. C., Crosswhite, F. J., Dossey, J. A., Kifer, E., Swafford, J. O., Travers, K. J., & Cooney, T. J. (1987). *The underachieving curriculum: Assessing U.S. school mathematics from an international perspective.* Champaign, IL: Stipes Publishing Company.

National Commission on Teaching and America's Future. (in press). *What matters most: Teaching for America's future.* New York: Author.

National Data Resources Center (NDRC). (1993). [Schools and staffing survey, 1990–1991]. Unpublished tabulations of data.

Newmann, F., & Wehlage, G. (1995). *Successful school restructuring.* Madison, WI: Center on Organization and Restructuring of Schools.

Oakes, J. (1985). *Keeping track: How schools structure inequality.* New Haven, CT: Yale University Press.

Oakes, J. (1990). *Multiplying inequalities: The effects of race, social class, and tracking on opportunities to learn mathematics and science.* Santa Monica, CA: The RAND Corporation.

Orfield, G. F., Monfort, F., & Aaron, M. (1989). *Status of school desegregation: 1968–1986.* Alexandria, VA: National School Boards Association.

Peterson, P. (1979). Direct instruction reconsidered. In P. Peterson & H. Walberg (Eds.), *Research on teaching: Concepts, findings, and implications* (pp. 57–69). Berkeley, CA: McCutchan.

Shavelson, R. J. (1988). Contributions of educational research to policy and practice: Constructing, challenging, changing cognition. *Educational Researcher, 17*(7), 4–12.

Shepard, L., & Smith, M. L. (1986). Synthesis of research on school readiness and kindergarten retention. *Educational Leadership, 44*(3), 78–86.

Shulman, L. (1986). Those who understand: Knowledge growth in teaching. *Educational Researcher, 15*(2), 4–14.

Smith, E., & Tyler, R. (1942). *Adventure in American education: Vol. 3. Appraising and recording student progress.* New York: Harper & Brothers.

Tyack, D. (1974). *The one best system.* Cambridge, MA: Harvard University Press.

Wehlage, G., Rutter, R. A., Smith, G. A., Lesko, N., & Fernandez, R. R. (1990). *Reducing the risk: Schools as communities of support.* Philadelphia: Falmer Press.

William T. Grant Foundation, Commission on Work, Family, and Citizenship. (1988). *The forgotten half: Non-college youth in America.* Washington, DC: Author.

Wise, A. E. (1972). *Rich schools, poor schools: The promise of equal educational opportunity.* Chicago: University of Chicago Press.

PART 2

CONCEPTUALIZATIONS OF
MULTICULTURAL EDUCATION POLICY

CHAPTER 7

NO ONE MODEL AMERICAN (1973)

A statement on multicultural education

American Association of Colleges for Teacher Education,
Commission on Multicultural Education

Multicultural education is education which values cultural pluralism. Multi-cultural education rejects the view that schools should seek to melt away cultural differences or the view that schools should merely tolerate cultural pluralism. Instead, multicultural education affirms that schools should be oriented toward the cultural enrichment of all children and youth through programs rooted to the preservation and extension of cultural alternatives. Multicultural education recognizes cultural diversity as a fact of life in American society, and it affirms that this cultural diversity is a valuable resource that should be preserved and extended. It affirms that major education institutions should strive to preserve and enhance cultural pluralism.

To endorse cultural pluralism is to endorse the principle that there is no one model American. To endorse cultural pluralism is to understand and appreciate the differences that exist among the nation's citizens. It is to see these differences as a positive force in the continuing development of a society which professes a wholesome respect for the intrinsic worth of every individual. Cultural pluralism is more than a temporary accommodation to placate racial and ethnic minorities. It is a concept that aims toward a heightened sense of being and of wholeness of the entire society based on the unique strengths of each of its parts.

Cultural pluralism rejects both assimilation and separatism as ultimate goals. The positive elements of a culturally pluralistic society will be realized only if there is a healthy interaction among the diverse groups which comprise the nation's citizenry. Such interaction enables all to share in the richness of America's multi-cultural heritage. Such interaction provides a means for coping with intercultural tensions that are natural and cannot be avoided in a growing, dynamic society. To accept cultural pluralism is to recognize that no group lives in a vacaum—that each group exists as part of an interrelated whole.

If cultural pluralism is so basic a quality of our culture, it must become an integral part of the educational process at every level. Education for cultural pluralism includes four major thrusts: (1) the teaching of values which support cultural diversity and individual uniqueness; (2) the encouragement of the qualita-tive expansion of existing ethnic cultures and their incorporation into the mainstream of American socioeconomic and political life; (3) the support of explorations in alternative and emerging life styles; and (4) the encouragement of multiculturalism, multilingualism, and multidialectism. While schools must insure that all students are assisted in developing their skills to function effectively in society, such a commitment should not imply or permit the denigration of cultural differences.

Educational institutions play a major role in shaping the attitudes and beliefs of the nation's youth. These institutions bear the heavy task of preparing each generation to assume the rights and responsibilities of adult life. In helping the transition to a society that values cultural pluralism, educational institutions must provide leadership for the development of individual commitment to a social system where individual worth and dignity are fundamental tenets. This provision means that schools and colleges must assure that their total educational process and educational content reflect a commitment to cultural pluralism. In addition, special emphasis programs must be provided where all students are helped to understand that being different connotes neither superiority nor inferiority; programs where students of various social and ethnic backgrounds may learn freely from one another; programs that help different minority students understand who they are, where they are going, and how they can make their contribution to the society in which they live.

Colleges and universities engaged in the preparation of teachers have a central role in the positive development of our culturally pluralistic society. If cultural pluralism is to become an integral part of the educational process, teachers and personnel must be prepared in an environment where the commitment to multicultural education is evident. Evidence of this commitment includes such factors as a faculty and staff of multiethnic and multiracial character, a student body that is representative of the culturally diverse nature of the community being served, and a culturally pluralistic curriculum that accurately represents the diverse multicultural nature of American society.

Multicultural education programs for teachers are more than special courses or special learning experiences grafted onto the standard program. The commitment to cultural pluralism must permeate all areas of the educational experience provided for prospective teachers.

Multicultural education reaches beyond awareness and understanding of cultural differences. More important than the acceptance and support of these differences is the recognition of the right of these different cultures to exist. The goal of cultural pluralism can be achieved *only* if there is full recognition of cultural differences and an effective educational program that makes cultural equality real and meaningful. The attainment of this goal will bring a richness and quality of life that would be a long step toward realizing the democratic ideals so nobly proclaimed by the founding fathers of this nation.

CHAPTER 8

BILINGUAL/BICULTURAL EDUCATION (1983)
Its legacy and its future
Carlos J. Ovando

Like the intricate baobab tree of Africa, which is a natural haven for myriad fauna, bilingual/bicultural education has become an educational phenomenon that serves many different groups. Beyond this point, however, the simile takes a different turn. For, unlike the baobab tree, with its largely self-regulating web of life, bilingual/bicultural education has many wardens who monitor its status with a great deal of interest. At one extreme are parents who (understandably) want to know what is going on inside the bilingual or English-as-a-second-language (ESL) classroom in terms of curricular content, first- and second-language development, and cultural emphasis. At the other extreme are politicians and journalists who are eager to extract a great deal of mileage from a topic that has consistently, during the past 15 years, touched some of the most sensitive sociopolitical and pedagogical nerves in U.S. society.

Both participants and observers view bilingual/bicultural education in a variety of ways. Some embrace with zeal the revitalization of languages and cultures through the public schools. They see bilingual education as a natural consequence of the sociocultural realities of a pluralistic society. For them, dual language instruction is a logical vehicle for cognitive and language development for those students with limited proficiency in English—and for those students whose first language is English, as well. They believe that bilingual/bicultural education will be personally satisfying to all students and that it will help them to develop the interpersonal skills and attitudes that are essential to a healthy society. Students with limited proficiency in English, these advocates would argue, are entitled to a fair share of the goods and services of the society, and this includes equal access to high-quality educational opportunities through the use of the language spoken in each student's home.

Those individuals at the other extreme argue that the positive effects of bilingual education on academic achievement, dual language development, cultural affirmation, national integration, and psychological well-being have been exaggerated. Such critics often suggest that support for bilingual education springs from faith, not from empirical evidence. They fear that the institutionalization of bilingual education in the public schools will further fracture social cohesion by encouraging youngsters to depend on languages other than English and to adhere to cultural patterns that may be in conflict with the mainstream U.S. culture. Such results, these critics argue, will only hamper upward mobility for students with limited proficiency in English.

Somewhere between these two extremes are those individuals who concede, on ideological and pedagogical grounds, that students with limited proficiency in English are entitled to schooling in their primary language until such time as they can assume the demands of an all-English curriculum—but the sooner, the better. Where this view of bilingual education is dominant, students with limited proficiency in English are generally removed from the bilingual program—somewhat arbitrarily—after one or two years of instruction. Bilingual education is only a means of pushing and pulling the speaker of limited English as quickly as possible into the mainstream American culture (whatever that is).

Finally, some individuals believe in the importance of nurturing ancestral languages and cultures, but they also believe that such endeavors should take place somewhere other than in the public schools. Consider, for example, the Korean community of about 2,000 in Anchorage, Alaska. Sensitive to the fact that its children were forgetting their mother tongue, becoming alienated from their culture, and having trouble communicating with their parents (who speak limited English), the Korean community, with help from the Korean consulate, started a Saturday school to teach these youngsters the Korean culture and language. The Japanese community in Anchorage also operates such a school, as do many other ethnic groups throughout the U.S.

Although it is useful to isolate and examine the myriad voices competing for attention on the topic of bilingual/bicultural education, the debate is much less clear in reality. The formulation of a national policy on language would compel the articulation and examination of language-related issues. Such a policy could function as a sounding board for debates on the homogenization or the pluralization of U.S. society. To what extent, why, how, and by what means should we move in one direction or the other? A national policy on language would resolve the often conflicting language policies that the U.S. has randomly and almost unconsciously followed to date. The National Defense Education Act (NDEA) of 1957 and the Title VII bilingual education legislation of 1968 epitomize this conflict. The NDEA affirmed the significance of foreign languages as integral components of national security; the bilingual education legislation, by contrast, was designed to allow the rich linguistic experiences of the immigrant and indigenous minority communities in the U.S. to atrophy.

To establish the need for a national policy on language, we must look back at the pedagogical and the sociopolitical development of bilingual/bicultural education since the late 1960s. By isolating these two closely interrelated strands of development, we can see that both the pedagogy and the sociopolitics of bilingual education have suffered from a general lack of direction. The usual approach has been one of ad hoc experimentation. This is natural in the early stages of developing a new program, but it also demonstrates more clearly the need for a national policy on language.

Bilingual pedagogy

Pedagogically, bilingual education was based on the assumption that building instruction on what students with limited proficiency in English already knew would result in more learning than would total instruction in a second language. Those who held this view also assumed that cognitive skills acquired in one language can be transferred to other languages and cultures. The general objective of bilingual education was to open up two-way communication between the world of the limited-English-speaking student and the school in subject-area content, in first- and second-language development, and in cultural awareness. The long-term goal was to improve the academic achievement of students with limited proficiency in English.

The partial institutionalization of bilingual education in U.S. public schools was an admission that defects in the regular curriculum accounted, at least in part, for the poor academic showing of limited-English-speaking students. Through bilingual/bicultural education, educators, parents, and policy makers expected to improve the marginal academic achievement and the equally marginal sociocultural status of these students.

But those educators charged with carrying out this dual mission had no reliable research to guide them. In fact, not until federally sponsored bilingual education was 10 years old, in 1978, did the now-defunct Department of Health, Education, and Welfare direct a Title VII committee to monitor a research agenda in the following areas: 1) assessment of national needs for bilingual education, 2) improvement in the effectiveness of services for students, and 3) improvement in Title VII program management and operations.[1] The data from these research efforts were to be ready for the congressional hearings for reauthorization of Title VII in 1983.

Approaches to language delivery illustrate the experimental nature of bilingual education during the Seventies. Teachers who were bilingual themselves often used the concurrent method—switching back and forth between two languages during lessons—for delivery of content and development of students' language. The concurrent method was a commonly prescribed mode of delivery in early Title VII programs. More recently, this approach has come into disrepute, however. Teachers have found it time-consuming, tedious, and—more important—not conducive to the development of a second language. Rather than actively listening to the second language, students learn to wait passively until the teacher returns to their first language. Similarly, teachers tried and then often discarded many varieties of the alternate and preview/review models for delivering language.

As with modes of language delivery, approaches for developing literacy skills in the bilingual classroom have varied tremendously. Some programs have introduced reading skills exclusively through the first language, while English as a second language is developed separately. Other programs have chosen to immerse children in English exclusively. Still others have experimented with introducing reading and writing simultaneously in students' first and second languages.[2]

Two of the most debated issues in bilingual education have concerned *who* should participate and *for how long*. Educators have used a wide variety of instruments to assess the language skills of learners slated for entry into or exit from bilingual or English-as-a-second-language programs. Some educators have been interested in instruments that would identify only those students most in need of bilingual instruction—and that would deem these youngsters ready for exit from such programs as quickly as possible. Others have looked for instruments that would identify many students with diverse language needs and that would demand higher levels of achievement in the areas of language and literacy before returning these youngsters to regular instructional programs. It was not until 1978 that Title VII made provisions to assess all four language skills— listening, speaking, reading, and writing. Even then, a gap existed between this policy and the availability of instruments to carry out these tasks with sufficient validity and reliability.

The policy regarding which youngsters to include in bilingual/bicultural programs has also been subject to change. The major intent of early bilingual legislation, for example, was to address the needs of limited-English speakers, who were frequently children of poverty. But a 1978 amendment to Title VII encouraged the inclusion of other students, provided that they did not exceed 40% of the total classroom population. Thus it was possible to have in one classroom indigenous minority students whose parents wanted them to reclaim their ancestral languages, English-dominant majority students whose parents saw the benefits of acquiring a second language, highly bilingual children whose parents wanted them to develop in both languages, and students with limited proficiency in English. The instructional implications for each of these groups are quite different. For instance, indigenous minority students whose dominant—or only—language is English may have endured negative experiences associated with their linguistic or cultural identities. To focus in the classroom on a language or culture that a student has rejected may be a delicate endeavor. Furthermore, such children—even though their dominant language is English—may in fact speak a nonstandard version of English. Often, their needs are overshadowed by the glaring language deficits of limited-English-speaking students—and thus not given the attention they deserve.

Such instructional problems stem in part from the shortage of classroom-tested research findings to shape and buttress program designs. Bilingual teachers, many of them novices, have been given a complex charge. They must 1) provide literacy instruction in two languages for a variety of students; 2) understand and apply theories of language acquisition; 3) organize their classrooms for the triple goals of language development, cognitive growth, and intercultural awareness; 4) stay abreast of the latest research findings; and 5) keep up to date on the constantly changing federal, state, and school district regulations. Simultaneously, bilingual teachers must manage their classes, which are characterized by linguistic, cultural, and academic diversity.

What have we learned during the past 15 years that can help us realize more fully the promise of bilingual education? To begin with, linguists have made important progress in understanding first- and second-language acquisition. Their research suggests that the developmental process is similar and predictable for both children and adults. Thus the acquisition of a second language requires time and experiences that are tailored to a learner's developmental stage.

One stage is manifested in the informal language that we all use as we deal with our immediate environments. Because the context is clear, this level of language is characterized by incomplete responses, a limited vocabulary, and many non-verbal cues. An average non-English-speaking student learns to communicate at this level after about two years of instruction.

A second developmental level consists of the language used in school and in many facets of adult life. Here the context is less clear; instead, communication depends on a speaker's (or writer's) ability to manipulate the vocabulary and syntax with precision. Students with limited proficiency in English need at least five to seven years of instruction to master this formal language.[3]

The implications for timing the exit of students from bilingual programs into the regular curriculum are clear. In assessing the language proficiency of such students, we must be certain that they can handle this formal (i.e., context-reduced) language. However, assessments during the Seventies of children with limited proficiency in English often measured only context-embedded communication, not the formal language that students need for sustained academic growth.

During the past 15 years we have also learned that certain methods promote natural acquisition of language, while other methods promote only a mechanical ability to manipulate rules of grammar. Moreover, because learners follow a neurologically programmed sequence of stages in acquiring a second language, we now recognize that our expectations for second-language production should follow that sequence. Likewise, the language to which teachers expose learners during language lessons should reflect those stages. To be comprehensible, teachers should begin with concrete objects, firsthand experiences, and visual contexts. In other words, students with limited proficiency in English are likely to make more progress in one hour of carefully designed, *comprehensible* input than in many hours of simply sitting in a regular classroom listening to what, to them, is "noise." In addition, Stephen Krashen has found that students' attitudes toward the second language are as important as their talents for learning languages; the students' ages, their previous exposures to the second language, and their levels of acculturation are also factors that teachers must take into account.[4]

We have also learned that bilingualism and biculturalism are not detrimental to cognitive development, and that cognitive skills are transferable across cultures and languages. In fact, some evidence suggests that bilingualism may encourage the development of divergent thinking and creativity.[5] This new view of bilingualism challenges the view that researchers held from the Thirties through the Fifties: that bilingualism hindered cognitive and linguistic development because the brain could not deal with multiple linguistic tracks.

The evolution of bilingual education has caused us to recognize the fact that social context affects learning outcomes in bilingual setting. For example, programs that immerse youngsters in a second language are successful only when they do not stigmatize the students' primary languages and home cultures. Thus the attitudes of the host society toward groups that speak another language have an enormous impact on minority students' perceptions of themselves and of the school.

Much pedagogical experimentation and learning took place during the Seventies in the areas of language and cognitive development, but not all the findings were pleasant. The most publicized negative findings were those of the report by the American Institutes of Research (AIR),[6] which suggested that students enrolled in Title VII bilingual programs did not achieve at a higher level than counterparts who were not enrolled in such programs. However, Doris Gunderson points out that:

> Although there is insufficient research documenting the effects of bilingual education, there is no research to substantiate the claim that bilingual education and bilingualism are harmful. Moreover, the available research indicates that bilingual education is either beneficial or neutral in terms of scholastic achievement, giving the student the added advantage of exposure to two languages.[7]

A variety of longitudinal studies have also revealed positive academic gains for students who have been enrolled in bilingual programs for at least four years.[8]

To date, many students who would qualify for bilingual or English-as-a-second-language programs have not received such instruction—and, in general, such students are still not achieving on a par with students whose native language is English. There is still much work to be done. As bilingual educators become better acquainted with theories of language acquisition and the methods they imply, with the relationships that research is disclosing between cognition and language, and with the findings related to the optimal organization of classroom programs and resources, bilingual education will become increasingly effective. But better bilingual education also depends on a supportive sociopolitical environment.

The war of words regarding bilingual/bicultural education has centered on three disputed issues: 1) the use of public funds for special educational programs for students with limited proficiency in English, 2) the function of language as a bonding or polarizing force in society, and 3) the extent to which language—and not other socioeconomic and cultural factors—is responsible for academic failure. Historically, bilingual programs emerged in the U.S. wherever ethnic communities believed that it was in their interest to create such programs. But 1968 marked the beginning of an uneasy relationship between the federal government and such ethnic communities, brought about by the enactment of Title VII of the Elementary and Secondary Education Act. The primary purpose of Title VII was to improve the academic performance of economically deprived children who also had difficulty with English. Congress appropriated the initial funds to teach such students in their home languages, but these students were to transfer into the all-English curriculum as soon as they were able to handle such instruction. Congress did not intend the legislation either to promote minority languages or to pluralize society. Rather, the intention was to use the home languages and firsthand experiences of these students to assimilate them as rapidly as possible into the regular (i.e., English-dominant) school program. Congress supported Title VII on the premise that these low-income youngsters needed all the help they could get to overcome their linguistic, cultural, and environmental handicaps and thus to equalize their opportunities for success in U.S. society.

Title VII recognized the importance of building on what the students already knew. However, this legislation was not intended to maintain the rich linguistic resources that these children represented. Much of the debate about bilingual education during the Seventies focused on this issue. One side favored prolonged attempts by the schools to maintain children's home languages; the other side believed that the period of bilingual instruction should be as short as possible. As the debate on the length of programs grew more heated, participants focused less attention on the quality of bilingual instruction.

From the debate about language maintenance versus rapid transition to English, a second question arose that the public found more worrisome: would bilingual education cause students to develop divided linguistic and cultural loyalties? The federal guidelines for Title VII implied that the schools would encourage a common culture, since they would eventually return bilingual students to regular classes. At the community level, however, ethnic minorities were beginning to see that they could join the societal mainstream politically, educationally, and economically without forgetting their first languages and their cultural traditions.

Should linguistic minority groups have the right to participate fully in American life without being completely assimilated into the mainstream culture? This issue is still not resolved. Court decisions have consistently affirmed the civil rights of all residents without regard to race, language, or national origin.[9] However, many defenders of monolingualism and monoculturalism have argued that, with respect to bilingual education, the courts have limited the rights of local communities to run their schools as they see fit. Therefore, even though the intent of the courts has been to protect the civil rights of all students, many individuals have interpreted these decisions as invidious vehicles for social engineering.

Moreover, bilingual education is intertwined with such sensitive issues as governmental attitudes toward immigrants and indigenous minorities. The U.S. has received in the recent past large numbers of political refugees, economic refugees, and undocumented workers. But consistent policies regarding who can enter the U.S. and on what criteria are nonexistent. Nor do clear policies exist with regard to trade relations with the developing nations or political relations with oppressive regimes. It is hard to examine the pedagogical value of bilingual instruction without becoming entangled in such sensitive political issues as the rights and status of undocumented workers.

Given these tensions and the current trend toward less federal involvement in education, some observers feel that bilingual programs are doomed to extinction. However, the 1982 cutbacks in bilingual education were no more severe than those in other federal programs, and it looks as though Congress will reauthorize funding in 1983. Furthermore, extensive state legislation is now in place to continue the funding of bilingual education. It would be pedagogically unsound and sociopolitically imprudent to return to the sink-or-swim methods of the past. Bilingual education is a reality that even Nathan Glazer, one of its most ardent critics, admits is here to stay.[10]

This does not mean that bilingual education will have smooth sailing. As we reflect on the experiences of the past 15 years and consider the political, demographic, and economic realities of the future, we must recognize the need to define more clearly the mission of bilingual education. This mission is to meet— rationally and realistically—the linguistic and cognitive needs of students with limited proficiency in English. This mission assumes greater importance when we consider that the non-English-speaking population in the U.S. is expected to increase from 30 million in 1980 to about 39.5 million in the year 2000.[11] There will never be a more appropriate time for the U.S. to develop a clear language policy.

An official language policy toward ethnolinguistic minorities would create a better balance between the learning needs of students with limited proficiency in English and the national interest. Such a policy would stress the universal language needs of all learners; it would also consider both the importance of breaking down the social barriers between ethnic groups and the potential for cognitive development of intracultural and cross-cultural affirmation. Likewise, such a policy would recognize the role of language in the promotion of academic excellence, and it would encourage the development of multilingualism in the larger society. In this era of global interdependence, such multilingualism would help to advance U.S. trade and political interests. Although it is difficult to quantify, the humanistic rationale for encouraging individuals to maintain or acquire a second language is also important. Through language, human beings discover one another's worlds.

The public is still somewhat uncertain today about the content and the process of bilingual education, about its posture regarding goals for national unity, and about the balance that bilingual education strikes between benefits and costs. But despite these uncertainties, most Americans seem to agree that language development and cross-cultural studies advance national interests. The final report of the President's Commission on Foreign Language and International Studies, *Strength Through Wisdom: A Critique of U.S. Capability*,[12] confirms this positive attitude. Largely as a result of the commission's recommendations, a consortium of 10 organizations involved in language instruction—called the Joint National Committee for Languages—has begun to assess governmental support for a more coherent national policy on language.

Such a language policy must be responsive to the desires and needs of local communities. As it relates to the education of children with limited proficiency in

English, however, this policy could aim to accomplish three general goals: 1) the affirmation of children's right to maintain their home languages, 2) the collection and dissemination of research findings on the role of the home language in cognitive development, and 3) the collection and dissemination of research findings that compare the outcomes of carefully designed bilingual education programs with those of undifferentiated instruction in an all-English environment.

The U.S. should nurture the rich linguistic resources that ethnic minorities provide. A national language policy will increase the likelihood of a flexible support system for children whose home language is other than English. Such a policy will also foster the acquisition of second languages among English-speaking students and can be adjusted to meet the needs of local communities.

Notes

1   Betty J. Mace-Matluck, *Literacy Instruction in Bilingual Settings: A Synthesis of Current Research* (Los Alamitos, Calif.: National Center for Bilingual Research, 1982), pp. 19–20.
2   Eleanor W. Thonis, "Reading Instruction for Language Minority Students," in *Schooling and Language Minority Students: A Theoretical Framework* (Los Angeles: Evaluation, Dissemination, and Assessment Center, California State University, 1981), pp. 162–67.
3   Jim Cummins, "Four Misconceptions About Language Proficiency in Bilingual Education," *NABE Journal*, Spring 1981, pp. 31–44.
4   Stephen D. Krashen, "Bilingual Education and Second Language Acquisition Theory," in *Schooling and Language Minority Students . . .*, pp. 76–77.
5   Elizabeth Peal and Wallace E. Lambert, "The Relation of Bilingualism to Intelligence," *Psychological Monographs: General and Applied*, no. 76, 1962, pp. 1–23.
6   Malcolm Danoff, *Evaluation of the Impact of ESEA Title VII Spanish/English Bilingual Education Program* (Palo Alto, Calif.: American Institutes for Research, 1978), pp. 1–19.
7   Doris V. Gunderson, "Bilingual Education," in Harold E. Mitzel, ed., *Encyclopedia of Educational Research*, Vol. 1, 5th ed. (New York: Free Press, 1982), p. 210.
8   See, for example, Wallace E. Lambert and Richard Tucker, *Bilingual Education of Children: The St. Lambert Experiment* (Rowley, Mass.: Newbury House, 1972); William Mackey and Von Nieda Beebe, *Bilingual Schools for a Bicultural Community: Miami's Adaptation to the Cuban Refugees* (Rowley, Mass.: Newbury House, 1977); and Bernard Spolsky, "Bilingual Education in the United States," in James E. Alatis, ed., *Georgetown University Round Table on Languages and Linguistics: International Dimensions of Bilingual Education* (Washington, D.C.: Georgetown University Press, 1978).
9   See, for example, *Aspira of New York v. Board of Education of the City of New York*, 423 F. Supp. 647 (S.D.N.Y. 1967); *Lau v. Nichols*, 414 U.S. 563, 566 (1974); and *Castañeda v. Pickard*, 648 F. 2d 989 (5th Cir., 1981).
10 Nathan Glazer, "Pluralism and Ethnicity," in Martin Ridge, ed., *The New Bilingualism: An American Dilemma* (Los Angeles: University of Southern California Press, 1982), p. 58.
11 *The Prospects for Bilingual Education in the Nation: Fifth Annual Report of the National Advisory Council for Bilingual Education, 1980–81*, p. xii.
12 President's Commission on Foreign Language and International Studies, *Strength Through Wisdom: A Critique of U.S. Capability* (Washington, D.C.: U.S. Government Printing Office, 1979).

CHAPTER 9

MULTICULTURAL EDUCATION AND RACISM IN AMERICAN SCHOOLS (1984)

Charles Payne

The events, both legal and illegal, that have led to the miseducation of American groups, particularly minorities of visible distinction, have been many and span centuries. Some of these occurrences were carried out in conjunction with a doctrine that had as its basis a premise of racial superiority. Consequently, our schools of today, whether by design or due to a lack of awareness on the part of many educators, are a product of this doctrine of racial superiority.

The purpose of this paper is to review how racism, expressed through attitudes and court decisions, has come to demand the antidote of multicultural education, and to offer suggestions as to how multicultural education can be invaluable in overcoming the miseducation of Americans. (It is also recognized that there are many who work in today's schools who do not hold a racist attitude. However, unless all educators become aware and knowledgeable of how racism has influenced American education, we run the risk of perpetuating rather than eradicating the effects of racism.)

Racism in American education has had a devastating effect on generations of Americans. Its results cannot be removed simply by busing or by providing so-called "equal opportunity." To be sure, equal opportunity is desirable, but equal opportunity must not be used interchangeably with equal chance. The distinction is crucial. Equal opportunity can be granted through court decisions and thus is legal in nature, whereas equal chance is probabilistic and therefore depends on many nonlegal aspects such as prior training. In this instance prior training has to do with family background—with the experiences and success of parents, grandparents, etc., in school. Thus, while it is true that equality of educational opportunity for all Americans appears to be within reach, equal chance of successful experiences for a majority of members from certain American groups is far from being achieved. Perhaps multicultural education can become one of the equalizers by increasing the individual's and group's chance for success.

A historical review

While it is common to associate racial and/or ethnic discrimination with blacks in the United States, it must be pointed out that there are other groups which have experienced legislated segregated education. Native Americans, Mexican Americans and Puerto Ricans, and to a lesser extent Asian-Americans, particularly Chinese, were subjected to the same restrictions as blacks. It must also be mentioned that many white European groups suffered prejudice and discrimination within the schools. However, there were never specific laws related to educational opportunity that separated them from the dominant group.

An example of a court decision involving an Asian-American is *Gong Lum v. Rice.* Alexander (1980) notes: "In 1927 the Supreme Court held that states could segregate a Mongolian child from the Caucasian schools and compel her to attend a school for black children. Segregation of the Gong Lum type was formed in many states, both North and South" (p. 458).

Regarding the Mexican-American, "during the first third of the 20th century, a number of Texas counties failed to provide any public schools for them. In more cases, extralegally segregated schools were made available ... In many Texas communities the black schools were in better shape than those of the Mexican-Americans before the 1930s. Not until the 1960s, as a consequence of widespread protest movements among Mexican-Americans, did the schools begin to reexamine their practices with respect to this group" (Cross, Baker, & Stiles, 1977).

Moreover, the many tribes of Native Americans did not have one unified school system. The various Indian schools ranged in scope from those of the Cherokee nation to government controlled schools. The latter had as one of their tenets the destruction of the Indian culture: the only acceptable behaviors were those of white people. Again, not until the 1960s was this position reviewed. The following quotation illustrates the effects of such schooling on the Cherokee nation:

> One of the most remarkable examples of adaptation and accomplishment by any Indian tribe in the United States is that of the Cherokees. Their record provides evidence of the kind of results which ensue when Indians truly have the power of self-determination: A constitution which provided for court representation, jury trial, and a right to vote for all those over 18; a system of taxation which supported such services as education and road construction; an educational system which produced a Cherokee population 90 percent literate in its native language and used bilingual materials to such an extent that Oklahoma Cherokees had a higher literacy rate than the white population of either Texas or Arkansas; a system of higher education which was together with the Choctaw nation and had more than 200 schools and academies, and sent numerous graduates to Eastern colleges; the publication of a widely-read bilingual newspaper—that was in the 1800s before the federal government took control of the Cherokee's affairs.
>
> The record of Cherokees today is proof of the tragic results of 60 years of white control over their affairs: Ninety percent of the Cherokee families of Adair County, Oklahoma, are on welfare; 90 percent of the Choctaw Indian population in McCurtain County, Oklahoma, live below the poverty line; 40 percent of adult Cherokees are functionally illiterate; and the Cherokee dropout rate in public schools is as high as 75 percent. (Hilliard, 1976, pp. 66–67)

Yet, it is the blacks who are most often associated with school discrimination. This is probably due to three factors: 1) except for Native Americans, blacks are the oldest minority group in the country; 2) blacks are the largest minority group of visible distinction with some residents represented in every state; and 3) there is the lingering reminder of slave status, a dubious distinction.

For blacks the dehumanizing process began early in the 17th century. However, a review of the number of laws prohibiting the instruction of blacks gives the impression that it was not an easy task to keep blacks from learning. Hilliard has cited the following chronology of blacks in American education:

> From 1830 to 1832 many state laws were enacted forbidding instruction of slaves, limiting black preachers, forbidding the assembly of blacks except when supervised by whites, limiting slave hiring, forbidding drums, whistles, and musical instruments.
>
> In Louisiana the law provided imprisonment and hard labor for life or the death penalty for writing, printing, publishing, or distributing anything having a tendency to produce discontent among the free black population or insubordination among the slaves. It also provided the penalty of one month to one year imprisonment for teaching or permitting or causing to be taught any slaves to read or write. In Kentucky in the same year, blacks were not allowed to vote or to use schools although they paid taxes. In Mississippi the law forbade the employment of blacks in printing offices, and prohibited blacks from keeping a house of entertainment. (Hilliard, 1976, p. 67)

After the Civil War and Reconstruction, the court decision which greatly limited school participation for blacks for over a half-century was *Plessy v. Ferguson* (1896). In this case, the Supreme Court upheld a Louisiana law entitled "An Act to Promote the Comfort of Passengers" which provided that "all railway companies carrying passengers in their coaches in this State, shall provide equal but separate accommodations for the white and colored races ..." (Alexander, 1980, p. 457). After this decision separation of the races was quickly transferred to formal education and beyond. Moreover, it expanded to include not only black and white, but also yellow, brown, and red as well.

Two other important cases that helped to stigmatize the education of blacks with inferiority status were *Cumming v. Richmond County (Georgia) Board of Education* (1899) and *Berea College v. Kentucky* (1908). The Cumming case simply stated that school boards could use discretion in providing equal-but-separate facilities. Thus, in some cases schools for blacks were legally closed; in others, little or no building repairs took place; and there were lower teacher salaries and split school sessions. The result was an inferior education for blacks (Alexander, 1980, p. 457).

Berea College, a small private college founded in 1859 to provide nondiscriminatory education for needy students, both Negro and Caucasian, represented the last hope for blacks to receive integrated schooling. The Berea Case stated that blacks and whites may not be educated together even where it is a private school (Alexander, 1980, p. 458).

These three decisions dominated formal education with respect to minorities until *Brown v. Board of Education of Topeka* (1954). In the Brown decision the Supreme Court ruled that separate-but-equal facilities are inherently unequal. This decision included cases from the states of Kansas, South Carolina, Virginia, Delaware, and the District of Columbia. Each of the cases had originated in the lower courts, and they served to impact a large geographical area of the United States as well as to strike a severe blow at the numerous legal practices used to prevent school integration.

In terms of this history, I would like to share a brief first-hand summary of my experiences as a student and teacher in a separate-but-equal southern school district in Mississippi during the 1950s and 1960s. The "notable" elements that present themselves are:

1. An all black teaching staff, including the principal, but a white superintendent, whom we rarely saw but who still dictated our educational experiences.
2. No libraries, gymnasiums, swimming pools, etc., either at school or in the local community. However, they were available for the whites.
3. Not enough textbooks to go around for an entire class.
4. Our textbooks were hand-me-downs, after having been used for approximately five or six years by the white students. Book cards were pasted on the front and the back of the books. The white students used the front book card and black students the back. This book card always had *nigger* written in the space for "race." I recall that one black teacher attempted to avoid writing *nigger* and wrote a capital N for Negro. This avoidance was recognized by the superintendent and the teacher was reprimanded. All teachers had to write *nigger* in the books or be fired. Our books normally ran 10 to 15 years behind publication.
5. Class size was usually above the thirty-to-one ratio because of the ADA (average daily attendance). Even though teachers were required to keep attendance, the ADA was based on what the state auditors would find. They seemed to visit our school only during the height of the farming season in the autumn and spring, as well as on rainy days when all of the bridges and roads were washed out. A high percentage of the students were the children of sharecroppers and therefore the landlord's work came before attending school. On more than one occasion, the state auditor called the principal and said he or she would visit on a certain day. The teaching staff would write letters and make visitations to families, begging them to let their children come to school on that day. We usually would get good attendance, but no auditor, and the parents would then be angry with the teachers. During my first year of teaching, there were 82 students in my first period seventh and eighth grade mathematics class.
6. Even though busing was practiced for practical reasons as well as for racial balance (100 percent white and 100 percent black), blacks always were given the old worn-out buses. Hence, on school related trips, such as athletic events, the buses would break down and students either spent the night or long hours on the road. Buses commonly were without heaters and/or windows.

The above summary is presented only as a personal mini-capsule of separate-but-equal schooling and not as a comprehensive history. The reader should also keep in mind that the above description was of the 1950s and early 1960s in Mississippi. But the important point is that this took place only two decades ago, and many young blacks, as well as members of other minority groups, suffer today from the consequences of racial discrimination.

For at least a decade after the Brown decision there was no rush to carry out the ruling. However, there were isolated incidents. For example, there was the Little Rock, Arkansas, desegregation of Central High School. Also, Alabama and Mississippi admitted under the supervision of federal marshals one black undergraduate student each, and Georgia, two. In the case of Alabama and Mississippi, the governors stood in doorways to prevent black enrollment. One way state officials avoided providing certain courses and/or programs at black schools was to use what was known as out-of-state aid. For example, during my initial graduate school days, Mississippi would pay (reimburse) the expense for any black person attending graduate school outside the state. Of course blacks were not admitted to that state's graduate schools, and today many black professionals from the South are products of that system.

The next significant case was the *Griffin v. County School Board of Prince Edward County (Virginia)* (1964). This decision stated that the state closing of public schools and contributing to the support of private segregated schools is unconstitutional (Alexander, 1980, p. 470). Despite this, schools for blacks were actually closed in some states in the 1960s. While many states had massive school building programs for blacks at a cost of millions of dollars, these programs did not reflect the spirit of the Brown decision. Rather, they were belated attempts to carry out the separate-but-equal doctrine.

Between the years of the Brown decision and the Green decision the so-called "freedom of choice" principle existed. In many states freedom of choice did exist concomitantly with the burning of the homes and churches of blacks, and black beatings and murders. In *Green v. County School Board of New Kent County, Virginia* (1968), the Supreme Court ruled that states must institute affirmative action where "freedom of choice" fails to create a unitary system (Alexander, 1980, p. 475). Approximately 15 years after the Brown decision, lightning suddenly and forcefully struck. Indeed, in *Alexander v. Holmes* (1969) the Court declared that dual school systems were to be terminated at once and unitary systems were to begin immediately (Alexander, 1980, p. 478). With little warning school systems in southern states, in the middle of the school term, had to start massive school desegregation. In some instances many of the new buildings mentioned earlier were used, but in most cases those new buildings went to waste and trailers were purchased or additions were made to buildings previously used for only white students. Many of these new buildings stand empty today; not used since 1968.

More commonly, however, school districts in other sections of the country used housing patterns as a justification for segregated schools. As a result, the court decision *Keyes v. School District No. 1, Denver* (1973) stated that school board actions may have the effect of creating unconstitutional *dejure* segregation (Alexander, 1980, p. 480). Correspondingly, the final piece of the implementation strategy of nationwide school desegregation is found in *Swann v. Charlotte-Mecklenburg Board of Education* (1971). This decision states that busing to overcome racial segregation is a judicially acceptable alternative where dejure segregation has existed (Alexander, 1980, p. 489).

Why multicultural education and what is it?

The foregoing historical review of the influence and legacy of racism on American educational policy and practices should make the need for multicultural education apparent. Although the events of the past are important and must be overcome, multicultural education should not be allowed to focus primarily on past events: it must be a force which propels us into the future as well. In short, multicultural education should entail good teaching and good education. Why, then, the term multicultural education? Until recently, good teaching and good education have meant the type of lessons described by Woodson (1933) in *The Mis-Education of the Negro*.

The people who maintained schools for the education of certain Negroes before the Civil War were certainly sincere; and so were the missionary workers who went South to enlighten the freed men after the results of that conflict had given the Negroes a new status. These earnest workers, however, had more enthusiasm than knowledge. They did not understand the task before them. This undertaking, too, was more of an effort toward social uplift than actual education. Their aim was to transform the Negroes, not to develop them. (p. 17)

From the teaching of science the Negro was likewise eliminated. The beginnings of science in various parts of the Orient were mentioned, but the Africans' early advancement in this field was omitted. (p. 18)

In the study of language in schools pupils were made to scoff at the Negro dialect as some peculiar possession of the Negro which they should despise rather than direct to study the background of this language as a broken-down African tongue. (p. 19)

In the teaching of fine arts these instructors usually started with Greece by showing how that art was influenced from without, but they omitted the African influence which scientists now regard as significant and dominant in early Hellas. (pp. 19–20)

Negro law students were told that they belonged to the most criminal element in the country; and an effort was made to justify the procedure in the seats of injustice where law was interpreted as being one thing for the white man and a different thing for the Negro. (p. 20)

In medical schools Negroes were likewise convinced of their inferiority in being reminded of their role as germ carriers. The prevalance of syphilis and tuberculosis among Negroes was especially emphasized without showing that these maladies are more deadly among the Negroes for the reason that they are Caucasian diseases; and since these plagues are new to Negroes, these sufferers have not had time to develop against them the immunity which time has permitted in the Caucasian. (pp. 20–21)

The status of the Negro, then, was justly fixed as that of an inferior. Teachers of Negroes in their first schools after Emancipation did not proclaim any such doctrine, but the content of their curricula justified these inferences. (p. 22)

The above observations make it clear that racism had permeated the entire school system through teacher preparation, textbooks, methodologies, and instructional examples. Therefore multicultural education will have to be equally broad in scope and inclusive in its application if it is to counteract racism.

When the concept of multicultural education is discussed, the focus of the discussion usually takes one of the following three emphases, either singularly or in combination. The first of these views is multicultural education as product, whereby emphasis is given to the study of ethnicity; namely the contributions of, and the unusualness or surface aspects (the pow wow, rain dance, "dozens," piñatas, etc.) of ethnic groups. Since this view reflects the teaching about different ethnic and cultural groups, it could best be labeled "ethnic studies."

The second view of multicultural education emphasizes the role of oppression and the atonement or compensation for past injustices. While this approach involves a study of historical data and an analysis of sociological relationships, its emphasis is primarily on certain targeted oppressed groups, and an amelioration of their condition. This view of multicultural education limits the study of selected cultural activities to these targeted groups and, thus, multicultural education is viewed as only a concern of minorities.

The third perception, and the least utilized, is that of multicultural education as a teaching process. Proper implementation of this approach includes the aspects of multicultural education as product and entitlement. However, it goes beyond these two aspects in that the primary attribute of this approach is that it requires the teacher, when planning instruction, to focus on the concept of culture as a separate entity from ethnicity. It also highlights the intrinsic aspects of culture, and the influence of culture on the everyday classroom instructional process. This approach to multicultural education as process recognizes the entitlement aspect through the fact that to obtain what one is entitled to begins, first, with a fair system, and second, with an equal chance to acquire social and academic skills. It incorporates the product view in that (a) certain historical facts and events must be taught and (b) an adequate understanding of present conditions as well as human behavior is aided by a knowledge of historical facts. The idea of multicultural education as process includes the understanding by educators of such essential educational variables as methodology, curriculum, subject examples, and instructional techniques; in other words, the total process of teaching. Again, another way of stating this view is that multicultural education is simply good teaching and good education. Last, the process approach to multicultural education has its emphasis on the activities involved in teaching all of the disciplines (mathematics, science, language, fine arts) to members of different ethnic and/or cultural groups, as opposed to basically teaching historical facts about various ethnic and cultural groups. Multicultural education should regard cultural behaviors and cultural differences as teaching and learning tools to be used in the classroom.

If the elimination of racist behavior is our goal, then we must view racism and racist behavior as developmental aspects of personality. The formation of personalities is, among other variables, a product of our experiences, which leads to the fact that racism is embedded in the personality. Therefore, we must use not only those topics that in the past have been used to cover this area but we must also look for those areas and topics where multicultural content is a natural part of the lesson. With that in mind the following section presents examples of instructional methods for multicultural education.

Multicultural education: selected instructional methods

The decision to use a particular teaching method is based upon one's assumptions regarding the role of the teacher, the role of the student, the nature of the content, the nature of the learning process, and the result intended. The unit (methods and materials) described in Table 10.1 is a reflection of a commitment to a view of multicultural education aimed at eradicating the vestiges of racism. That is, it is assumed that the primary goal or aim of multicultural education is to develop intellectually autonomous students who buttress a commitment to racial equality with skills, knowledge, attitudes, and values requisite to living in a democracy.

The unit, covering five ethnic groups, consists of an outline and material resources which can be easily adapted to the secondary classroom in dealing with the topics of oppression, prejudice, stereotypes, and racism.

Table 10.1 A multicultural education unit

I. Rationale

In most classes, oppression is dealt with only from the standpoint of how people are oppressed and not why people feel the need to be oppressors. It is important to understand the reasons people want to oppress others rather than solely studying the effects of oppression. If these reasons are not understood, they are most likely to continue to result in new forms of oppressions.

Students must understand that prejudice and stereotypic attitudes lead to oppressive interactions between people. They should be aware that they may be oppressors of other students and teachers as well as being oppressed by others in the classroom setting.

II. Statement of Specific Objectives

A. To introduce the meaning of culture, ethnic groups, prejudice, and oppression through the use of definition and examples.

B. To develop an awareness of oppression through small group studies pertaining to oppression of different ethnic groups.

C. To reinforce group participation through the technique of group studies.

D. To study and discuss why people feel the need to oppress others.

E. To study and discuss means by which people oppress others, i.e., slavery, holocaust, and internment.

F. Through viewing a film, to gain an awareness of the meaning of stereotype and its effect upon people.

G. To gain an awareness of the relationship between stereotypic beliefs and the willingness to oppress others.

H. To gain an awareness of the presence of oppression in the classroom through actual classroom experiments.

I. To experience and discuss the feeling of oppression.

III. Procedure

A. Day One

1. The experience of oppression
   a. Discussion of definition of terms
      (1) prejudice
      (2) culture
      (3) ethnic group
      (4) oppression
   b. Handout on the comparison between factual information and prejudice
   c. Discussion on feelings experienced during the classroom experiment on oppression

B. Day Two

1. Introduction to group activities
   a. divide students into groups
   b. independent group study work

C. Day Three

1. Continuation of Day Two

D. Day Four

1. Presentation of group studies
   a. discussion of questions and answers pertaining to group studies on oppression

       b. discussion of extraneous ideas or comments as a result of class participation

   2. Summation of group presentations

 E. Day Five

   1. Introduction to prejudice and stereotypes

       a. role playing exemplifying cultural differences

       b. discussion of role playing

   2. Presentation of film, "Bill Cosby on Prejudice"

   3. Discussion of film and summation of unit

IV. Materials

 A. A list of questions assigned for group studies:

   1. The Japanese Group (see Daniels, 1972; Yin, 1973)

       a. List some of the lessons the Japanese have taught us. (Include other lessons that could be learned, but have not.)

       b. Before the evacuation of the Japanese from the West Coast, there were many stereotypes concerning the Japanese. Write a paragraph, summarizing each of the following stereotypes:

          (1) the Chinese legacy

          (2) the "Yellow Peril"

          (3) Hollywood and the Oriental

       c. Describe General DeWitt's feelings and position concerning the evacuation of the Japanese

       d. Describe in detail the evacuation (include living conditions in the concentration camps, jobs, and income)

       e. In December of 1944, the army changed its control over the Japanese from "mass exclusion" to "individual exclusion." Describe individual exclusion and detention. (Include in your description explanations of expatriation and renunciation.)

   2. The Mexican American Group

       a. In the book, *Aztecas Del Norte* (DeForbes, 1973), the author speaks in the chapter, "Life in the U.S.: The experience of a Mexican—1929," as one of the immigrants. Read the chapter and include in your summary the following:

          (1) jobs, wages, and availability

          (2) education

          (3) the Mexican contribution to agricultural and industrial expansion

       b. In the book *Ando sangrando (I am Bleeding)* (Morales, 1972), Chapter Four states many stereotypes given to Mexican Americans by different groups. Read the chapter and list several stereotypes. Be sure to include some of the developmental history of the stereotypes.

       c. In the book, *Viva la raza* (Nava, 1973), the last chapter describes and conveys a feeling of triumph for the Mexican American. Read the chapter and describe the Mexican American's triumph and feelings.

       d. In the book, *Ando sangrando* (Morales, 1972), "The Problem of Passivity" is discussed in the first chapter. Read the chapter and write a description stating the thesis of the "passive" nature of the Mexican American. Also list other stereotypes. Be critical!

   3. The Black Group

       a. In the book, *The nature of prejudice* (Allport, 1954), the author states several stereotypes given to blacks. List 10 stereotypes and also compare

(Continued overleaf)

Table 10.1 continued

the difference between children's stereotypes of blacks to that of adult stereotypes.

b. In the book, *Race, creed, color, or national origin* (Yin, 1973), read "The Treatment of Negro Families in American Scholarship." Write a summary of the article, including the following:
   (1) a critical description of the Moynihan Report
   (2) a brief outline on the different phases of studies done on Negro families

c. In the book, *Race, Creed, Color, or National Origin*, read the article, "Can a Black Man Get a Fair Trial?" Write a brief summary.

d. In the book, *White racism and black Americans* (Bromley & Longino, 1972), the authors attempt to define *white racism*. They divide the term into three subgroups, individual racism, institutional racism, and cultural racism. Read and briefly discuss each subgroup.

e. In the book, *The challenge of blackness* (Bennett, 1972), read the following chapter "Reading, 'Riting, and Racism," and write a brief summary. Include the following:
   (1) education and its relationship to racial oppressions
   (2) the injustices forced upon the blacks by the educational system
   (3) strategy of reform in education to aid the blacks

4. The Jewish Group
   a. In the book, *The Nature of Prejudice* (Allport, 1954), the author states several stereotypes and an example of contradictory stereotypes.
   b. There are four main phases in the history of the Jewish ghettos. Briefly describe each phase and its intended outcome.
   c. Describe the Jewish labor camps. Include in your description the following:
      (1) who was given the opportunity to work?
      (2) what type of work was provided?
      (3) how was the Jewish worker treated?
   d. In the book, *Anthology of holocaust literature* (Glatstein, Knox, & Margoshets, 1973), read "The Death Train" and write a summary of the true story.
   e. What did Hitler mean by "the Jewish problem" and what did he feel would be the outcome for the Jews if Germany was the victor of a second World War?

5. The Indian Group (see Wissler, 1966)
   a. Describe life on the Indian reservation. Include in your description the following:
      (1) the high death rate and its cause.
      (2) describe the power of the "agent" on the reservation.
      (3) explain how the Indians rebelled on the reservations.
   b. List some achievements made by the Indians.
   c. The white man gave the Indian three "gifts", the gun, the horse, and liquor. Describe the effects of each gift and what that gift meant to the Indian.
   d. Describe how you think the Indian must have felt. (There are many stereotypes placed on the Indians due to their actions.) Read and find the *real* reasons behind their actions.

e. Stories give the impression that the Indian lived a simple life, enjoyed ideal freedom, and was always happy, and therefore lived the most desirable life. Find some contradictions to this.

B. Conclusion

The following was included in all five group studies as the final question:

Why were and are the _____ oppressed?

(Payne & Davis, 1978)

Conclusion

I have attempted to explicate the major problems of racism and the objective of multicultural education. My primary assumption is that multicultural education can be a field of inquiry contributive to an amelioration of racism in the United States today. My strategy has been to briefly trace the basic steps in the legal process which have promoted equality of educational opportunity, and then to demonstrate how multicultural education can represent a vehicle for helping students gain an equal chance for success. It is hoped that the unit example will provide insights into the critical link between racism and multicultural education.

References

Alexander, K. (1980). *School law*. St. Paul: West Publishing.

Cross, D.E., Baker, G.C., & Stiles, L.J. (1977). *Teaching in a multicultural society*. New York: The Free Press.

Hilliard, A. (1976). Conference summary. In C. Payne & D. Redburn (Eds.), *Multicultural education clinic papers*. Muncie, IN: Ball State University.

Payne, C.R., & Davis, T. (1978). *A unit on oppression, prejudice, stereotypes and racism*. A lesson plan developed at the Laboratory School at Ball State University.

Woodson, C.G. (1933). *The mis-education of the Negro*. Washington, DC: The Associated Publishers.

Books listed in unit

Allport, G.W. (1954). *The nature of prejudice*. Reading, MA: Addison Wesley.

Bennett, L. (1972). *The challenge of blackness*. Chicago: Johnson Publications.

Bromley, D.G., & Longino, C.F., Jr. (1972). *White racism and black Americans*. Cambridge, MA: Schenkman.

Daniels, R. (1972). *Concentration camps U.S.A.: Japanese Americans and World War II*. New York: Holt, Rinehart & Winston.

DeForbes, J. (1973). *Aztecas Del Norte: The Chicanos of Aztlan*. Greenwich, CT: Fawcett Publications.

Glatstein, J., Knox, I., & Margoshets, S. (1973). *Anthology of holocaust literature*. New York: Atheneum.

Morales, A. (1972). *Ando sangrando*. LePuente, CA: Perspective Publications.

Nava, J. (1973). *Viva la raza: Readings on Mexican Americans. New York: Von Nostrand*.

Wissler, C. (1966). *Indians of the United States*. Garden City, NY: Doubleday.

Yin, R.K. (1973). *Race, creed, color, or national origin*. Itasca, IL: F.E. Peacock Publishers.

CHAPTER 10

ETHNOCENTRIC PEDAGOGY AND MINORITY STUDENT GROWTH (1984)

Implications for the common school

Robert A. Cervantes

Any discussion of the common school in a multicultural society provokes varying judgments about the inadequacy of our educational system to serve multicultural groups. Indeed, to appreciate the full significance of the topic requires attention to such interdependent issues as demographic trends, historical patterns, social stratification, school governance, institutional change, racism, program funding, and educational practices, theories, legislation, and litigation. I shall limit my contribution to (1) a conceptualization of the "common school" and its underlying ideology, (2) the status of minority student demographic trends, and (3) immediate and long-range policy implications.

The common school

I define the common school as the K-12 public school system. It is a highly institutionalized system, which performs two essential functions: It socializes students to the values of the dominant society, and it provides students with essential literacy skills to function in society. In fulfilling these functions the common school instills in our children and youth those social, economic, and political values that support our cherished institutions.

The common school reflects a Judeo-Christian model of education implying specific value orientations, role expectations, and task behaviors. The common school today is believed to reflect an idealized, monolithic value system dominated by the notions of democracy and equality. The purported mission of the common school is to develop in our youth humanism and individualism, scientific rationality in the tradition of John Locke, and social and technical skills necessary to function in an increasingly technologically complex society.

With respect to indigenous and immigrant minority groups in the American Southwest, the history of the common school has not been auspicious. While the common school may well have facilitated the acculturation of some northern and western European immigrants, non-Europeans such as Mexican Americans, Blacks, American Indians, and Southest Asian groups have not fared well. Ethnolinguistic minorities compared to their Anglo peers have received less than equitable education in the United States (Cervantes, 1981). The common school cannot legitimately claim to provide equitable quality education.

The inequality of educational opportunity and continued discriminatory school practices toward ethnic and language minorities have had the following effects.

- low educational achievement within these groups
- high absenteeism, dropouts, and ingrade retention
- overrepresentation in low ability groups and in special education
- de jure and de facto segregation
- cultural exclusion and distortion
- inequality in school financing

The pernicious effects of these practices have been extensively documented and reported (Carter and Segura, 1979; Brown, 1980; Sanchez, 1966; Romano-V, 1967).

What are the antecedent conditions in the common school that result in pernicious school practices for ethnolinguistic minorities? The answer lies partly in what I call the enthnocentric ideology of the common school.

The contemporary Judeo-Christian model of the common school stresses two principal philosophies: humanism and rationality. Through humanism one strives to understand one's self for the purpose of enlightenment, self-fulfillment, individual dignity, and freedom. Through rationality one arrives at scientific objectivity—hard data, facts, and classifications—which serve to explain various phenomena and assure the central importance of human beings. The educational and social manifestations of this duality depend on ethnocentric pedagogy.

By ethnocentric pedagogy I mean preconceived, idealized, and monolithic values, behaviors, and characteristics that students should exhibit to succeed in school. These are most frequently exemplified by Anglo-Saxon middle-class values and experiences. The closer one reflects the idealized, the higher the probability of school success. The common school has not recognized ethnolinguistic minorities—students of varying cultural and linguistic backgrounds—as a resource but, rather, has treated them as a deficit, something to be changed if they are to be educated. History provides ample evidence of this position: the exclusionary policies of the late 1800s, the segregationist doctrine of the early to mid-1900s, and the cultural deprivation dogma since the mid-1960s.

The ethnocentric pedagogy served as a rationale in the mid-1800s to exclude ethnic and racial minorities from public school. In 1856, for example, California State Superintendent Hubbs established an "English only" policy in public schools arguing that "Anglo-Saxons came from the Fatherland of our race . . . [a] race that has towered over all other races." This policy was followed in 1859 by the prohibition of the admission of "Negroes, Mongolians and Indians to Public Schools." ("Indians," incidentally, included Mexicans and Mexican Americans.) Galarza (1972) noted that the elimination of the original bilingual provisions of the California constitution in 1878 "marked the end of true biculturalism, as it did of bilingualism, in school, courts, newspapers, and public administration." By the 1890s strong anti-Catholic, anti-German, and anti-Oriental feelings fostered promotion of "America" as "White man's country." It was supported by the total exclusion of anything "foreign" in schools.

The period between 1910 and the advent of World War II was marked by social and economic upheaval—the Mexican Revolution of 1916, World War I, the "Boom or Bust" economy of the 1920s, the depression and so-called repatriation of Mexican nationals in the 1930s. In education there were three important developments. First, this period saw the beginning of attention to and growing consciousness of minorities. During this period there first appeared studies on underprivileged groups and "racial and cultural minorities." They were, however, simplist and assimilationist, with such titles as the "Americanization of Mexicans."

Second, charitable and religious organizations began to provide limited social and educational services to minorities, as exemplified by the settlement houses of that period. Third, segregationist doctrine in schools—separate and unequal—as the natural order of society was fully implemented.

The mid-1940s and 1950s witnessed the initial affirmation of minority group rights before the law if not in fact. Three cases will illustrate this development. In 1944 in *Mo Hock Ke Lok Po v. Stainback*, the U.S. Supreme Court affirmed an earlier lower-court decision that parents had a right to have their children taught a foreign language. The Court noted that "in today's world of the United Nations there has been added an equally profound international need for understanding between the peoples of a world of different languages." In 1945 there was a little-known but critical case in Westminister in which the court rules that segregation of Mexican Americans was unconstitutional. This set an important precedent for the famous 1954 decision of *Brown v. State Board of Education*, which declared the separate-but-equal doctorine unconstitutional. There was, of course, also the G.I. Bill of Rights, which provided educational access to thousands of minority group veterans for the first time, despite the prevalence of segregationist practices.

The 1960s and 1970s saw educational experimentation intended to achieve educational "equity" through the enactment of remedial and compensatory educational programs. Of course, extensive litigation—the most notable of which were the *Lau v. Nichols* and *Serrano* cases—continued. Characteristic of ethnocentric pedagogy of this period was the naive pseudopedagogical assumption exemplified by the cultural deprivationist theory embodied in the "culture of poverty." Inherent cultural and language traits of ethnolinguistic groups were seen as the cause for their school failure. The social sciences during this period created an entirely new vocabulary to explain the school failure of minorities. They were described as apathetic, fatalistic, non-goal oriented, underachieving, unacculturated, and culturally deprived. Everything seemed right with the system, it's just that "those damn minority kids fail to learn."

This brief review is not intended as an exercise in indignation; rather it serves to exemplify several points:

- Prevailing social ideology cannot be viewed as distinct from educational ideology. The extent to which society accepts or rejects students of different languages and cultures will be reflected in educational practices—hence ethnocentric pedagogy.
- The state of the national economy affects both social and educational services for minorities. In relatively affluent periods progressive legislation and educational programs are developed; conversely, economic recession results in removal or decreased funding of educational programs, and conservative (if not totally repressive) legislation toward minorities.
- The educational system fails to utilize the intrinsic attributes of minorities in the educational process.

In brief, schools, as Carter and Maestas (1984) wrote, perpetuate the "cherished belief in the concept of the melting pot" and of a monolingual society. Schools are viewed as a vehicle of acculturation for minorities that requires the replacement of language and culture with "American truths, values, norms, and languages." Those who conform in behavior, dress, and language are praised for becoming "True Americans," while those who do not are viewed as "uncooperative, un-American, and . . . subversive."

Ethnocentric pedagogy is self-serving. It mandates liberating minorities from their language and culture in order to lift them from their poverty, ignorance, and oppression. The paradox of ethnocentric pedagogy is apparent: It requires minorities to divest themselves of their past and characteristics and become something they are not in a society that does not fully accept them.

So long as racial, ethnic, and linguistic minorities remain minorities—5%, 10%, or 15% of the population—without economic or political power, they do not threaten the majority group, nor the role of the common school reflecting the values, expectations, or perceptions of the dominant society. What happens, however, when the "minority" becomes the "majority"? Will the philosophy, role, ideology, or governing structure of the common school be altered? The question is threatening to many. A brief review of demographic trends in California is revealing.

Demographic trends

Within the past decade and a half the composition of the public school population has changed dramatically throughout the nation and in California. From 1967 to 1981, for example, the number of minority group pupils increased in California from 25% to 44%, while the nonminority group population declined from 75% to 56%. Concurrent with the minority pupil growth, limited-English proficient (LEP) pupils and refugee students have also increased. Simultaneously, the incidence of racial isolation and problems related to social and educational equity have grown. These trends, coupled with declining state and federal revenues for education, are straining available education program services. Equally important, the growth in the number of minority pupils suggests the need for immediate program planning.

Between 1970 and 1980, California's population increased by 3.7 million (18.5%), from 19.95 to 23.67 million. During this period the combined minority group population increased by 6.09 million while the white population decreased by 2.38 million (see Table 11.1).

In effect, the combined minority group population increased from 20.5% in 1970 to 43.6% in 1980. This trend can be expected to accelerate. One report (Council on Intergroup Relations, 1977) estimates that 1990 minority population will reach 64%.

The dramatic increase in the minority population—in particular, the Hispanic and Asian groups—may be attributed primarily to their fertility rates. The minority population is relatively younger, with larger households and a higher fertility rate than those of the White population.

Table 11.1 Population change in California

	1970	1977	1980	Net changes (1970–80)
Total population	19,953,000	22,700,000	23,668,362	+ 3,715,362
Anglo	15,867,000	15,665,000	13,487,911	– 2,379,089
Combined minority	4,086,000	7,035,000	10,180,651	+ 6,094,651

Immigration has also contributed to minority population growth. It accounts for about one-fourth of the net population growth nationally (Coates, 1978). Since 1970, non-European immigrants were more than 50% of all immigrants to the United States (see Table 11.2). The influx of Vietnamese due to the end of the Vietnam conflict has been particularly dramatic.

Another issue that cannot be ignored is the proximity of Mexico. Social and economic changes in Mexico and other central and southern Latin American countries have an impact on California and the southwestern states. Mexico's population is projected to double every 21 years, while the United States population doubles every 116 years. There will be larger migrations from Mexico, increasing the numbers of both documented and undocumented workers.[1]

Thus California has experienced a significant shift in the ethnic/racial composition of the population. The combined minority population increased 20% between 1970 and 1980 and now constitutes 43.6% of the population. By about 1985 the minority population can be expected to equal or surpass the state's White population, making California the first Third World state in the continental United States.[2]

This shift is particularly evident in the school-age population (see Table 11.3). There has been a gradual decline in the number of White students from 3.31 million in 1967 to 2.28 million in 1981. Simultaneously there has been an increase from 25.3% to 43.6% in the minority student population over the last thirteen years, with simultaneous decrease in White student enrollment from 74.7% to 56.4%.

Examination of the grade distribution data of pupils reveals that in grades K-3 the combined minority population either exceeds or equals the White student population (see Table 11.4). The combined minority population in grades 4–9 ranges from a low of 40.9% to 46.6%, and in grades 11–12 from 33.9% to 37.6%. Within the next two school years it may be expected that throughout grades K-4 the minority group students will be prominent. Given current population trends, within the next decade grades K-10 will be composed primarily of minority groups.

Student attrition

While the school population is becoming increasingly minority, student attrition in the secondary grades reveals considerable disparity. The number of pupils in grade 9 as compared to grade 11 three years later indicates that significantly fewer Hispanic students remain in school than do their White student peers (see Table 11.5). The attrition rate of Black and Hispanic students in grades 10–12 and 11–12 is far in excess of White students. Only the Asian group has more students entering school in grades 9–11 and 10–12 (which may be due in part to the influx of Indochinese refugees) than all other groups. These data would suggest an attrition rate between grades 9–12 for Hispanics on the order of about 45%, for Blacks 41%, for American Indians 28%, for Whites 21%, and for Asians 11%. These data suggest a minority attrition of 162,000 pupils between grades 9–12. This is equivalent to 5,400 classrooms of 30 pupils each and 135 schools of 1,000 students. No doubt a number of socioeconomic factors play a critical role in the attrition of students, but such great disparity is dismaying.

The number of LEP pupils identified since the enactment of mandated bilingual education legislation has also increased dramatically. In part this is due to improvement in census-taking methods, a change in definitions (i.e., use of proficiency instead of dominance), and population increases in language minority

Table 11.2 Immigrants into the United States, by region and years

Region	1820–60	1861–1900	1901–30	1931–60	1961–70	1971–76	1977–79
Northern and Western Europe	95%	68%	23%	41%	17%	7%	5%
North America	3%	7%	11%	21%	12%	4%	3%
Southern and Eastern Europe	–	22%	58%	17%	16%	13%	8%
Latin America	–	–	5%	15%	39%	41%	42%
Asia	–	2%	3%	5%	13%	32%	39%
Other	3%	1%	–	1%	3%	3%	3%

Source: *PRB Population Bulletin*, Vol. 32, No. 4.

Table 11.3 California student enrollment population (in millions)

	Years									
	1967	1968	1969	1970	1971	1973	1977	1979*	1981
Anglo student population	3.31 (74.7%)	3.36 (74.5%)	3.36 (73.7%)	3.29 (72.1%)	3.23 (71.1%)	3.09 (69.6%)	2.70 (63.1%)	2.38 (63.1%)	2.28 (59.9%)
Combined minority student population	1.12 (25.3%)	1.15 (25.5%)	1.20 (26.3%)	1.27 (27.9%)	1.31 (28.9%)	1.35 (30.4%)	1.58 (36.9%)	1.59 (40.1%)	1.76 (43.6%)
TOTAL	4.43 (100%)	4.51 (100%)	4.56 (100%)	4.56 (100%)	4.54 (100%)	4.44 (100%)	4.28 (100%)	3.97 (100%)	3.94 (100%)

Source: California State Department of Education Racial and Ethnic Survey 1967–1971, 1973, 1977, 1979, 1981.
* Excludes special and continuation schools and institutional enrollees.

Table 11.4 Racial/ethnic distribution, by grade, by percentage (California 1981)

Grade	Total student population	American Indian	Asian	Filipino	Hispanic	Black	White	Total minority
K	300,239	0.5	5.1	1.7	34.1	9.1	49.5	50.5
1	298,341	0.6	5.5	1.6	33.1	9.7	49.5	50.5
2	287,652	0.7	5.7	1.7	31.6	9.7	50.7	49.3
3	282,464	0.7	5.9	1.8	30.4	9.6	51.5	48.5
4	290,323	0.8	5.9	1.8	28.5	9.6	53.4	46.6
5	310,874	0.8	5.6	1.7	26.5	9.7	55.7	44.3
6	324,324	0.8	5.4	1.6	24.5	9.8	57.9	42.1
7	322,264	0.9	5.1	1.5	23.8	10.1	58.6	41.4
8	307,429	0.9	5.1	1.5	23.2	9.9	59.3	40.7
9	326,143	0.9	5.3	1.5	23.0	10.2	59.1	40.9
10	334,287	0.9	5.9	1.5	22.1	10.7	58.9	41.1
11	311,518	0.9	5.8	1.5	19.2	10.1	62.2	37.6
12	280,811	0.9	5.5	1.4	16.9	9.2	66.1	33.9
Other*	69,480	0.7	3.1	1.0	26.2	12.8	56.2	43.8

* Institutional and Special Education.

pupils. Of the 1983 California school-age population of 3.9 million pupils, about one million were language minority, and of these 436,000 LEP pupils (see Table 11.6). Approximately 80% of all LEP pupils are Spanish language speakers, 10% Asian language speakers, and 10% other language speakers. In grades K-6 there are about 65% LEP pupils, and in grades 7–12 there are about 35%. Nationally the non-English background population was 30 million in 1980 and expected to grow to about 40 million in the year 2000; the LEP pupil population was about 2.4 million in 1980 and is expected to increase to 3.4 million by the year 2000 (National Center for Educational Statistics, 1981).

Given the growth trends of both the general and the student population in California, the number of LEP pupils in 1985 will surpass the .5 million mark, with corresponding increases nationally. The Hispanics' concentration would appear to constitute at least 75% of the LEP population and Asian language groups another 10%. Among the Asian languages, it is anticipated that Korean and Vietnamese will show the greatest gains.

While the character and composition of the school population has undergone significant changes, the ethnicity of public school staff remains predominately White (see Table 11.7). Although the combined minority student population is 43.6%, the White professional school staff was, in 1979, 84% of teachers, 84% of principals and assistant principals, and 83% of other professionals. There are no appreciable differences between these data and those of 1981 (less than 1%). Nor is there any evidence of any significant age shift of staff between 1979 and 1981, suggesting little, if any, accelerating influx of younger teachers into public school teaching. This does suggest, however, that when the present 40–50-year-old cohort reaches retirement in the next decade there may well be a general teacher shortage in addition to the continuing need for bilingual, math, and science teachers. The large ethnic disparity between students and teachers raises apprehension about adequately reflecting minority group educational interests and meeting their sociocultural and linguistic needs (Richards, 1982).

Table 11.5 California high school student attrition rate, by ethnicity, 1979–1981

	Comparison of ninth graders (1979) and eleventh graders (1981)			Comparison of tenth graders (1979) and twelfth graders (1981)			Comparison of eleventh graders (1979) and high school graduates (1981)			Attrition of combined classes (9th, 10th and 11th graders) by ethnicity		
	Number in 9th grade (1979)	Number in 11th grade (1981)	% Change	Number in 10th grade (1979)	Number in 12th grade (1981)	% Change	Number in 11th grade (1979)	Number of graduates (1981)	% Change	Combined enroll-ment (1979)	Attrition 1981	% Attrition
American Indian	3,232 (.96%)	2,924 (.94%)	−308 (−9.5%)	3,089 (0.9%)	2,410 (.86%)	−679 (−22%)	2,818 (.9%)	2,338 (.96%)	−480 (−17%)	9,139	−1,467	(16.05)
Asian	13,667 (4.08%)	18,124 (5.82%)	+4,457 (+32.6%)	14,646 (4.26%)	15,569 (5.54%)	+923 (+6.3%)	13,678 (4.3%)	12,146 (5%)	−1,532 (−11%)	41,991	+3,848	(9.16)
Filipino	4,335 (1.29%)	4,615 (1.48%)	+280 (+6.5%)	4,343 (1.26%)	3,999 (1.42%)	−344 (−7.9%)	4,005 (1.3%)	3,014 (1.2%)	−991 (−25%)	12,683	−1,055	(8.32)
Hispanic	69,748 (20.81%)	59,833 (19.21%)	−9,915 (−14.2%)	66,812 (19.44%)	47,575 (16.94%)	−19,237 (−28.8%)	55,875 (17.5%)	38,714 (15.9%)	−17,161 (−31%)	192,435	−46,313	(24.07)
Black	34,936 (10.42%)	31,547 (10.13%)	−3,389 (−9.7%)	35,568 (10.35%)	25,702 (9.15%)	−9,863 (−27.7%)	31,793 (10%)	20,628 (8.5%)	−11,165 (−35%)	102,297	−24,417	(23.87)
White	209,291 (62.44%)	194,475 (62.43%)	−14,816 (−7.1%)	219,189 (63.78%)	185,563 (66.08%)	−33,626 (−15.3%)	210,445 (66%)	165,923 (68.4%)	−44,522 (−21%)	638,925	−92,964	(14.55)
TOTAL	335,209 (100%)	311,518 (100%)	−23,691 (−7.1%)	343,647 (100%)	280,818 (100%)	−62,826 (−18.3%)	318,614 (100%)	242,172 (100%)	−75,851 (−24%)	997,470	−162,368	(16.28)

Source: CBEDS 1979 and CBEDS 1981, California State Department of Education.

Table 11.6 Limited English proficient students in California, 1977, 1979–1982

Language	1977	1979	1980	1981	1982
Spanish	195,673	235,073	257,033	285,567	322,526
Cantonese	4,390	7,219	10,174	14,196	16,096
Mandarin	1,310	2,244	2,298	3,370	3,775
Vietnamese	5,819	7,426	14,018	22,826	27,773
Korean	4,271	6,054	6,599	7,508	7,980
Japanese	2,032	2,199	2,713	2,788	3,023
Tagalog	5,670	5,979	6,658	6,752	8,569
Llocano	919	808			
Samoan	1,152	1,260	*	*	*
Portuguese	1,882	2,246	2,230	2,332	2,357
Native American	218	399	*	*	*
Cambodian	*	*	1,071	2,474	5,166
Lao	*	*	2,652	5,585	7,129
All others	10,108	17,520	20,302	23,396	27,095
TOTAL	233,444	288,427	325,748	376,794	431,489

Source: Office of Bilingual Education, California State Department of Education, Language Census Reports, 1977–1982.
* Included in "All others" category for year reported.

Table 11.7 Distribution of students and school staff, by ethnicity, in California, 1979

Ethnic group	Students	Teachers	Principals & Assistant Principals	Other full-time professionals	Paraprofessionals
White	2,441,120 (60.0%)	139,813 (84.0%)	8,590 (83.8%)	12,052 (82.6%)	35,406 (64.3%)
Hispanic	953,295 (23.4%)	9,205 (5.5%)	612 (6.0%)	897 (6.2%)	12,452 (22.6%)
Black	405,938 (10.0%)	10,367 (6.2%)	798 (7.8%)	1,147 (7.9%)	5,017 (9.1%)
Asian	172,956 (4.3%)	5,217 (3.1%)	155 (1.5%)	345 (2.4%)	1,359 (2.5%)
Filipino	57,917 (1.4%)	820 (0.5%)	22 (0.2%)	64 (0.4%)	405 (0.7%)
American Indian	36,794 (0.9%)	1,018 (0.6%)	71 (0.7%)	79 (0.5%)	388 (0.7%)
TOTALS	4,068,029	166,440	10,248	14,584	55,027

There has been a tremendous increase in the number of schools and districts that have become racially isolated. In the 12-year period from 1967–1979, the number of schools exceeding 50% minority concentration more than doubled, from 977 to 1943 (see Tables 11.8 and 11.9). Reduced efforts to achieve integration, "white flight," housing costs, and the marginal socioeconomic status of minorities will continue to exacerbate the trend. Public rejection of efforts to achieve desegregation, such as busing, limit alternatives. The large numbers of racially isolated schools suggests reexamination of existing desegregation remedies. Heretofore, remedies have been too static, and obviously ineffective.

Policy implications

The dramatic shift in the characteristics of the student population in the common schools can be summarized as follows: There is

- continued and accelerated increase in the number of racial and language minorities;
- significant increase in racial segregation;

Table 11.8 Number of schools that are 50 percent or more minority, 1967–1979

	Number of schools	Number of districts	Minority enrollment	Total enrollment
Fall 1979	1,943	287	997,527	1,296,504
Fall 1977	1,755	264	921,052	1,196,198
Fall 1973	1,344	215	722,259	936,063
Fall 1971	1,215	215	683,957	884,818
Fall 1969	1,015	202	612,169	775,196
Fall 1967	987	212	553,182	692,705

Note: There was no racial and ethnic survey of California public schools in 1975.

Table 11.9 Proportion of students in 20 percent and 50 percent minority concentrated schools in California, fall 1979

Group	N	+20%	+50%
White	2,441,120	12%	15%
Hispanics	453,295	22%	62%
Black	405,938	30%	72%
Asian	172,956	9%	43%
Filipino	57,917	13%	57%
American Indian	36,794	6%	23%
Total minority	1,626,900	10%	61%
Total students	4,068,020	10%	32%

Source: *Racial and Ethnic Distribution of Students and Staff in California Public Schools, Fall 1979.* (Figures 6 and 8). Sacramento: Office of Intergroup Relations, California State Department of Education.

- significant increase in the number of unserved and underserved minorities in regular and categorical programs;
- an increasing disparity between the racial/ethnic composition of students and school staff;
- increasing pressure for teachers trained in sociolinguistic and multi-cultural competencies; and
- increasing pressure for minority group representation in the governance structure.

It is tempting to call for increased funding, more responsive teacher preparation programs, more research, and the like. Even assuming consensus on reforms, they may represent nothing less than a "headstart up a short alley" as notes Galarza. The fundamental problem, in my judgment, remains. It is the pervasive ethnocentric pedagogy.

I find it difficult as an educator to be sanguine about the gap between full realization of educational equity, equalization of status for all groups, and participatory democracy in educational policies and programs, on one hand, and the social reality of educational inequality and the pernicious effects of ethnocentric pedagogy on the other.

We lament the need to develop foreign language capabilities in our youth, yet society begrudges bilingual education. We agree that the special educational needs of minority pupils are essential to improving their educational performance, yet the needed educational reforms are opposed, and categorical programs are continually underfunded. We concur that intergroup harmony is essential to our social well-being, yet school segregation continues.

Revisions in the existing educational philosophy and pedagogy are essential. It is socially dysfunctional to maintain educational institutions that absolve themselves from responsibility for a failure rate of 40% among minority groups. Continued neglect can only result in increasing numbers of people excluded as contributors to the socioeconomic order of society. The common school can and should become the instrument of constructive progressive change, reflecting the interests of a concerned society.

The period from about 1985–1990 will be critical because of the changes in the student population. The forthcoming demand on educators is really an old demand—the full acceptance of minorities into the social and economic mainstream. Several courses of action present themselves.

(1) There must be a recognition that California—indeed the United States—is neither monolingual nor monocultural. The imprint of cultural richness is not an abstraction but a reality—in place names, vocabulary, customs, food, religion, agricultural methods, and law. We must recognize the internal attributes of culture—perceptions, beliefs, values, and motivations. We must also recognize and allow to flourish, in our national interest, the linguistic richness of our young people—Spanish, Vietnamese, Cantonese, Russian, and more. Sanchez (1966: 14) characterized the absurdity of the present situation when he noted,

> We extol the virtues of foreign languages in the development and the achievements of an educated man; we decry their decline in public education; we view with alarm our backwardness when we compare ourselves with the Russians and others; we subsidize the teaching of foreign languages. Yet in the Southwest, one of the world's great languages is suppressed. It does not make sense!

As Kloss noted, our country is bilingual: In 40 of the 50 states a language other than English is actively spoken and in 21 states over 20% of the population is bilingual. Rather than attempting to eradicate culture, the common school would embrace it, one would think. The significance of language, customs, and heritage in personality formation, motivation, and learning demands recognition. In many ways bilingual-multicultural education has been a vanguard. Bona fide bilingual programs have produced significant accomplishments: increased school attendance, English language acquisition, and improved school achievement. These efforts obviously need to be expanded.

(2) Minority group representation in policy making must increase. As more and more Blacks, Chicanos, and Asians enter school during the 1980s, increased pressure on the present governance system can be expected. The extent to which a nonminority superintendent, a school board member, or a legislator can or should represent minority group interests will be challenged. Increasingly minority groups will seek to represent their own interests. The tug-of-war exemplified by Hispanic interests to maintain and expand bilingual education against conservative nonminority interests is a foretaste of more such struggles in the future. The mid-1980s and beyond will become a period of coalition politics; nowhere will this become more apparent than on school boards.

(3) We must concentrate on our failures in school; the successes will take care of themselves. As previously noted, minorities currently experience a high failure rate. Contrary to popular opinion, early European immigrants did not, according to Greer (1972) do much better than today's Blacks, Chicanos, or Puerto Ricans. Only after successive generations have European immigrants achieved an economic security that in turn has brought school success. But the nature of our economic system has changed drastically, and we cannot allow three to four generations to pass before the same thing occurs with Blacks, Chicanos, and other minority groups. Early theories to explain the failure of Italian, Irish, Polish, and other immigrants are much the same as those used today; latter-day variations are more exotic and seductive. Deficiency theories to explain away school failure are an attempt only to excuse our own role as silent co-conspirators.

I would venture to say that the failure rate of minorities would be dramatically reduced by simply putting into practice the lessons learned from studies of effective Black (Glenn and McLean, 1981) and Chicano schools (Carter and Maestas, 1984). Particularly important are enlightened support, leadership, humane instruction, and the teacher's conviction that minority groups have a vast pool of talents, resources, and experiences. Recent studies of model bilingual programs traced extraordinary pupil gains to the fact the teachers in those programs did not believe in deficiency theories, but viewed their pupils positively.

(4) It is imperative to place the role of schools in the broader social and economic context. Children learn in the home and the community and from their peers. The influence of the media is equally profound. I believe schools should be extended into the home and community through active, responsible parent involvement. I am well aware of the lip service that educators pay to the issue of community and parent participation, and to the use of "advisory committees." No doubt some educators are afraid of parents, or regard advisory committees as necessary evils in the administration of programs directed at minority groups. To the degree that educators provide open and meaningful parental involvement through the use of schools as community centers for health, language, and vocational courses, they will gain community interest and support. Courses in

how the school systems operate and how parents can participate in the system are particularly critical.

(5) We should implement alternative approaches to instruction. The frontiers of education must constantly be extended through the use of cooperative learning models, language status equalization, teacher training in sociolinguistic and multicultural education, and the like.

(6) The issue of testing must be faced. In particular, its pernicious labeling, dividing, and sorting of minority children must be addressed. The focus needs to change from testing children to assessing the effects of particular programs on children. The difference is significant and important.

In summary, it is clear that we have an imperfect educational system, one that has ignored the cultural and linguistic attributes of minority pupils. For large percentages of minority pupils the product of the common school has been an unconscionably high failure rate, bitterness, and frustration. There is no justification for the fear that minority groups are going to alter radically the role or the function of the common school. Rather, I seen change as a matter of degree involving reconstruction in curriculum, staffing, governance, and ethnic composition. Needed changes to make our school more responsive to the multi-cultural reality of the pupil population cannot occur too soon. In the end we will all benefit.

Notes

1   The Immigration and Naturalization Service, U.S. Department of Justice, places the number of registered legal aliens in California at 940,000, of whom 637,200 are Spanish speaking. The Council on Intergroup Relations report estimated 1.2 million undocumented workers in California in 1977.
2   The trend in the ethnic/racial composition appears to be undergoing similar changes in major metropolitan areas, particularly in the southern and eastern states.

References

Brown, G. et al. (1980) The Condition of Education for Hispanic Americans. Washington, DC: National Center for Education Statistics.
Carter, T. and L. Maestas (1984) Model Bilingual Education Programs. Sacramento: Office of Bilingual Education, California State Department of Education.
Carter, T. P. and R. D. Segura (1979) Mexican Americans in School: A Decade of Change. New York: College Entrance Board.
Cervantes, R. A. (1981) "Bilingual education: the best of times, the worst of times," in K. Cirincione-Coles (ed.) The Future of Education. Beverly Hills, CA: Sage.
Coates, J. (1978) "Population and education: how demographic trends will shape the U.S." The Futurist (February).
Council on Intergroup Relations (1977) Third World Population in California. Sacramento: Office of the Lieutenant Governor, State of California (June 10).
Galarza, E. (1972) "Mexicans in the Southwest: a culture in process," in E. Spicer and R. Thompson (eds.) Plural Society in the Southwest. New York: Weathead Foundation, Interbook.
Glenn, B. C. and T. McLean (1981) What Works? An Examination of Effective Schools for Poor Black Children. Cambridge, MA: Center for Law and Education, Harvard University (August).
Greer, C. (1972) The Great School Legend. New York: Basic Books.
Kloss, H. (1977) The American Bilingual Tradition. Rowley, MA: Newbury House.
National Center for Educational Statistics (1981) Projections of Non-English Language

Background and Limited English Proficient Persons in the United States to the Year 2000. Washington, DC: Author.

Richards, C. (1982) Employment Reform on Pupil Control? Desegregation, Bilingualism and Hispanic Staffing in the California Public Schools. Project Report 82-A9. Palo Alto, CA: Institute for Research on Educational Finance and Governance, Stanford University (April):

Romano-V, O. I. (1976) "Minorities, history, and the cultural mystique." El Grito 1, 1 (Fail).

Sanchez, G. I. (1966) "History, culture and education," in J. Samora (ed.) La Raza: Forgotten Americans. South Bend: University of Notre Dame Press.

Weinberg, C. (1975) Education is a Shuck. New York: Morrow.

CHAPTER 11

THE "AT-RISK" LABEL AND THE PROBLEM OF URBAN SCHOOL REFORM (1989)

Larry Cuban

Unless policy makers and practitioners begin to consider how problems involving schools are framed, they will continue to lunge for quick solutions without considering the fit between the solution and the problem. In doing so, well-intentioned educators may perpetuate lies that harm children, rather than help them. As Georges Bernanos warned: "There is no worse lie than a problem poorly stated."[1]

Consider how the problem of at-risk students is framed today. Many families live in poverty. Even though parents try hard to make ends meet, the corrosive effects of long-term poverty splinter families. Children in these families often lack care; to survive, they lie, steal, and fight. They lead stunted lives. Without help, these children will continue their destructive behavior as adults. Thus, if some parents cannot rear their children properly, the public schools must intervene to avert substantial future costs to society and to help each child become a productive citizen.

This description of at-risk students and their families should be familiar. After all, it is almost 200 years old, and it remains today, as it was when it first appeared, a formula used by reformers to arouse the public to action.

In 1805, before there were public schools in New York, the New York City Free School Society asked the state legislature to establish a school for poor children. This is how that group framed its request:

> [We] have viewed with painful anxiety the multiplied evils which have accrued . . . to this city from the neglected education of the children of the poor. . . . The condition of this class is deplorable indeed; reared up by parents who . . . are . . . either indifferent to the best interests of their off-spring, or, through intemperate lives . . . these miserable and almost friendless objects are ushered upon the stage of life, inheriting those vices which idleness and the bad example of their parents naturally produce. The consequences of this neglect of education are ignorance and vice, and all those manifold evils resulting from every species of immorality by which public hospitals and alms-houses are filled with objects of disease and poverty.[2]

In 1898, after public schools had been established and compulsory attendance laws had been passed, a staff member of the board of education in Chicago reported to a committee of board members the following concern about truant children:

All good citizens desire to have these children educated, and we certainly should not permit a reckless and indifferent part of our population to rear [its] children in ignorance to become a criminal and lawless class within our community. We should rightfully have the power to arrest all these little beggars, loafers, and vagabonds that infest our city, take them from the streets and place them in schools where they are compelled to receive education and learn moral principles.[3]

In 1961 former Harvard University President James Conant studied affluent suburban schools and city schools in which most of the students were poor and black. Conant concluded:

I am convinced we are allowing social dynamite to accumulate in our large cities. I am not nearly so concerned about the plight of suburban parents whose offspring are having difficulty finding places in prestige colleges as I am about the plight of parents in the slums whose children either drop out or graduate from school without prospects of either further education or employment. In some slum neighborhoods I have no doubt that over half of the boys between sixteen and twenty-one are out of school and out of work. Leaving aside human tragedies, I submit that a continuation of this situation is a menace to the social and political health of the large cities.[4]

For almost two centuries, poor children—often nonwhite and from other cultures—have been seen to pose a threat to the larger society because neither parents nor existing community institutions could control their unacceptable behavior. Fear of having to spend more for welfare payments and prisons drove public officials to compel attendance in schools as a solution to the problem of children we would today label "at risk." Since the early 19th century, this way of framing the problem and this view of compulsory schooling as its solution have reflected an abiding political consensus among federal, state, and local policy makers.

During these years, some poor children from various ethnic and racial backgrounds achieved well in school, but many did not. Why did so many fail to meet the school's standards for academic performance and behavior? Why were so many placed in special classes and segregated from the rest of the school? Why did so many drop out?

Framing the problem

Compulsory schooling, proposed as a solution to the social problems of children in poverty, produced another problem: growing numbers of children performing poorly in classrooms. Over the last century, educators and public officials have most often defined the problem of low achievement by at-risk children in the following two ways:

- Students who perform poorly in school are responsible for their performance; that is, they lack ability, character, or motivation.
- Families from certain cultural backgrounds fail to prepare their children for school and provide little support for them in school; they are poor, lack education, and don't teach their children what is proper and improper in the dominant culture.

Two alternative views of the problem have been proposed, though much less frequently:

- Children often fail because the culture of the school ignores or degrades their family and community backgrounds. Middle-class teachers, reflecting the school's values, single out for criticism differences in children's behavior and values; they crush the self-esteem of students and neglect the strengths that these students bring to school.
- The structure of the school is not flexible enough to accommodate the diverse abilities and interests of a heterogeneous student body. Programs are seldom adapted to children's individual differences. Instead, schools seek uniformity, and departures from the norm in achievement and behavior are defined as problems. Social, racial, and ethnic discrimination are embedded in the routine practices of schools and districts.

Note that the two most popular explanations for low academic achievement of at-risk children locate the problem in the children themselves or in their families. As evidence of the popularity of these explanations, recall the labels applied to such children over the last 20 years: disadvantaged, culturally deprived, marginal, and dropouts. Almost a century ago, such students were labeled as backward, retarded, or laggards. In short, since the beginnings of public education, poor academic performance and deviant behavior have been defined as problems of individual children or of their families.[5]

When the problems have been attributed to deficits in children, the solutions have involved more intense doses of what the children were already getting or should have been getting: academic preschools, compensatory education, longer school days, higher academic standards, and so on. When the problems have been attributed to deficits of families, the solutions have focused on training adults to do a proper job of rearing their children.

In the 1980s the barrenness of such definitions and solutions is apparent in soaring retention rates and in dropout rates approaching one out of two among the ethnic poor. It is time to consider a less popular way of framing the problem: that the inflexible structure of the school itself contributes to the conditions that breed academic failure and unsatisfactory student performance.

One of the most inflexible of the structures of schooling is the graded school. The graded school categorizes, segregates, and, as a last resort, eliminates those whose performance and behavior deviate too sharply from the norm. The graded school—consisting of one teacher and one class of 30 or so students of roughly the same age who spend about 36 weeks together before moving on to another grade or class—assumes that students possess equal mental and physical capacities, have equal amounts of help available from their families, and will be taught by teachers with equal skills and knowledge. The implicit theory underlying the graded school is that educational quality comes through uniformity. If a teacher teaches a group of students for a certain amount of time, according to the theory, almost all of these students will learn the required amount of knowledge at roughly the same rate and will move on to the next teacher. Those who don't keep pace will simply take a little longer to master the standard course of study.

Hence, the graded school requires a curriculum divided into equal segments, tests to determine whether the knowledge and skills have been learned, and promotion only for those who have attained the minimum levels set for each grade. This organizational scaffolding holds the graded school together.

Such an impulse to standardize student achievement and behavior also nourishes negative beliefs about children on the part of teachers, administrators, and parents. For example, deviations in children's performance or behavior are commonly ascribed to genetic deficits in the child. To end these deviations, children must be grouped by ability. Separate classrooms or programs are established to "remediate" those who deviate too far from the norm. Ultimately, if students' unacceptable performance persists; school officials either terminate the careers of these students or allow the students to drop out.

Despite these problems, the graded school has succeeded beyond the dreams of the 19th-century reformers who invented it. By the early 1900s the graded school was *the* way to organize education, and so it has remained. It is no accident that the education systems in most developed nations are built on the graded school.

My point should be self-evident. Although the graded school may have moved large numbers of students through a system of compulsory schooling for many decades when a growing economy could absorb early leavers, a substantial number of today's young people from low-income ethnic and racial minorities are unequipped to find jobs when they leave school. Such a waste of human potential is damaging to a society committed to equal opportunity. I believe that one of the unquestioned and unexamined reasons for this waste of individual and social potential stems from the imperatives of the graded school.[6]

I am *not* arguing that graded schools are solely responsible for the academic failure that can result from attaching labels to students and segregating students in special classes that stigmatize them in the minds of adults and other children. Until recently, blacks, Hispanics, and Native Americans who attended legally segregated public schools were already viewed by the larger society as different from whites and unworthy to sit in classrooms with them. Migrants and immigrants from other cultures—marked as different by language, culture, religion, and poverty—have always worn badges of difference and have had to cope with categories created by the school. Finally, over the last 150 years, those children who were physically and mentally impaired have faced a similar process of labeling, segregation, and elimination. For members of these groups, the differences were present before they met their first teacher.

Beyond overt racism, the effects of long-term poverty can disfigure families and children. The grim outcomes of poverty—such as malnutrition, physical abuse, parental neglect, and living in neighborhoods where crime and violence are commonplace—also mark children early and deeply. Children carry these marks to school.

I argue that the graded school unintentionally worsens these social disadvantages by branding students for the duration of their careers through the mechanisms of separate classes and programs. The graded school, with its imperative to sort out differences in order to preserve uniformity, hardens low-status labels (derived from poverty and racism) in the minds of well-meaning teachers and administrators and makes it more difficult for the students to succeed. For those labeled "at risk," graded schools are poised to produce failure.

In generalizing about groups, I do not wish to minimize or ignore the many students who have succeeded by dint of personal resilience and the luck of having one or more teachers who could see strengths when the school saw only failure. My point is that the structure of the school is viewed as legitimate by the community. Thus that structure helps to shape not only the attitudes and behavior of administrators and teachers, but also those of students.

The case against the graded school

What evidence is there for my claims that labeling, segregation, and elimination are inherent to the graded school? Let me begin my answer with a brief historical excursion.

The labels I have been discussing refer almost exclusively to children and families. We seldom say that a teacher is culturally deprived, that a school is at risk, or that a school district is disadvantaged or backward. The child and the family are labeled. And, in the last half-century, more efficient ways of blaming the young have been found, especially through the use of intelligence testing and achievement testing.

Invented by leading psychologists in the early 1900s and clothed in the aura of modern science, both types of testing made it possible for schools in the 1920s to respond efficiently to the enormous cultural diversity among their students. Test results were converted into new labels and attached to groups of children. Mentally defective, dull, average, superior, and gifted children were assigned to separate classes in an effort to enable all children to reach their potential. As two reformers in a low-income elementary school in New York City in the 1920s explained, "It seemed fairly obvious to us that, if enough groups were created within a grade, each moving at different rates of speed, every type of child could find his own place."[7]

Even in the 1920s the children who were sent to classes for "dull" and "defective" students came from immigrant, Mexican-American, and black families. Their labels became badges—filed away in cumulative folders to follow them every step of the way through public school. That pattern has continued until the present. Although group intelligence testing is now out of favor in many districts, the impulse to classify differences still demands categories.[8]

More recently, Jane Mercer investigated classes for mentally retarded children. In one community she found more than 2,500 children who were attending Catholic schools in which there were no special classes for mentally retarded children, although many of these children scored low enough on intelligence tests to qualify them for special classes in the public schools. However, the Catholic schools in this community labeled no one "mentally retarded." The public schools had created this label, but it simply did not exist in the parochial schools.[9]

Finally, if such labeling leads to separate classes and programs and if students seldom shake these labels, the cumulative effect will be that fewer of them will complete high school. In the early decades of this century, most students who had been tagged dull or backward left school for good by the age of 14 or after completion of eighth grade. They found jobs, and the labels were left in files and forgotten. The expanding economy in the decades before and immediately after World War I absorbed hundreds of thousands of young men and women who had limited education and strong backs. Just before World War II, the dropout rate was 60% for *all students*.[10] However, the economic and social penalties for dropping out were not as severe as they are today.

With its mechanisms for labeling, segregating, and ultimately driving out certain students, the graded public school contributes unintentionally to the problem of deviant performance and behavior among children identified as at risk. Unknowingly working in partnership with social and economic forces in a larger culture marked by racial discrimination, unemployment, inadequate housing, and a social safety net that is barely adequate, the graded school is ill-equipped to erase these social effects; it is an organization that, through no ill intent on the part of the people who work within it, is designed to fail most of the children who have historically been labeled at risk.

Past efforts to redesign schools

In the early decades of this century, reformers expanded the role of the school beyond teaching the basic skills. Reformers wanted to broaden the narrow academic curriculum and end the regimentation and tedious drill that marked public schools in the early 1900s. If the curriculum was too uniform and the mission too narrow for schools in an urban, industrialized society, the solution was to fit the school to the child's needs.

In those decades, reformers introduced such innovations as gymnasiums, lunch-rooms, vocational education, medical checkups, extracurricular activities; field trips, greater informality in relations between teachers and students, rugs, rocking chairs in primary classrooms, and movable desks in the upper grades. However, fitting the school to the student also fed the passion for testing and ability grouping.

Framing the problem in terms of both the child *and* the school widened the focus from solutions involving the child alone to solutions in which teachers, administrators, and policy makers assumed responsibility for altering their practices to accommodate differences among children and within a changing society. The actual changes that occurred in these decades, however, often intensified the sorting of children. New tests, more ability grouping, expanded curricula, better counseling, and different promotion policies were designed to fit the school to the child, but seldom were beliefs or practices seriously questioned or redesigned. Seldom was the graded school itself seen as a source of the problem.

Schools have indeed adapted to children over the last half-century. But the core processes, what we might think of as the DNA of the graded school—labeling, segregating, and eliminating those who do not fit—have largely endured in the persistent practices of testing, ability grouping, differentiated curricula, and periodic promotions.[11] By the late 1970s a coalition of practitioners, researchers, and policy makers was beginning to examine the influence of teacher expectations on learning and the influence of the principal in shaping a school's culture. This new approach, termed the effective schools movement, shifted the focus of efforts to deal with poor academic performance among low-income minorities from the child to the school.

Reformers, embracing the ideology of the effective schools movement, tried to convince school professionals that all children can learn—regardless of background—and that schools can raise individual achievement and group esteem. They argued persuasively that the school—not the classroom or the district—is the basic unit of change. Advocates of effective schools, however, seldom questioned the core structures of the graded schools within which they worked. Their passion was (and is) for making those structures more efficient.[12]

We are now in the midst of those reforms. School-based change, restructuring, and school-site management are hot phrases that few can resist. Yet the results for at-risk children seem minimal. Urban schools have been bypassed by current reforms: dropout rates continue to climb, low academic achievement persists, and measurement-driven instruction geared to minimal skills continues to gain in popularity.[13]

In saying this, I am *not* criticizing those hard-working teachers, principals, and superintendents who have created schools that expect the best from children—

and get it. Nor am I criticizing school staffs that can point with pride to the improved academic achievement of children who seldom did well in school. These staffs have, in effect, seen the problem as one of making a better school in order to make a better child, and they have made substantial contributions to the lives of their students.

At the heart of the effective schools movement, however, is the unexamined assumption that the graded school best serves all at-risk students. And efforts to shift the responsibility for change from the shoulders of at-risk children to the backs of school professionals have frequently exhausted those professionals, have often been limited to small numbers of schools, and have seldom spread throughout school systems.

The difficulty of redesign

There are several reasons why redesigning schools is so difficult. First, the acute pressure to educate all children requires efficient and inexpensive means of managing students as they move through 12 or more years of public education. The graded school has proved to be a durable mechanism for handling large numbers of children over long periods of time because it has succeeded in standardizing expectations and procedures at a fairly low cost.

Second, many citizens and educators consider the process successful. Some point to the increasing numbers of students who complete high school: three out of four today, as opposed to one out of nine a century ago. Others cite the correlation between expanded schooling in the 20th century and the nation's economic growth, high standard of living, and status as a world power. Whether or not schooling actually causes growth in wealth and power, the connections between the two are deeply embedded in our thinking. Thus there is little apparent desire and even less political will to investigate other ways to provide schooling for American children.

Except, I should add, in national emergencies. Political coalitions do arise to question the status quo when the security or economic health of the nation is threatened. Recall the Soviet gains in science and technology in the 1950s, and consider the current concern over America's loss of economic productivity and our trade deficit. In both cases, national concern about the quality of schools led to legislation, innovation, and increased funding. However, then as now, we simply assumed that the graded school would be the vehicle for improvement; it simply had to work better. Few, if any, questioned the structure or processes that were embedded in this mid-19th-century invention, and fewer still seriously considered alternatives.

Over the last 60 years, only during the civil rights movement of the 1960s have students been seen as poorly served by schools and undeserving of blame. The spillover of that movement from urban slums into affluent suburbs touched many middle-class, nonminority students. Serious questions were raised about who was teaching, about what these teachers believed about students, about what and how they taught, about how they grouped students, and about what effect that grouping had. Finally, questions were asked about the graded school itself. Alternative ways of teaching, organizing the curriculum, and structuring the school were explored and developed. Many of these alternatives persist today in special education, in Head Start, in dropout-prevention programs, in alternative schools, and in a variety of similar inventions. Many other alternatives failed to endure because of their own inadequacies; most have simply disappeared.

Alarms are sounding again about at-risk children being ill-served by schools, about low academic performance, and about high dropout rates. The current passion for restructuring schools comes from unlikely coalitions of corporate executives, foundation officials, governors, and union presidents—all of whom wish to improve schooling for at-risk children by substituting new arrangements (e.g., teacher-run schools, mentor and lead teachers, more parental choice in selecting schools) for the current ways in which schools are governed.

The reformers mean well, but they miss the target: the graded school itself and the ways in which it contributes to the very problem they seek to solve. No significant improvement will occur in the school careers of at-risk students without fundamental changes in the graded school, and current restructuring proposals will not achieve that end.

Alternatives to the graded school have slipped in and out of fashion but have never disappeared. There have always been one-room schoolhouses in isolated rural areas, but nongraded urban elementary schools have been operating since 1934. Milwaukee introduced nongraded schools in 1942. After World War II, interest in nongraded elementary schools increased. The publication of *The Nongraded Elementary School*, by John Goodlad and Robert Anderson, coincided with rapid growth in the number of schools that were trying the innovation. Between 1960 and the early 1970s nongraded elementary schools (along with a smattering of secondary schools) gained visibility as an alternative to the dominant model. Since the mid-1970s, however, nongraded schools have lapsed into obscurity.[14]

Talk of restructuring has rekindled interest in nongraded schools, grouping across age and ability, team teaching, core curricula, and cooperative learning. However, abolishing grades and changing nothing else would be simple-minded folly; grouping, teaching, and curricular practices also need to be reexamined. Such fundamental changes require endorsement, if not visible support, from the gatekeepers of change within a district: the school board and the superintendent. Such changes will also require time, and the planning and implementation must include teachers, principals, and parents.

Incremental change

What if teachers, principals, and district administrators are overwhelmed by the mere thought—much less the task—of redesigning the graded school? Or what if educators are not persuaded that the graded school is a substantial source of academic failure among at-risk students? Whether overwhelmed or unpersuaded, suppose that these very same educators are still convinced that some changes must be made within mainstream elementary and secondary schools. What can they do?

To answer these questions, practitioners would need to know whether there is sufficient knowledge available to make smaller changes that fall short of a complete redesign. They would need to know what, if any, common markers characterize those schools, programs, and classrooms that are successfully serving at-risk students.

Is there enough knowledge of this kind available to practitioners? From both the wisdom accumulated by practitioners over decades of experience and from the knowledge produced by research, enough is known to make substantial changes in schools and classrooms. Some of that wisdom is captured in the work of gifted principals and teachers who have figured out what has to be done and have done it. Some of it occasionally appears in syntheses of research aimed at lay and professional audiences, such as *Schools That Work: Educating Disadvantaged Children*, the booklet prepared by the U.S. Department of Education.[15]

However, no formulas exist as yet to explain how to put together the right combination of people, things, and ideas to create a particular setting that succeeds with at-risk students. All that is currently available is general advice: build commitment among those involved in school-based change, help practitioners strengthen their skills in working together, and remember that change should be viewed as a process rather than as a product.

What common markers characterize those successful schools, programs, and classrooms that practitioners have created for at-risk students? By *successful* I mean schools and classrooms that motivate students to complete school, that increase students' desire to learn, and that build self-esteem and enhance academic performance. Certain features of such schools and classrooms have appeared repeatedly in the research literature, and they coincide with practitioners' wisdom about what works with at-risk students.

1. *Size.* Successful programs serve as few as 50 students and seldom more than a few hundred. All adults and students know one another at some level. In secondary schools these successful programs might be schools-within-a-school or housed apart from the main building. The face-to-face contact cultivates enduring, rather than passing, relationships between old and young. Small programs are also more likely to involve students in program activities, and smaller class size permits more personalized instruction.[16]

2. *Staff.* Teachers volunteer for these programs and classes and make a commitment to educating at-risk students. Teachers develop camaraderie when they share a commitment, personal and cultural knowledge about students, and a willingness to learn from failure.[17]

3. *Program flexibility.* Because these schools and programs are small and are committed to rescuing students from what appears to be inevitable failure, they share a willingness to try different approaches. Ability grouping is uncommon; few, if any, distinctions are made among students; tests are used only to match students with appropriate materials. Passing and failing are personal benchmarks along a clearly marked road of achievable goals, not public displays in which some move ahead and others stay behind.

Time and scheduling are handled differently in these schools. Secondary teachers frequently spend more time each day with students, and the same teacher may work with a group of students for two or even three years.

Teaching is flexible, as well. Working with small groups of students and individuals is common; team teaching is widespread. The same high school teacher may teach three subjects and serve as advisor for a handful of students. In-school activity is frequently mixed with paid employment outside the school building. Finally, many of these programs link students with a wide array of social services through teachers, advisors, or special staff members. Hence, teaching is an uncommon mix of many tasks.[18]

4. *Classroom communities.* In these successful schools, the school, program, or classroom becomes a kind of extended family, and achievement and caring for one another are both important. A sense of belonging to a group—in effect, a different culture—is created as a means of increasing self-esteem and achievement. Of course, the community model exists in some special programs in regular schools, in small elementary schools, and in high school athletics, clubs, bands, drill teams, and the like. But this model tends to be rare in large schools and is

further limited by the structure of the school schedule, by ability grouping, and by a host of other factors.[19]

These features of schools, programs, and classrooms that have succeeded with at-risk children add up to teachers and administrators working together to make *what is* into *what ought to be.* They must change the size, structure, staffing, and relationships between students and adults. They must alter—dramatically and fundamentally—what occurs routinely between teachers and students.

What about individual teachers in their classrooms? There are at least three directions that teachers could take. First, research on teacher effectiveness links certain teaching practices to gains on test scores. Proponents of the approach called "direct instruction" or "active teaching," for example, claim that test scores rise when teachers of at-risk students use such an approach to teach reading and math in certain elementary grades. These research findings have frequently been wedded to larger efforts to create effective schools.[20]

Critics of direct instruction have focused on the small amount of subject matter covered; the tedious, routine work; the emphasis on test scores; the inappropriateness of the approach for secondary school subjects; and the low expectations for the teaching of reasoning and critical thinking at the elementary level. Yet, for elementary teachers concerned about the skills of their at-risk students, this research—harnessed to the folk wisdom of veteran teachers—suggests that familiar techniques of managing a class and of introducing and explaining material will pay off in rising test scores—if that is a goal.[21]

Other choices are available, as well. There are instructional approaches that build on the strengths that at-risk children bring to school. Teachers can make connections with the life experiences of students from diverse cultural groups and can exploit what we know about active learning and student involvement to develop students' reasoning skills. Such approaches enhance the home language of children and connect children's experiences with school concepts and abstract ideas.[22]

Finally, teachers can turn to the growing body of evidence that mixed-ability and mixed-age groupings within and across classrooms have positive effects on student motivation and learning. Evidence drawn from the classrooms of at-risk students regarding the benefits of nongraded early primary units, combination classes, and cooperative learning suggests that there is a technology of instruction to fit heterogeneous classrooms.[23] In order to move in this direction, teachers will need to know the cultural backgrounds and experiences of students. If they are part of a larger school effort, they will need to manage several groups of students of varied abilities during the school day.

Are schools and classrooms that embrace these approaches very different from mainstream schools, where silence, reprimands, worksheets, and uniformity dominate the school day? Indeed, they are. Does this mean more work for the principal and teacher? Indeed, it does. Will this produce deep satisfaction from overseeing student growth? Indeed, it will.

Many teachers and principals have made these kinds of changes. The work is both exhilarating and exhausting. It helps, of course, if colleagues share similar aims for improving classrooms. It is far better if the principal endorses such classroom changes and provides material and emotional support. Even better is the situation in which the district office, the superintendent, and the school board not only endorse, but actively nourish, such schools and classrooms. Going it alone is tough but not impossible. Others have done it, but they have paid a high price. The rewards are intensely personal and sharply felt, and they last a lifetime. There is, then, a tiny window of opportunity open to teachers and principals who, unaided by state and district policy makers, nonetheless wish to improve the lives of at-risk children.

How sad it is, though, that so much rhetoric about fundamental change has produced so little energy for redesigning the graded school. The message I must close with has often been conveyed by well-intentioned citizens and educators: in the absence of fundamental reform, teachers and principals who desire genuine reform will have to go the extra mile.

The larger issue and my central point, however, is this: the basic design of the graded school has trapped both staff members and at-risk students in a web of shared failure. We must reexamine the institution of the graded school and determine the degree to which *it* is the source of high rates of academic failure among at-risk students. The popular understanding of the problem, which locates the source of failure within the children and their families, is bankrupt. There is, after all, no worse lie than a problem poorly stated.

Notes

1 Georges Bernanos, *Last Essays of Georges Bernanos* (Chicago: Henry Regnery Co., 1955), p. 153.
2 Emerson Palmer, *The New York Public School: Being a History of Free Education in the City of New York* (New York: Macmillan, 1905), p. 19.
3 *Forty-Fourth Annual Report of the Board of Education* (Chicago: Public Schools of the City of Chicago, 1898), p. 170.
4 James B. Conant, *Slums and Suburbs* (New York: McGraw-Hill, 1961), p. 2.
5 Stanley Zehm, "Educational Misfits: A Study of Poor Performers in the English Class, 1825–1925" (Doctoral dissertation, Stanford University, 1973).
6 For early evidence of the connection between the graded school and dropouts, see William T. Harris, "The Early Withdrawal of Pupils from School: Its Causes and Its Remedies," *Addresses and Journal of Proceedings, National Educational Association* (Peoria, Ill.: N.C. Nason, 1873), p. 266; and E. E. White, "Several Problems in Graded School Management," *Addresses and Journal of Proceedings, National Educational Association* (Worcester, Mass.: Charles Hamilton, 1874), p. 34.
7 Elisabeth Irwin and Louis Marks, *Fitting the School to the Child* (New York: Macmillan, 1924), p. 70.
8 Seymour Sarason and John Doris, *Educational Handicap, Public Policy, and Social History* (New York: Free Press, 1979), pp. 296–354.
9 Jane Mercer, *Labeling the Mentally Retarded* (Berkeley: University of California Press, 1973).
10 Russell W. Rumberger, "High School Dropouts: A Review of Issues and Evidence," *Review of Educational Research*, Summer 1987, p. 101. For examples of the literature that connects school processes to dropping out, see Michelle Fine, "Why Urban Adolescents Drop Into and Out of Public High School," in Gary Natriello, ed., *School Dropouts* (New York: Teachers College Press, 1987), pp. 89–105; and Gary Wehlage and Robert Rutter, "Dropping Out: How Much Do Schools Contribute to the Problem?" in Natriello, pp. 70–88.
11 For a discussion of the persistence of 19th-century policies and practices, see John Goodlad and Robert Anderson, *The Nongraded Elementary School* (New York: Harcourt, Brace and World, 1963), Chs. 1, 2.
12 See, for example, Kenneth Clark, *Dark Ghetto: Dilemmas of Social Power* (New York: Harper & Row, 1964); and Ronald Edmonds, "Effective Schools for the Urban Poor," *Educational Leadership*, October 1979, pp. 15–24.
13 *An Imperiled Generation: Saving Urban Schools* (Princeton, N.J.: Carnegie Foundation for the Advancement of Teaching, 1988).

14 See, for example, Charles Silberman, *Crisis in the Classroom* (New York: Random House, 1971); and Goodlad and Anderson, op. cit.
15 U.S. Department of Education, *Schools That Work: Educating Disadvantaged Children* (Washington, D.C.: U.S. Government Printing Office, 1987). See also Ken Macrorie, *20 Teachers* (New York: Oxford University Press, 1984).
16 *An Imperiled Generation . . .*, pp. 21–24.
17 See Shirley Brice Heath, *Ways with Words* (New York: Cambridge University Press, 1983); and Mary Anne Raywid, "Drawing Educators to Choice," *Metropolitan Education*, Fall 1987, pp. 7–23.
18 U.S. Department of Education, *Dealing with Dropouts* (Washington, D.C.: Office of Educational Research and Improvement, 1987); and *An Imperiled Generation . . .*, pp. 24–33.
19 James Comer, *School Power* (New York: Free Press, 1980); idem, "Home-School Relationships as They Affect the Academic Success of Children," *Education and Urban Society*, vol. 16, 1984, pp. 323–37; Peggy Farber, "Central Park East: High School with a Human Face," *Rethinking Schools*, May/June 1988, pp. 6–7; and Lisbeth Schorr, *Within Our Reach* (New York: Anchor Press, 1988), pp. 241–45.
20 Jere Brophy and Thomas Good, "Teacher Behavior and Student Achievement," in Merlin Wittrock, ed., *Handbook of Research on Teaching* (New York: Macmillan, 1986), pp. 328–75.
21 Ibid.
22 James Banks, "Ethnicity, Class, and Cognitive Styles: Research and Teaching Implications," paper presented at the annual meeting of the American Educational Research Association, Washington, D.C., 1987; and Kathryn Au, "Participation Structures in a Reading Lesson with Hawaiian Children: Analysis of a Culturally Appropriate Instructional Event," *Anthropology and Education Quarterly*, vol. 11, 1980, pp. 91–115.
23 Robert Slavin, *Cooperative Learning* (New York: Longman, 1983); and Gaea Leinhardt and William Bickel, "Instruction's the Thing Wherein to Catch the Mind That Falls Behind," *Educational Psychologist*, vol. 22, 1987, pp. 177–207.

PART 3

ACTIONS TO POLICY

CHAPTER 12

POLITICS, THE COURTS, AND EDUCATIONAL POLICY (1973)

Donna E. Shalala and James A. Kelly

Over the past two decades, race, religion, and the allocation of public money for education have reshaped the politics of education. In all three areas particular interest groups have pressed for unambiguous definitions of "equality of opportunity" especially as the phrase is realized in American public school systems. For each public policy issue—school desegregation and busing, public financing of parochial and nonpublic schools, and the growing awareness that our system of educational finance promotes a maximal separation between resources and areas of greatest educational need—most of the political conflict has been over the definition and, more painfully, the application of that phrase.

It is not surprising, therefore, that the courts have become increasingly a major focus for interest groups concerned with education. Consequently, any analysis of the current status of educational politics must focus in large part on past and present judicial activity affecting education.

School desegregation

In the 1954 *Brown v. Board of Education*[1] case, the United States Supreme Court ruled that a child's constitutional right to equal protection of the laws under the Fourteenth Amendment was denied when a state-supported school system required the child to attend racially segregated schools.[2] Nineteen years after this decision, which overturned the prevailing "separate but equal" doctrine, the controversy over segregation persists and has been inflamed by the issue of busing to achieve racial balance.

Until 1964 the Court's ruling was slowly enforced by private civil rights lawyers, chiefly in the South, with financial and technical assistance from the NAACP Legal Defense Fund. The Civil Rights Act of 1964 assigned the federal government the responsibility to bring about school desegregation. Under Title IV, Title VI, and Title IX, that act offered the federal government three means of accomplishing elimination of the dual school system and other educational discriminations based on race, color, or national origin.

Title IV allowed the Department of Justice to file suits in federal courts upon receipt of a parent's complaint alleging discrimination against his children in local schools. It also authorized the Department of Health, Education, and Welfare to provide technical assistance to desegregating school systems upon the request of local school officials. Title VI forbade the use of federal funds for any program or activity which discriminated on the basis of race, color, or national origin. Title IX empowered the Justice Department to intervene in school desegregation suits on the side of the aggrieved plaintiffs.

By the time the Democrats left office in January 1969, all three of these school desegregation tools of the Civil Rights Act of 1964 had been thoroughly developed and put to work. Used by HEW, Title VI proved most effective. The desegregation plans HEW required of former dual school systems if they were to be eligible for federal funds caused significant desegregation, particularly in rural areas and small cities of the South.

The Justice Department used its Title IV authority against the most recalcitrant school systems, also located chiefly in southern rural areas. Federal action was not so urgently needed in southern cities. Nonetheless, under Title IX of the 1964 Civil Rights Act, the Justice Department could intervene in suits brought by private parties. On a number of occasions the Justice Department did enter cases on the side of the Legal Defense Fund and other civil rights attorneys.

Beginning in the 1966–67 school year, HEW issued successive guidelines under Title VI. These guidelines required local school systems to submit voluntary desegregation plans as a prerequisite for federal funding and outlined yearly steps whereby the plans would abolish the dual school system. At first HEW required progressive yearly performance under free-choice desegregation plans. Early in 1968, the Department required the submission of complete or terminal plans to eliminate totally the dual school structure by September 1969, or, given certain unique conditions, September 1970, at the latest. While HEW was requesting and negotiating terminal plans for most school systems, it was moving against systems that refused to make such commitments by using the administrative enforcement process of Title VI, which could result in termination of federal funds. In other words, to back its requirements, HEW invoked the sanction of the federal purse.

This process of clear policy requirements, negotiation, and the use of available sanctions was carefully developed. Consistently, though not without controversy, it brought positive results. With few exceptions the entire process was almost completely removed from the political crosscurrents of the White House, the Cabinet, and Congress.

Under the administration of President Nixon the desegregation situation changed dramatically. During its first year in office the Republican administration hesitantly followed the earlier pattern. While student desegregation took a large statistical jump by 1970, the increase was largely the result of Legal Defense Fund success in several big-city school desegregation suits and of earlier plans enforced by HEW. By 1972, Title VI enforcement was nearly dormant, the Justice Department had ceased filing desegregation suits on behalf of minority students, and almost no technical assistance to local school systems was forthcoming from HEW. More important, the issue of busing had been pushed into the political arena by the President himself. Siding with the opponents of busing, he ordered administration officials to cut off funds for any such program. The strategy of the administration, seen in a series of management decisions and the passage of additional special aid programs to areas which faced the implementation of desegregation plans, has been to shift the responsibility for desegregation from the Executive branch (i.e., HEW jurisdiction) to the "neutral courts." This shift allowed the Executive branch to lead the attack against busing and court requirements. By switching the focus to the courts, the administration could fix responsibility for controlling the courts in school desegregation cases on the Democratic Congress.

The 1954 *Brown* decision of the U.S. Supreme Court and the subsequent federal court actions implementing that opinion represent, by any standards, an intervention of historic proportions in the status quo of American education. Twenty years of passionate attempts by southern blacks and liberal whites to desegregate schools are paying dividends in the South, but outside the South there are more segregated classrooms today than in 1954.

Since that decision, the courts have become more and more enmeshed in education policy. By developing new constitutional theories as well as carefully monitoring existing statutes, activist lawyers generate new court cases even before prior rulings have been fully implemented. The difficulties of translating the *Brown* decision into specific plans for desegregation are being encountered anew in efforts to reform school financing systems consonant with new judicial decisions, such as California's landmark case, *Serrano v. Priest*.[3] Although resolving these problems in specific terms is partly a political function, it will also involve careful judicial scrutiny of legislative and administrative action to ensure that new financing plans are fully compatible with constitutional principles.

The racial politics of education since 1954 has thus been dominated by federal court decisions, federal administrative and legislative action, and at the local level, by persistent conflict as school boards and administrators struggle between the frequently contradictory thrusts of court orders and community conservatism. States—the legal locus of authority to establish education policy—have been strangely by-passed in this federal-local action and with only a few exceptions have taken no initiative to become involved directly. The complexity of education politics is nowhere better illustrated than by the dominance of federal initiative and absence of state involvement in the most emotionally intensive local education issue of the past twenty years.

Church and state in education

Another issue in which court action has significantly affected the politics of education is public aid to parochial schools. For the past twenty years this issue has been the major focus of the perennial church-state debate. The political history of efforts to obtain tax-raised funds for religious schools largely chronicles attempts to evade prohibitions of state and federal constitutions.

Other issues have occasionally surfaced. A constitutional school prayer amendment was vigorously debated in Congress in the early seventies but failed to get the necessary two-thirds majority. The Tennessee legislature in early 1973 was embroiled again in the issues of the Scopes trial, recast as a proposal to include both the Biblical and evolutionary theories of human origins in school curricula. In 1972 California was thrashing about in a similar conflict.

The controversy over federal aid to parochial schools was in part resolved during the maneuverings that surrounded passage of the federal Elementary and Secondary Education Act of 1965. The device primarily responsible for the enactment of ESEA in 1965 was the so-called child benefit theory. According to this principle, aid would be provided directly to poor and educationally deprived children enrolled in both public and nonpublic schools. Both the National Catholic Welfare Conference, which had long opposed federal school aid without some aid to parochial schools, and the National Education Association, which had long opposed aid to parochial schools, accepted the child benefit concept. On its face, there was nothing unconstitutional in ESEA. It did not explicitly mention schools or church institutions. However, the act's legislative history clearly demonstrates that Congress intended parochial schools to become beneficiaries of aid, and this intent gave ESEA the votes of legislators with Catholic constituencies.

Since ESEA's passage in 1965, numerous disputes have arisen over its constitutionality, and again the courts intervened with widespread effects on the politics of education. The most important court test came in 1966 in *Flast v. Cohen*,[4] a suit brought by New York City's United Parents Association, the New York Civil Liberties Union, the United Federation of Teachers, and the American Jewish Congress. The defendants named in the suit were the Secretary of Health, Education, and Welfare and the United States Commissioner of Education.

Predictably, religious and sectarian school interests strenuously opposed the suit. The federal government moved to dismiss the complaint on the grounds that the plaintiffs, suing as taxpayers, did not have standing to challenge the legality of the expenditures of federal funds. The Supreme Court, ruling only on the issue of the litigants' standing, voted 8–1 in favor of the plaintiffs. The Court held that federal taxpayers have the right to initiate a suit in a federal court challenging the expenditures of federal funds to sectarian schools on the ground that such institutions violate the establishment clause of the First Amendment. A special three-judge panel was directed to hear the substance of the suit. The sponsors of *Flast* are currently investigating alleged misuse of Title I funds across the country, but have not yet decided when to move on the case.

Since the passage of ESEA, other Congressional activity in the field of education has reawakened the church-state controversy. A school prayer constitutional amendment was defeated in 1971, as mentioned above. Tax credit legislation was introduced in 1972 which would allow a credit against individual income taxes for tuition paid toward the elementary or secondary education of dependents. Although the legislation has the powerful support of Representative Wilbur Mills in the House, it is doubtful such a bill could pass the Senate.

Nonpublic schools and the state

Early attempts to gain state aid for nonpublic schools by incorporating parochial schools into a public school system were declared unconstitutional. Later, however, demands in many states for free textbooks, bus transportation, free lunches, and other welfare services for nonpublic school children were granted. Until the decade of the sixties, parochial school interests had not sought direct public aid in view of state constitutional and Supreme Court rulings. They have actively lobbied for such support in the last ten years. Since 1968, twenty-seven statutes in thirteen states have awarded public aid to parochial and other nonpublic schools. Of these "parochaid" measures, thirteen have since been nullified by repeal, court action, popular referenda, or replacement. The remaining fourteen laws are being challenged in the courts; several cases are pending with the U.S. Supreme Court.

The Supreme Court has handed down decisions in two major cases involving parochaid to primary and secondary education. In June 1971, ruling on *Lemon v. Kurtzman*[5] and *Earley v. DiCenso*,[6] the Court held that Pennsylvania in the former case and Rhode Island in the latter had unconstitutional laws which allowed special kinds of aid to parochial schools. Despite a series of unfavourable rulings from the courts, New York State has continued to seek ways to use public funds for parochial schools.[7] Interestingly, despite the fact that many parochaid measures have been passed by state legislatures, voters have consistently opposed them when given the opportunity to do so. Thus, for example, in 1967, New York voters defeated a proposed comprehensive revision of the state's constitution primarily because it would have repealed specific language prohibiting state aid to religious institutions, substituting the general language of the First Amendment.[8] In 1970, Michigan voters approved a constitutional amendment that comprehensively prohibited numerous means of promoting state aid to sectarian schools.[9] In 1972 statutes favorable to the parochaid concept were defeated by referenda in Maryland, Idaho, and Oregon.

States have thus been drawn much more directly into the church-state politics of education than they were in the area of school desegregation. In church-state relations, federal courts define the basic rules of the game even more definitely than in school desegregation, but unlike the desegregation area, interest groups have focused more of their energies on the state than on the local level. State legislatures have repeatedly responded to pleas for aid to parochial schools only to have plan after plan struck down as unconstitutional by federal courts. Parochial school advocates and legislators may soon exhaust their supply of new, possibly constitutional wrinkles on old, already unconstitutional arrangements. If this is so, the 1970s may witness a gradual diminution of state legislative activity with continuing attention to judicial determinations of whether and in what ways localities either may or must channel to nonpublic schools some part of their federal aid.

The political economy of education

In addition to race and religion, economic issues are becoming increasingly enmeshed in the politics of education. The metropolitanization process—the movement of people and economic activities from city to suburb—current local, state, and federal educational finance policies, and social-science research on educational finance and related issues have all shaped the politics of education. The implications of each can be seen by examining recent trends in six aspects of the fiscal politics of education.

Schools and general politics

The first trend indicates that the politics of education, never actually separate from politics at large, is being clearly drawn into general politics by the growing competition for scarce public resources. Between 1960 and 1970, school expenditures more than doubled, increasing from $16.8 billion to $42.4 billion, a rise of 153 percent.[10] During the same period, pupil enrollment increased by only 30 percent.[11] Similarly, between 1960 and 1970, GNP increased at an average annual rate of 7.0 percent, while school expenditures rose at an average rate of 9.8 percent.

Expenditures for other public sector activities such as highways, welfare, health, national defense, and higher education have also risen rapidly. In reality, schools compete with all other agencies of government for public money. This competition may be seen in battles over tax rates between the private and public sectors of the economy, between educational and noneducational activities in the public sector, and between public schools and institutions of higher education. Despite a facade of separate financing, schools compete with other governmental agencies for public dollars through a process which throws education into general politics.

Troubling implications emerge as one watches school systems compete for dollars. In half of the nation's urban school districts (those that are fiscally "dependent"), mayors and city councils increasingly exercise their authority to control school budgets on a line-by-line basis. In other large school districts and virtually all nonurban districts, the requirement that school taxes (unlike other taxes) can be increased only by referendum makes schools particularly vulnerable to general taxpayer resistance. In California, 60 percent of school tax and bond elections were defeated in 1971. In 1971–72, over half of the school bond issues submitted in the nation were defeated.

Within large cities, black populations frequently support higher school taxes, reflecting an unquenched faith that somehow schools can help children toward a better life; simultaneously, large numbers of whites oppose increases in school taxes, no doubt reflecting both antiblack "backlash" sentiments as well as the growing *proportion* of urban white children who attend nonpublic schools (many white public school families having departed for nearby suburbs). Urban public schools are thus peculiarly dependent for local political support on the steadily growing nonwhite proportion of urban populations, a condition that exacerbates the traditional weakness of city schools in state legislative appropriations battles. Rural and suburban legislators seem even less likely to aid predominantly non-white urban schools than they were to aid the mostly white schools of ten or twenty years ago.

Teachers' organizations

The emergence of teachers' organizations as a potent political force is a second fiscal trend in the politics of education. Long organized into politically passive professional associations, teachers have come to an extraordinary realization of the potential power of teachers' organizations, particularly regarding educational finance. The beginning of this trend was signalled by the United Federation of Teachers under Albert Shanker, who successfully bargained collectively with the New York City Board of Education in the mid-1960s. Suddenly blossoming as the largest local in the AFL-CIO, the UFT captured the imagination of young and aggressive teachers across the nation whose orientation toward leadership and politics had been conditioned more by the activism of the civil rights movement than by the traditional low-keyed norms of professionalism. By 1973 approximately thirty-five states required local boards of education to bargain with teachers' organizations. Of those states all but California mandated exclusive bargaining with one teacher organization. In a remarkably short time, that once sleepy giant, the NEA, abandoned its previously iron-clad prohibitions against strikes and collective bargaining. Although teacher strikes are permitted by law in only three states (Hawaii, Pennsylvania, and Vermont), teachers in impressively large numbers have accepted the "work stoppage" as a legitimate, if ultimate, weapon in the annual war of nerves called collective bargaining.

Confronted by this united phalanx of teachers, the influence of school boards over education policy has waned. At first boards appeared willing to agree to *any* financial settlement in order to avoid strikes. Several large-city boards, and boards in some smaller districts in Michigan, signed contracts promising salary increases for which there was no revenue. Legislatures, city councils, and voters were asked *ex post facto* to bail out the school boards by providing the needed revenue. In a few cases, banks loaned boards money to keep schools open, but in many instances school boards lacked the administrative will and the fiscal means to cope with the teachers at the bargaining table. Teachers quickly learned to bypass school boards, dealing directly with mayors and even governors to work out settlements.

Early teacher bargaining dealt primarily with salaries and fringe benefits, but in recent years teacher organizations appear equally interested in working conditions and nonfiscal education policy.

While boards were clearly on the defensive in their negotiations during the late 1960s, they will vigorously resist further erosion of their management powers through collective bargaining. In this regard their hand is strategically strengthened by the oversupply of teachers; many boards are simply inundated with teacher applications, a condition likely to give pause to untenured teachers. One should not underestimate, however, the achievement of teachers during the past years in wresting from boards and administrators a hefty share of their power over local resource management.

School boards

A brief review of the historical evolution of school boards suggests that their waning power over fiscal policy is not a new trend and has deeper roots than recent collective bargaining trends. Significant changes in the functions and powers of school boards have accompanied a decline—100,000 to 15,000—in the number of school districts since 1930. One hundred years ago, school board members were elected by relatively small constituencies. Elections were typically structured so that board members represented particular precincts or wards within a school district, rather than representing all citizens in an at-large capacity. School board members themselves made most of the decisions necessary to operate the schools, including the purchase of supplies, the selection and promotion of school personnel, the setting of curriculum standards and content, and the legal inspection of schools. Before the development of administrative staffs and personnel tenure policies, individual school board members wielded great authority over the most trivial aspects of school operation.

In the late nineteenth and early twentieth centuries, it became common for school boards to employ professional administrators who handled many of the detailed operations previously supervised exclusively by board members. During this period school boards transferred much of their executive power to school administrators and teachers. For their part, both administrators and teachers were not loathe to seek tenured job security and less "political interference" in the conduct of school affairs.

As the number of school districts declined, local boards of education and superintendents found that their decision-making powers were giving way to an increasing body of regulation and law developed by other governmental agencies. State education codes became a thicket of detailed stipulations that today impede local decision-making discretion. More than twenty major federal programs of assistance to public schools contain their own specific guidelines and requirements which local districts must meet in order to participate in the federal program. After the Supreme Court's 1954 desegregation decision, courts played an increasingly important role in setting educational policy—thus further diminishing the discretionary authority of boards. The California State Supreme Court's *Serrano* decision in 1971 declared unconstitutional school finance plans in which local wealth is allowed to determine school expenditures, a decision likely to enhance state initiative and influence in the 1970s. State restrictions on school district personnel and expenditure policies continue to expand in volume and specificity, while municipal police powers further restrict the local school board. Beyond these legal and quasi-legal factors, socioeconomic conditions and the nature of the local school district's revenue structure severely reduce alternatives for action. As much as three-fourths of the variance in educational expenditures among local school districts can be explained by measures of community socioeconomic differences alone, ignoring local board of education policies.

Today local boards respond to initiatives from teachers, administrators, courts, and legislatures, but spend much of their time performing routine institutional maintenance functions such as paying bills. Occasionally, they must adjudicate disputes, but the old adage that "boards make policy" is now more anachronistic than accurate.

Government and Congress in education

The federal government and the Congress are a third source of influence over the politics of education. At last count, no fewer than forty-two departments, agencies, and bureaus of the executive branch of the federal government administer about 111 different educational programs. Many of these programs became law during the presidency of Lyndon Johnson, when over sixty education bills were passed by the Congress in less than four years.

The most visible federal agency for educational programs is obviously the United States Office of Education. Shaken up vigorously by the legislative spasms of the Great Society, as well as the personal leadership of Commissioners Francis Keppel and Harold Howe, USOE has now settled back into more comfortable bureaucratic routines of program administration. USOE continues to enjoy the most intimate cooperation with state and local education agencies. Many permanent USOE staff members are civil servants who have neither formal training nor experience in education, but who have pretty much been running the store during the past four years. Many key jobs have been vacant for months—some for two years.

Both the federal politics and administration of education are fractionated along program lines. USOE itself administers several key programs, such as ESEA, vocational education, National Defense Education Act, special education, and P.L. 874. But other federal programs are administered outside USOE, including the new National Institute of Education, Job Corps, Head Start, Vista, Manpower Development Training Programs, Neighborhood Youth Corps, and daycare efforts. Further fractionation is observed among federal, state, and local levels as federal dollars agonizingly trickle down through layers of stolid bureaucracy in state education departments and local school districts.

Similarly, the Congress' ability to generate coordinated responses to educational problems also suffers from fragmentation of structure. Consider for a moment the substantive committees in the House of Representatives that pass upon education legislation: Education and Labor, Agriculture (school lunch program), Veterans' Affairs (G.I. Bill of Rights), and District of Columbia (the *real* school board of Washington, D.C.). Of course, bills from these committees are considered by the House only after being scheduled for floor consideration by the Rules Committee. Money is appropriated separately through the Appropriations Committee, which in turn depends partially on the Ways and Means Committee to raise the taxes needed for its appropriations. The dependence of the entire process on tax policy is particularly relevant in a period like the past decade when Congress has been cutting tax rates.

Structural fragmentation is not the only problem. Congressional leadership and composition frequently do not reflect the increasingly metropolitan character of the American population. Five of the seven House committees named above are chaired by representatives whose congressional district does not contain a city of 250,000 people or more. The chairman of the Education and Labor Committee, Carl Perkins, represents a predominantly rural area of Kentucky; Ashland, the largest town in his district, had a population of 29,245 in 1970. In the 91st Congress, the eighteen Senators from the nine least populous states represented only 2 percent of the American people, but the eighteen Senators from the nine most populous states represented 52 percent of the American people—graphic evidence of urban under-representation.[12]

The political pressures that move the Congress and Executive to action in education are programmatically focused. Vocational and special education, for example, have clearly defined constituencies that are effectively organized for lobbying in state and national capitals. Representatives of the special education and vocational education interests long ago cemented linkages to their respective bureaus within USOE and with counterpart bureaus in almost every state department of education. Such programmatic special interests have their champions on Capitol Hill, where key members of committees in both houses are long-established friends of these interests.

The constituents for vocational and special education are parents and educators. Parents of handicapped children are obviously difficult constituents for legislators to oppose; organized labor and large corporations alike are directly interested in the legislative success of vocational education programs. These constituencies may not be formally organized at the local level, but each has effective ties to special interest groups in state capitols and in Washington and remain in close communication with state and federal executive and legislative branches.

This state of affairs contrasts sharply with the chaotic relationships between the federal government and urban school districts *per se*. Large city districts must often bypass their state educational agencies and deal directly with Washington, but no effective coalition representing urban education interests exists in Washington. Effective liaison in behalf of urban education legislation is seldom observed among national organizations with urban orientations such as the Great Cities Research Council, the American Federation of Teachers, the Association of Large City School Boards, the superintendents of schools in cities over 300,000 in population, and the urban-based elements within the NEA family of organizations. The Emergency Committee for Full Funding of Education Laws, the most successful Washington lobbying effort by educators in recent years, placed greater priority on obtaining P.L. 874 funds than on shifting funds into programs such as Title I of the ESEA, which speaks directly to urban needs. This is understandable, for the real lobbying "muscle" of the Emergency Committee came initially from the well-disciplined P.L. 874 lobby, called by former HEW secretary Wilbur Cohen the most effective single lobby facing HEW.

Uses and misuses of social science

New patterns have recently emerged in the use of social-science research to formulate and rationalize education policies, and the politics of education has been correspondingly affected. The "Coleman Report" electrified the politics of education.[13] Coleman concluded that measures of social class and home environment were so closely correlated with school achievement scores that, once this correlation had been estimated, measures of schooling (e.g., libraries, expenditures, class size) were almost uncorrelated with achievement scores. This finding was itself debatable on grounds of data validity, sampling representativeness, and statistical procedure. But social scientists were disturbed by the gross misinterpretation of Coleman by politicians and journalists. Coleman's work has been perverted to mean that "schools make no difference," yet he did not ask whether, for example, the 90 percent of eighth graders who can read and count were helped by schools. He asked merely what differences exist *among eighth graders*, and concluded that social background appears to be a more important factor than schooling in determining those differences.

A distinction must thus be drawn between scientific and popular interpretations of Coleman. The politics of education since 1966 has been deeply influenced by the popular version. Daniel P. Moynihan, for one, mistook journalistic misinterpretations of Coleman for scientific fact. His view that further spending on schools is futile rested on his failure to recognize what Coleman did and did not study. But when Moynihan became counselor to the President in 1969, his views became national policy. The Nixon administration has steadfastly clung to this patently oversimplified policy. Veto after veto cut back Congressional spending bills in education. The policy won its most recent "vindication" from Jencks's recent press-release excursion into the effects of education on lifetime earnings.

The only cracks in the Nixon policy have been observed in connection with the President's Emergency School Assistance Act. At one point in the lengthy process of securing passage of this legislation and renewal of ESEA, HEW reversed engines and argued that schools *would* make a difference if only federal "compensatory" moneys totalled $300 per pupil per year!

The sorry history of policy interpretations of "Colemanesque" studies reveals serious flaws in the process—necessarily political—by which policy-makers learn of the various fields of knowledge (e.g., learning psychology or the economics of education) useful to the practice of education. Institutions such as the National Institute of Education, the Social Science Research Council, the American Educational Research Association, and the National Academy of Education, as well as the NEA and AFT, should apply their considerable resources to the urgent problem of helping policy-makers to distinguish fact from myth in educational research.

Courts and educational policies

It is difficult to exaggerate the growing importance of judicial action to educational politics in general. The most prominent current example of court influences is the school finance cases based on the *Serrano* prototype now in litigation in about forty states. These cases, where successful, will draw governors and legislators into a re-examination not only of educational policy but of the state's overall tax structure. Governors in many states now hold education financing as a pressing priority: Thomas L. McCall in Oregon, William G. Milliken in Michigan, Rubin Askew in Florida, William T. Cahill in New Jersey, and Wendell Anderson in Minnesota are leading recent examples. Although major legislative changes in school financing do not yet present definite patterns, it can be said that most plans call for state takeover or tighter control of the property tax, coupled with more stringent state restrictions on the salary and expenditure discretion of local districts.

There is much reason to believe that courts are still only at the threshold of defining educational rights. In a number of settings courts have held that each child has the same rights vis-à-vis public schools as every other child. But the courts and education authorities have only begun to define the criteria by which to determine whether the education offered to one child is qualitatively the same as that offered to another.

Moreover, the United States Supreme Court recently dealt the concept of equal educational opportunity under the federal Constitution a blow of uncertain proportions. In its decision in *San Antonio Independent School District v. Rodriguez*,[14] the Court ruled that a child's right to public education is not a "fundamental (federal) right" under the Fourteenth Amendment. While the Court then ruled that the school finance arrangements in Texas did not violate the Fourteenth Amendment of the Constitution, it suggested the possibility that numerous states had constitutions which explicitly guaranteed a child's right to an education.

As if responding to this cue, just two weeks after *Rodriguez*, the New Jersey Supreme Court, in *Robinson v. Cahill*,[15] struck down the state's school financing statutes on the ground that they failed to meet the state constitutional requirement of a "thorough and efficient system of free public schools for all the children in the State."

Judicial recognition that children have an enforceable state constitutional right to a certain qualitative standard of education has potential implications that extend far beyond the politics of public education, ultimately affecting state-local tax structures and the quality of education in the classroom. The implications of *Robinson* also extend beyond the geographic confines of New Jersey because thirty-eight other states have constitutional provisions which prescribe a required quantum of education. Many of these provisions are comparable to New Jersey's "thorough and efficient" clause.

The current legal issues ultimately query educational outcomes—what should students gain from their education? A set of related issues bears directly on the politics of education. These are process rather than outcome issues; they ask *how* educational decisions are made. Student rights in various permutations have been widely litigated. Students, it turns out, are citizens after all, and have taken an increasingly energetic part in the politics of education, especially at the local level. A second process issue—the openness of educational decision-making—is just beginning to emerge as crucial, partly through legal action to assure parental access to pupils' records. Other types of information, such as achievement test scores, are being made public more frequently. Heightened consumer awareness in other settings contributes to the new sensitivity of parents and students to the accuracy and availability of information. As more data become public, increased political attention too is drawn to the successes and failures of the educational system.

This growing importance of judicial rulings in educational policy-making is neglected in most major schools of education. University programs which prepare educational leaders concentrate heavily on administrative politics, occasionally on legislative politics, but almost never on the crucial role of the courts in shaping educational policies. Those who would understand the politics of education in the 1970s and who care about the realization of equality of opportunity will necessarily focus much of their attention on the judicial politics of education.

Notes

1 *Brown v. Board of Education*, 347 U.S. 483 (1954).
2 This entire section draws on a series of interviews with Cynthia Brown, senior research associate, Washington Research Project, Washington, D.C., June 1973.

3   *Serrano v. Priest*, 5 Cal. 3d 584, 96 Cal. Rptr. 601, 487 P.2d 1241 (1971).
4   *Flast v. Cohen*, 392 U.S. 83 (1968).
5   *Lemon v. Kurtzman*, 403 U.S. 602 (1971).
6   *Earley v. DiCenso*, 403 U.S. 602 (1971).
7   In January 1972, in *Committee for Public Education and Religious Liberty et al. v. Levitt et al.*, a three-judge panel, relying on the *Lemon* case, ruled that the New York State legislature's Secular Education Services Act was unconstitutional. A second piece of legislation passed in 1970 (Mandated Services Act) was ruled unconstitutional in April 1972 by a three-judge panel.
8   Donna E. Shalala. *The City and the Constitution*. New York: National Municipal League, 1972.
9   *The New York Times*, November 8, 1970, p. 56.
10   National Education Association. *Estimates of School Statistics 1970–71*. Washington, D.C., 1970, p. 19.
11   *Ibid.*, p. 8.
12   Bureau of the Census. *General Population Characteristics, 1970*, Final Report, United States Summary. Washington, D.C.: U.S. Department of Commerce, 1970.
13   James S. Coleman et al. *Equality of Educational Opportunity*. Washington, D.C.: United States Government Printing Office, 1966.
14   *Rodriguez v. San Antonio Independent School District*, Civil Action 68-175-SA, U.S. District Court, Western District of Texas, San Antonio Division (1971).
15   *Robinson v. Cahill*. Docket L-18704-69, Superior Court of New Jersey, Hudson County (1972), Appendix A.

CHAPTER 13

POLICY ISSUES IN MULTICULTURAL EDUCATION IN THE UNITED STATES (1979)

Gwendolyn C. Baker

Clarifying the concept

The beginnings of multicultural education can be traced to the founding of this nation. However, the development of what is known today as multicultural education has occurred during the last ten to fifteen years. A review of the literature of the early 1960s finds educators making references to "diversity," "cultural pluralism," and "ethnic content." Much of what was contributed to the exploration of these terms was confined to what was needed—i.e., change in teacher attitudes, curriculum, and textbook selection. Little was articulated that precisely gave direction and definition to specific concepts and/or approaches that could be applied to educational practice. The discussions that surrounded "ethnic content" in the curricula of schools tended to be limited to the study of Blacks, Mexican Americans, Native Americans, and Asians. During the middle part of the sixties, the literature began to reflect the terms "ethnic minority education," "ethnic education," and to a lesser degree "multicultural education." However, by the early seventies, "ethnic studies," "ethnic education," and "multiethnic education" were popular in the literature and had become acceptable terminology with reference to the inclusion of ethnic content into existing school curricula. Perhaps the most exciting publication on ethnic studies and ethnic education at that time was the January 1972 issue of *Phi Delta Kappan*, (vol. 53, no. 5), on *The Imperatives of Ethnic Education*, edited by James A. Banks. The authors who contributed to this publication used a myriad of terms, all implying basically the study of the history of ethnic groups in the United States.

To this writer, multiethnic education, in 1972, implied the utilization of a multiethnic approach to the curriculum. This approach was defined as a method of teaching that integrated into all aspects of the curriculum the influences and contributions of Black, Indian, Japanese, Jewish, and Mexican American culture to the culture of American society.[1] This approach means planning and organizing the learning experiences for children in the classroom so that these experiences reflect cultural diversity. This and similar definitions, in addition to what was implied in analogous terms, laid the foundation for what multicultural education means in this current discussion.

Jack Forbes can be credited as being one of the pioneers in the usage of the term "multicultural education." His 1969 publication entitled *The Education of the Culturally Different: A Multicultural Approach* (Berkeley, Ca.: Far West Laboratory for Educational Research and Development) was recognized as one of the most explicit contributions to the concept. In 1972, the American Association for Colleges of Teacher Education (AACTE), through its newly formed Commission on Multicultural Education, adopted a statement on multicultural education which has served as the foundation for much of the work in the area of teacher education. The official statement, *No One Model American*, is extended but for the purposes of analyses the introductory paragraph is cited:

> Multicultural education is education which values cultural pluralism. Multicultural education rejects the view that schools should seek to melt away cultural differences or the view that schools should merely tolerate cultural pluralism. Instead, multicultural education affirms that schools should be oriented toward the cultural enrichment of all children and youth through programs rooted to the preservation and extension of cultural diversity as a fact of life in American society, and it affirms that this cultural diversity is a valuable resource that should be preserved and extended. It affirms that major education institutions should strive to preserve and enhance cultural pluralism.[2]

It is not difficult to see that the intent from this broad perspective includes all children and speaks to cultural differences, not just to ethnic content. As the statement continues, it incorporates the encouragement of multiculturalism, multilingualism, and multidialectism.[3] Thus, bilingualism is supported. This is a significant point that will be elaborated on later in this paper because what is included in multicultural education has implications for the issue of policy as well as legislative acts in this area.

As early as 1969, the Association for Supervision and Curriculum Development (ASCD) began addressing multiethnic education. However, it was not until a few years later that this association's recognition of cultural pluralism was labeled "multicultural education." The interpretation of the term by ASCD is as follows:

> ... is a humanistic concept based on the strength of diversity, human rights, social justice, and alternative life choices for all people. It is mandatory for quality education. It includes curricular, instructional, administrative, and environmental efforts to help students avail themselves of as many models, alternatives, and opportunities as possible from the full spectrum of our cultures. This education permits individual development in any culture. Each individual simultaneously becomes aware that every group (ethnic, cultural, social, and racial) exists autonomously as a part of an interrelated and interdependent societal whole. Thus, the individual is encouraged to develop social skills that will enable movement among and cooperation with other cultural communities and groups.[4]

This statement by ASCD is inclusive and all encompassing. The following sentence taken from further explanations of the term shows how it parallels the AACTE statement with reference to the intended audience: "If multicultural education is to achieve its goals, the concepts that constitute its foundations must pervade the educational experiences of all students." This point, the intent for benefiting all students, along with the inclusion of bilingual efforts have implications for advocating policy decisions.

The authors of *Teaching in a Multicultural Society* offer the following definition:

Thus, a multicultural concept is an inevitable reality in any society where there are people of various cultural backgrounds who are changing, moving about, and learning. The multicultural concept implies a view of life in which we recognize and cherish the differences among groups of people and search for ways to help such traits to be positive influences on both the individuals who possess them and all others with whom they associate in our society.[5]

This statement is much broader than those by AACTE or ASCD and allows for a greater degree of interpretation and application. This definition and the other preceding statements are similar to and supportive of the following definition that is offered at this point and will serve to establish common understandings as the topic is explored further.

Multicultural education in the context of this discussion is viewed as a process through which individuals are exposed to the diversity that exists in the United States and to the relationship of this diversity to the world. This diversity includes ethnic, racial minority populations as well as religious groups, language and sex differences. The exposure to diversity should be based on the foundation that every person in our society has the opportunity and option to support and maintain one or more cultures, i.e., value systems, life styles, sets of systems. However, the individual, as a citizen, has a responsibility to contribute to the maintenance of the common culture. This last concept of multicultural education is as inclusive as the previous examples but goes beyond in that it specifically includes religions and sex. This process can be illustrated by a three-circle model which contains a center or core circle, an inner circle, and an outer circle. The concepts involved in the model discussed here are not limited to the United States but are applicable to any country in the world, using a specific country as the reference point.

The *center circle* (core) in the model represents multiethnic education and refers to the content of ethnic studies. That is to say, it is concerned with the historical, economic, political, social and psychological perspectives, and involvements of a particular ethnic group. Within the development of a nation, it may also refer to all of the ethnic groups represented in the total society of a given country.

The *inner circle* refers to multicultural education and represents all cultural groups in the United States. This area contains the interaction and reactions among and between ethnic and cultural groups. The facets of the larger cultural group in the U.S. are affected, according to this concept, by the ethnic groups which collectively make up the larger cultural group. The reactions and interactions in the larger group are in part determined by the extent to which ethnic experiences are demonstrated by individual ethnic groups. For example, women and religious groups cannot or should not be thought of as ethnic groups but may be viewed as cultural groups. The study of women and religious groups as well as a myriad of other cultural groups can best be understood when the ethnic components and/or experiences are also analyzed. A study of women or religious groups in the United States should explore the relationship between various and/or specific ethnic groups. Ethnicity is a substantial portion of what is studied in the larger realm of culture.

To illustrate further, the feminist movement may be explored, but the full impact of this movement will be ignored completely unless we consider the interests, concerns, and responses to the issues involved by women of various ethnic groups. The value and interest which a Black, Native American or Hispanic woman places on the feminist movement are quite different from those of a white middle-class woman. The differences in perspectives and/or responses are primarily due to the ethnic experiences each has had in this country.[6]

To continue, the *outer circle* represents yet a third dimension and that is international education—education about another or other countries. So often, international education is taught in schools under the guise of multicultural education. International education does not become multicultural education until some aspects of what is being taught about a country can be linked to the behavior or life styles of ethnic groups who live in the United States but whose ancestors originated from the country being studied. In other words, a bridge must be established just as bridges have been established in the past to connect European cultures with Anglo-Saxon cultures in this country. In conclusion, from this reference point, it is possible to implement multiethnic education without multicultural education, but multicultural education cannot be implemented without involving multiethnic components. International education is neither multicultural nor multiethnic until bridges have been established.

Development of policy and legislation
Local education agencies

From a time perspective, it is not difficult to trace the development of multicultural education policy and legislation because most of it has occurred during the past decade. A natural approach to our discussion is to first look at what has taken place in local education agencies, then explore what has developed on the state, Federal and national levels. Unfortunately, there is no information available on local education agencies that is comprehensive enough to aid our discussion. Most of what is available is in piecemeal fashion. This fact alone tells us that there is a need for collecting this kind of data. It also tends to suggest that perhaps there is not as much activity on the local level as one would hope. There does exist some evidence of isolated situations where the activity within a local school district has affected the policy in that system. A case in point is the Ann Arbor, Michigan, public schools.

In response to racial discontent and disruption that occurred in their schools during the early seventies, the Ann Arbor Michigan Public School System adopted a report that specified the incorporation of multiethnic content, concepts, and principles throughout the entire educational system. The adoption of this report began to establish policy within and beyond the district. It is interesting to note that policy established on a local level had implications for developing policy in the surrounding teacher training institutions that placed pre-service teachers in the Ann Arbor public schools. The adoption of this report also caused the 1972–73 Master Agreement between the local board of education and the teacher's association to reflect new policy that directly affected teacher training. The policy read as follows:

> Beginning in the 1972–73 school year, no student teacher shall be accepted by the Ann Arbor Schools unless he can demonstrate attitudes necessary to support and create the multiethnic curriculum. Each such student teacher must provide a document or transcript which reflects training in or evidence of substantive understanding of the multiethnic or minority experience.[7]

This local school policy affected policy in at least two local teacher training institutions. Each institution developed policies within its respective training programs that required compliance with the policy set forth by the local school district. Other local districts in Michigan independently adopted similar policy. For example, the Jackson, Michigan Public School System established policy that required all teachers to have training in multicultural education prior to receiving tenure.

In other states, informal attempts to establish policies can be identified. For example, Wichita Public Schools, Wichita, Kansas, has not formerly adopted policy in multicultural education, but it is the practice of that district to provide training in multicultural education for all new teachers entering the system. Lake Washington School District, Kirkland, Washington, cooperates with Seattle Pacific University to provide multicultural instruction for teachers as the result of local initiative. What is being discussed here is the impact of local initiative on policy. There is some evidence of multicultural training taking place at the local level but in these situations the stimulus was provided by Federal legislation, i.e., Title IV of the 1964 Civil Rights Law and Title VII of the Elementary School Aid Act. Currently, local involvement as it relates to the initiation of local policy for the promotion of multicultural education needs to be encouraged.

State education agencies

Interesting and exciting aspects of the development of multicultural education policy and legislation have occurred on the state level. The variety of approaches used to accomplish either teacher in-service training or curriculum revision are many. They range from a more conservative approach such as the one included in the California Education Code to a more comprehensive and ambitious approach as that encouraged by the Iowa State Board of Education.

Article 3.3 of the California Education Code requires "multicultural education in school districts with one or more schools composed of at least 25% minority students ... [and] that districts provide teachers and other staff with in-service training in the history, culture and current problems of racial and ethnic minorities."[8] This legislation encourages multicultural education only for certain schools. It overlooks the important aspects that multicultural education is as important for the nonminority child as well as for the minority child. It also discriminates against the minority child who attends predominantly all-white schools. This legislation has the potential for encouraging the adoption of more extensive policy on the local level within the state of California.

The following approach used by the state of Iowa is more comprehensive:

> The Iowa State Board of Education encourages school districts to initiate in all subject areas, at all grade levels curriculum changes, teaching practices, and instructional materials which foster respect and appreciation for the cultural and racial pluralism of this country, and the achievement and contributions of minority groups, ethnic groups, and women as well as men.[9]

This approach is more inclusive and represents one of the few statements that is explicit as to the inclusion of women. These are but two examples of the kind of policy and/or legislation that exists on the state level.

The Multicultural Education Commission of the American Association of Colleges for Teacher Education, under a grant from the National Institute of Education, conducted a survey in 1976 of state legislation, provisions, and practices related to multicultural education. The survey was designed to solicit from state departments of education the degree to which each was involved in multicultural education. Recognizing the confusion that exists over the definition of "multicultural" and what is included, the survey instrument asked for responses to activities in the following specific areas: (1) provisions for multicultural education and ethnic studies, (2) provisions for bilingual/bicultural education, (3) teacher education requirements, (4) specific departments and persons assigned to coordinate multicultural education, (5) in-service training, and (6) curricular resources. As a result of the survey, the following information was obtained:

-   Thirty-four states address multicultural education through legislation, regulation, guidelines, and/or major policies.
-   Nineteen State Boards of Education have issued resolutions, position, and policy statements, or priority/goal statements related to multicultural education.
-   Twenty-one State Education Agencies (SEA's) have developed guidelines, regulations, or teacher certification requirements in order to comply with legislation or mandates from the State Board of Education.
-   In addition to the State Boards of Education and State Education Agencies, several states reported that other agencies had also produced Policy Statements related to the need for multicultural education, i.e., New York State Board of Regents provided a statement of policy on equal opportunity for women. The Vermont State Advisory Committee to the U.S. Commission on Civil Rights published a report that highlighted the need for teachers and teacher training related to human rights and minority groups.[10]

It is encouraging to note that at the time of this survey, sixty-eight per cent of the states had passed legislation, promulgated regulations and/or guidelines, and developed policy. Of these states, fifty-five per cent of the state boards of education have taken definite steps to adopt policy statements. Teacher certification is being affected in approximately fifty-five per cent of these thirty-four states.

In general, most of the activity that can be identified on the local school district level will be a result of legislation and policy that has been enacted on the state level. This suggests that multicultural policy decisions can be viewed as being interactive. In other words, in some cases, initiative from the local level can induce policy that can have a widespread effect. Certainly state policy directly affects local policy decisions as does Federal legislation. Policy decisions made in associations at the national level also affect the state and local involvement in multicultural education.

Federal government

Much of the multicultural education, however, is taking place perhaps because of recent Federal legislation. Even though that legislation has not been particularly aggressive or comprehensive, it has provided a stimulus for some activity. According to Giles and Gollnick,[11] there was little support for multicultural education on the Federal level prior to the passage of Title IX of the Elementary and Secondary Education Act of 1965 (ESEA). The Ethnic Heritage Program legislation in 1972, which emerged from ESEA, appears to have been the first to encourage the study of ethnic and racial minority culture by children in the United States.

Other Federal legislations that have implications for multicultural education have been primarily contained in Title IV of the 1964 Civil Rights Bill, Title VII of the Emergency School Aid Act of 1972, and in Title VII of the 1972 amendments of ESEA. Other legislations, such as the Title VI of the Civil Rights Act, are often cited as having enhanced multicultural education but these tend to fall more into the affirmative action or civil rights categories.

Many school districts have benefited from the provisions of Title IV of the Civil Rights Act of 1964. Title IV provides technical and financial assistance to desegregating school systems. However, the effect of this Act is limited because assistance can only be given when it is requested. With increased emphasis on the development of policy by the local level, it is possible that an increase in requests for the kind of services that Title IV can provide will be forthcoming.

The thrust of Title VII of the Emergency School Aid Act of 1972 is to meet the needs of students and faculty that have resulted from discrimination and group isolation. This piece of legislation could have a tremendous impact upon the development of policy in this area because it focuses upon the development and use of curricula and instructional methods, practices, and techniques that support a program of instruction for ethnic and racial minority children. School districts must also take the initiative in requesting assistance from Title VII.

Title VII, also known as the Bilingual Education Act, provides assistance to programs that are designed to address language differences. As indicated in our discussion on the definition of multicultural education, language differences are an important aspect of cultural diversity and, therefore, bilingual education is an important part of multicultural education.

The elimination of discrimination related to sex differences is also a very real part of multicultural education. For this reason, Title IX of the 1972 Education Amendments can be considered as another piece of legislation that supports multicultural education. This Act prohibits discrimination on the basis of sex in federally-assisted educational programs or activities.

While these legislative moves may not have been deliberate attempts on the part of the Federal Government to support multicultural education, it is perhaps accurate to say that they can have an impact on the development and promotion of multicultural education. There has been no specific lobbying effort directed at the Federal level to secure legislation that will precisely support multicultural education. Policy decisions at this level will need to be influenced and developed.

The impact that professional and related education organizations can have on multicultural education cannot be overlooked. As a part of the survey that was conducted by the Multicultural Education Commission, American Association for Teacher Education, and cited earlier in this discussion, a profile of multicultural education activities of professional and related education organizations was compiled. The following information was obtained from the profile:

- Thirty-three of the thirty-nine responding organizations indicated they had activities related to multicultural/bilingual education.
- Eighty per cent stated that the funding for this activity came from membership.
- Almost sixty per cent reported they had developed policy statements on multicultural or bilingual education.[12]

The profile makes it clear that although a large number of those responding to the survey have developed statements that promote multiculturalism, none outlines what the organization itself should do to bring about the changes implied. This is an example of how ineffective policy can be if commitment and procedures for monitoring the policy are not evident.

One of the organizations included in this profile has taken a major step toward the implementation of policy. The National Council for the Accreditation of Teacher Education (NCATE) is devoted to the evaluation and accreditation of teacher education programs throughout the country. The National Council has been authorized by the Council on Post-Secondary Accreditation (COPA) to adopt standards and procedures for accreditation and to determine the accreditation status of institutional programs for preparing teachers and other professional school personnel.[13]

Accreditation is determined by how an institution is assessed by the Standards used in conducting the evaluation of its teacher training program. Prior to 1979, these Standards did not include reference to multicultural education but the revised Standards, that went into effect as of January 1, 1979, do address multicultural teacher education. A new and separate Standard has been included and existing Standards have been revised so as to reflect appropriate multicultural approaches. This will have a major impact on schools, colleges, and departments of education because NCATE accredits approximately forty per cent of the teacher training institutions in the nation. It is also accurate to say that this change in reference to the NCATE Standards did not occur without a good deal of encouragement from external forces that organized to provide meaningful advocacy and assistance.

The proponents of multicultural education feel that the development of policy and legislation relevant to their interests has not occurred quickly enough, nor is the available support sufficient. If there is to be adequate and effective *policy* that will aid the development of multicultural education, strategies for accomplishing this is needed. If there is to be *legislation* that will support multicultural activity in the nation's schools, techniques for promoting it will also be needed.

Needed policy and legislation
National

One of the major recommendations of The Conference of Education and Teacher Education for Cultural Pluralism held in 1971 addressed an essential step crucial to policymaking at the national level. The recommendation states that:

> Cultural pluralism should be recognized in the selection of personnel for decision-making bodies in all federal education programs so that minority communities will have a policy role in such programs. This principle should be applied at all levels of a program, from top-level positions in the U.S. Office of Education (USOE) to the personnel of individual projects, and at the state and local levels.[14]

Other recommendations from this same conference speak to the importance of policy that would effect multicultural instructional materials, a clearinghouse for the dissemination of such materials and to an array of other issues that need to be effected by policy that would ensure multicultural approaches. What can be inferred from these recommendations and from what the previous discussion has suggested is that there needs to be national policy established that would permeate all decision making and practices in the United States Office of Education.

As was noted earlier, policy can exist; but without firm commitment to the content of such statements to enforcement, and to the provisions for monitoring the implementation of policy, it might as well be non-existent. That is to say, if policy were established on the national level, it follows that legislation would be needed to reinforce the implementation of multicultural education. The implementation could be reinforced via funding and monitoring provisions. A condition for Federal funding could be based on the degree to which the state and/or local district is committed to and involved in multicultural education for students and for teachers.

Policy and legislation at the national level could have a great impact on teacher training. Teacher training might look very different from its current pattern with regard to multicultural education if some means of accountability were encouraged. The development of curricula, selection of instructional materials, staffing patterns, and evaluation could be more effectively impacted if policy and legislation at the national level were directed to the issue of multicultural education.

State

On the state level, there exists a great need for more comprehensive policy and legislation that would support multicultural education. State education agencies and state boards of education could play important roles in providing effective policy through a number of avenues. Teacher certification could include provisions that would provide for training and experiences in this area. It is important to note that in some instances if only existing policy is enforced, nothing else would be needed. An example of this was cited by the State of Michigan:

> While the Guidelines for Multicultural Education seek to initiate innovation in the schools of Michigan, many of the crucial elements of multicultural education already exist in current policies and practices of the Michigan State Department of Education. Some of the current policies in which these elements can be found include: Common Goals of Michigan Education; Guidelines for Eliminating and Preventing Sex Discrimination; Guidelines for Providing Integrated Education Within School Districts; and Bilingual Education legislation.[15]

This document continues by illustrating the language contained in current policy. For example, in "The Common Goals of Michigan Education," the following is included:

> Michigan education must provide for each individual an understanding of the value systems, cultures, customs and histories of one's own heritage as well as others. Each student must learn to value human differences.[16]

In this instance, nothing more with regard to policy would be needed if this stated policy were implemented and monitored.

Comprehensive policy and legislation on the state level would ensure more effective teacher certification with regard to multicultural education. The content of the curricula of the schools through each state could also reflect that which would be appropriate for a given state. State endorsement of textbooks, the selection of personnel, and many other important areas in education, could be affected by state level action which is supportive of the principles inherent in multicultural education.

Local

The development of multicultural education at the local level would certainly be enhanced if local school boards committed themselves to the concept. Ann Arbor, Michigan, is an indication of the effect policy can have at this level. The selection of teachers, curriculum development, curriculum content, the development of evaluation instruments and procedures, selection of instructional materials, and many other areas at the local level, need to emerge from Board policy that will not only encourage the application of multicultural approaches but also enforce it.

Requisites for achieving policy and legislation

One of the most crucial aspects of attempting to encourage support on any issue, but certainly with respect to education, is the degree to which people can be convinced that what is being advocated will benefit them. In the 1977 Washington Policy Seminar,[17] one of the panelists stressed the importance of keeping in mind what the American people feel is worthy. It was reported that in a November, 1976, Louis Harris poll, eighty-nine per cent of those surveyed indicated that one of the most important aspects of the "quality of life" to them was "achieving quality education for children."[18] This fact is important to this discussion because it indicates that if multicultural education policy and legislation is to be advocated, then the value it has for providing quality education for all children must be stressed. The inclusiveness of the concept is an equally important point to be conveyed. The public as well as legislators are weary with the myriad of new thrusts and innovations they must respond to in the field of education. While multicultural education is not an innovation, it is a recent thrust designed to improve the education of *all* children. The "all" must be emphasized and the fact that what is being advocated is not only study about ethnicity and culture but includes bilingual education as well as efforts for the elimination of sexism. If policy and legislation that will make multicultural education become a reality is to be achieved, there must be advocacy that will accomplish the following: the acceptance of a comprehensive and unifying definition of the concept, the acceptance of the inclusiveness of multicultural education, and increased awareness of the importance of multicultural education for all children and their teachers. If we are to realize the benefits of advocacy, attention needs to be given to *organizing* efforts so that effective methods of lobbying for policy can be identified. Methods of attaining legislation at the national, state, and local levels also need to be identified and utilized.

A recognition of the importance and value of multicultural education is essential to the development of the approach. However, sensitivity and awareness on the part of a few will do little to promote the implementation on a grand scale unless that sensitivity, awareness, and interest is captured and transformed into meaningful support systems. In other words, the most effective way to ensure multicultural education in the schools of the nation is to organize for successful advocacy via policy and legislation.

Notes

1 Gwendolyn C. Baker, "The Effects of Training in Multi-ethnic Education on Preservice Teachers' Perceptions of Ethnic Groups" (Ph.D. diss., University of Michigan, 1972).

2 William A. Hunter (ed.), *Multicultural Education Through Competency-Based Teacher Education* (Washington, D.C.: American Association for Colleges of Teacher Education, 1977).

3 *Ibid.*, p. 22.

4 Carl A. Grant (ed.), *Multicultural Education: Commitments, Issues and Applications* (Washington, D.C.: Association for Supervision and Curriculum Development, 1977).

5 D. Cross, G. C. Baker, and L. J. Stiles, *Teaching in a Multicultural Society* (New York, Macmillan Publishing Co., 1977).

6 Gwendolyn C. Baker, "Cultural Diversity: Strength of the Nation," *Educational Leadership*, XXXIII (January, 1976), 257–59.

7 Gwendolyn C. Baker, "Development of the Multicultural Program: School of Education, University of Michigan," in *Pluralism and the American Teacher: Issues and Case Studies* (Washington, D.C.: American Association for Colleges of Teacher Education, 1977), pp. 163–69.

8 E.D. Cross and James Deslonde, "The Impact of Teacher In-Service Programs on Attitudes Toward Multicultural Education," *Educational Research Quarterly*, II (Winter, 1978), 96–105.

9 State Board of Public Instruction, *Guide to Implementing Multicultural Non-Sexist Curriculum Programs in Iowa Schools*, June, 1976.

10 American Association for Colleges of Teacher Education, *State Legislation, Provisions and Practices Related to Multicultural Education* (Washington, D.C.: AACTE, 1978).

11 Raymond Giles and Donna Gollnick, *Pluralism and the American Teacher: Issues and Case Studies* (Washington, D.C.: American Association for Colleges of Teacher Education, 1977), pp. 115–60.

12 *Profile of the Multicultural/Bilingual Education Activities of Professional and Related Education Organizations*, AACTE, May, 1978.

13 National Council for the Accreditation of Teacher Education, *Standards for the Accreditation of Teacher Education* (Washington, D.C.: NCATE, May, 1977).

14 Madelon D. Stent, *Cultural Pluralism in Education: A Mandate for Change* (New York: Appleton-Century-Crofts, 1973), pp. 153–58.

15 Michigan State Board of Education, *Guidelines for Providing Integrated Education Through Multicultural Education*, 1974, p. 6.

16 *Ibid.*, p. 7.

17 The Washington Policy Seminar, *Report of a Joint Activity of the Far West and California Teacher Corps Networks and Institution for Educational Leadership*, May, 1977.

18 *Ibid.*, p. 33.

CHAPTER 14

LEARNING FROM OUR LOSSES (1983)
Is school desegregation still feasible in the 1980s?
Derrick A. Bell

In 1901 W.E.B. Du Bois warned the world that the color line would be the major problem of the 20th century. More than 80 years later his words stand revealed as accurate prophecy – not only for the 20th century, but for the 21st.

Aided by the light of Du Bois's clear understanding, what predictions can we make about the future of the once-mighty drive to eliminate racial discrimination in U.S. public schools? The civil rights movement gained such momentum from the changes wrought by World War II that at one time only the most pessimistic doubted that the crusade fueled by the 1954 Supreme Court decision in *Brown v. Board of Education*[1] would eventually transform the nation's segregated schools. We would no longer have "a 'white' school or a 'Negro' school, but just schools."[2]

Whatever we may accomplish in the next two decades, few people are likely to be so blindly optimistic as to predict that the 21st century will be the last in which black Americans – in public schools or elsewhere – will feel, with Harriet Tubman, like "strangers in a strange land." That prediction is so disheartening that many people will deny what all who see must know. Such denials reveal a preference for the shock of surprise over the distress of disappointment.

Disappointment for those committed to racial equality is far from a new experience, however. Thaddeus Stevens, one of the most dedicated abolitionists of the 19th century, fought for years in the post-Civil War period for his plan to give land to the former slaves. But his effort to have Congress break up large plantations and distribute "Forty Acres and a Mule" to every freedman was never approved.

At age 74, aware that his reparations scheme would never be realized, Stevens rose in Congress and conceded defeat with a eulogy that fits only too well the hard-fought campaign to desegregate U.S. schools. "In my youth, in my manhood, in my old age," Stevens said, "I had fondly dreamed that when any fortunate chance should have broken up for a while the foundation of our institutions . . . [we would have] remodeled . . . [and] freed them from every vestige of human oppression, of inequality of rights. . . ." But, he admitted, "This bright dream has vanished like the baseless fabric of a dream."[3]

In the waning years of the 20th century, we have every reason to apply Thaddeus Stevens's eulogy to the more than 40-year campaign to desegregate public schools through court orders that aimed to place black and white children in the same schools. School desegregation litigation on what its opponents call the "racial balance" model has now exhausted its potential for improving the quality of schooling provided to the most needy nonwhite children.

The federal government and private civil rights groups continue to keep a number of school desegregation cases active. Hundreds of school districts remain under desegregation court orders, and it is likely that many of these cases will remain in the courts for the foreseeable future. But few new cases are being filed, and the issues litigated in existing cases are quite likely to involve school board plans and policies intended to reduce the obligation of the schools to achieve racial balance – or to replace or supplement desegregation to achieve racial balance with plans deemed more educationally effective.

Next year it will have been three decades since the *Brown* decision, but the statistical scorecard of school desegregation has been disappointing. Certainly, the once totally segregated school systems throughout the South are no more. Indeed, progress in southern states has outstripped that in northern and western regions where, if anything, the number of children attending predominantly minority schools has increased.

A recent analysis of school desegregation statistics gathered by a Congressional committee indicates that, during the 1980–81 school year, nearly half of the black students living in the Northeast attended schools that were at least 90% minority and that 63% of black students around the U.S. attended such schools.[4] Millions of black students in the South are enrolled in desegregated schools, but much of this change had been achieved by 1972. In recent years, the South has become slightly more segregated. School boards in several areas are in court trying to eliminate busing and other school desegregation procedures, and the Justice Department is supporting many of these attempts to undermine school desegregation plans.

But the reality of the failures of desegregation is even worse than the statistics – and the statistics are bad enough. They show intense segregation of blacks in areas of the Northeast, the Midwest, Washington, D.C., Maryland, the deep South, and California – areas where large numbers of blacks live in mainly black and often poverty-level neighborhoods. These are the areas where the need for effective education is greatest but where the schooling available is most inadequate.

Having given this brief but pessimistic overview, I can now try to discern – by examining the history of desegregation in more detail – a possible future course for school desegregation. Whatever the future holds, we should be determined not to repeat the errors of our disappointing past.

First, I will explore what went wrong with our expectation that the *Brown* decision, bolstered by federal civil rights laws and judicial support, would bring about the complete desegregation of the public schools. Second, it will do no harm to pose the somewhat irreverent question of whether greater progress in school desegregation might have been achieved if civil rights adherents had adopted or been forced to adopt different policies. And finally, from this examination of the past, we might discover strategies that could breathe new vigor into a school desegregation process rendered impotent both by greatly changed circumstances and by society's persistent willingness to deny black children the quality of public schooling without which, as Chief Justice Earl Warren wrote in *Brown*, "it is doubtful that any child may reasonably be expected to succeed in life. . . ."[5]

The derailing of Brown

Several years ago I suggested that, given the history of slavery and subordination that blacks have experienced in America, it was folly to view the *Brown* decision as a miraculous break with a 300-year past in which self-interest and the belief in white superiority dominated virtually every decision about racial policy, including the Emancipation Proclamation.[6]

It is not difficult to supply self-interested motives for the *Brown* decision. When the Court jettisoned the view that the 14th Amendment – intended to make blacks citizens – also permitted their exclusion from equal access to facilities available to whites,[7] it gave immediate credibility to America's struggle with communist countries for the allegiance of Third World countries. The *Brown* decision also provided long-awaited (and, as it turned out, premature) reassurance to American blacks that the precepts of equality and freedom so widely heralded during World War II might yet be given meaning at home. And, by ending state-sponsored segregation in public facilities, *Brown* opened the way for the industrialization of the South.

In the early 1950s these benefits seemed reason enough for policy makers to override the preferences of the mass of working-class whites who, half a century before, had insisted on segregation as one means to insure their societal status. However exploited these whites might be, Jim Crow laws reassured them that they were at least superior to blacks. The lot of poor whites had changed little since the Populist movement collapsed in the 1890s, precisely because working-class whites allowed the exclusion of blacks from power to become more important than their own fledgling efforts to achieve opportunities equal to those of upper-class whites. Thus many whites saw *Brown* as the betrayal of an unwritten agreement that had kept blacks "in their place" for decades. The white revolt against *Brown* has proved stronger and far more politically potent than the widely publicized but short-lived black revolt of the 1960s.

For more than a decade the concepts of judicial supremacy and federalism motivated the enforcement of the *Brown* decision despite state resistance. Even the racial balance remedies laid down by the Court in the 1970s, which brought about substantial compliance in many southern districts, were as much anti-defiance as equal educational opportunity remedies. Furthermore, when civil rights lawyers argued that meaningful desegregation in large, urban school districts would require the inclusion of suburban districts, the Court began more openly to balance the interests of blacks in desegregation against other well-established and highly valued interests, including local school board control and neighborhood schools.[8]

This new direction in determining when relief would be granted in school desegregation cases followed a lengthy review of desegregation cases by Justice Lewis Powell in the Denver case.[9] Powell urged the reconciliation of competing values in school cases through a balancing of the interests of blacks in desegregation against those of white parents in sending their children to nearby, locally governed schools.[10] What emerged during the years immediately following the Denver case was a difficult-to-meet requirement that blacks seeking compliance with *Brown* must prove that discriminatory policies were specifically intended to harm them.

The lessons of the first three decades following *Brown* were learned at great cost. They should not be ignored. We should have learned by now that, in the absence of shockingly overt racial discrimination, constitutional protections alone will not be read as authorizing an effective remedy for blacks when that remedy threatens the status of middle- and upper-class whites. The racial remedies that the courts impose tend not to be a response to the nature of harm suffered by blacks or the degree of liability proved against whites. Instead, court-ordered remedies rest on unspoken (and perhaps unconscious) conclusions that the remedies, if implemented, will advance societal interests deemed important by whites in policy-making positions.

As we have seen from time to time, racial justice may be counted among those interests deemed important by elite whites. But working-class whites, who tend to view any remedy for blacks as unfair and threatening, can be expected to challenge all racial remedies – even those that improve, their status as much as or more than that of blacks. Eventually, policy makers who must stand for election translate this white discontent and sense of betrayal into votes.

Equalization and school boards

In its second *Brown* decision, rendered in 1955, the Supreme Court refused to grant the request of the black petitioners that an immediate injunction be imposed on all segregated schools. The Court foresaw that serious resistance could arise in defiance of an immediate desegregation order. Thus it returned the school desegregation cases to the jurisdiction of the district courts and charged them to see that the schools were desegregated "with all deliberate speed."[11]

However, the district courts were located in communities in which the segregated way of life was deemed very close to godliness. The results of the High Court's delegation of authority to the district courts are laid out plainly in the pages of legal history, and (for proponents of civil rights, at least) they do not make pleasant reading.

What might have been the outcome had the Court instead specifically delayed any order requiring the dreaded "mixing of the races" for at least five years? Suppose that at the same time the Court had required the total equalization of school facilities and resources. It might have seemed cruel and unprecedented at the time, but more progress might have been made in the long run had the Court expressly deferred desegregation relief for a fairly long period.

It is still a little-known fact that many southern districts – hoping to forestall the invalidation of the "separate but equal" doctrine – had, by 1954, taken substantial steps to eliminate the most obvious and odious of the disparities between black schools and white schools. In the North, too, school officials hastily constructed buildings and found money for new textbooks, laboratories, libraries, and gymnasiums. The equalization programs were sufficiently far-reaching that the massive Coleman Report of 1966[12] failed to find the vast differences in buildings, books, and facilities between black and white schools that the researchers had expected.

Imagine that, in addition to requiring the equalization of all facilities and resources, the Court in 1955 had seen through the racist motivations of school segregation and had recognized that the separation of students by race was a means of perpetuating the real evil: white dominance over blacks in every important aspect of life. The Supreme Court might then have required that blacks be represented on school boards and other policy-making bodies in proportions equal to those of black students in each school district. This remedy would have given blacks meaningful access to decision making – a prerequisite to full equality still unattained in many predominantly black school systems. In addition, such an "equal representation" rule could have helped protect the thousands of black teachers and principals who were dismissed by school systems in the 1960s and 1970s, when school desegregation plans aimed at achieving racial balance were implemented.

This hypothetical Court would certainly have urged school districts to proceed with elimination of their dual school systems, as the Court actually did in *Brown*. But at the end of the five-year equalization period, it might have imposed a freedom-of-choice plan. Until that time, however, the major emphasis would have been placed, not on desegregating the children, but on desegregating the money and the control.

Advocates of school integration will complain that a judicial approach that did not give priority to pupil desegregation would have played into the hands of the segregationists by making black parents satisfied with all-black schools. But since the first public schools opened in Boston in the 1780s, black parents have sought not integrated schools, but schools in which their children could receive a good education.

Under the jurisdiction of my hypothetical High Court, all schools would not have remained strictly segregated. Many black parents would prefer to send their children to predominantly white schools either because they believed that such schools would better meet their children's educational needs or for reasons of convenience. Similarly, black schools with good academic reputations would have attracted some white children, just as such schools do today. Ideally, the quality of education provided to black children would have improved substantially.

But the course actually followed by the Court was far removed from the hypothetical course I have outlined above. With the exception of striking down instances of total recalcitrance, as in Little Rock in 1957,[13] the efforts of courts in the first 10 years of school desegregation after *Brown* were generally ineffectual and often counterproductive.

If civil rights groups and black parents had known in advance that the courts would not provide much help for 10 years, what might they have done? Certainly they might have become discouraged by the delay in student desegregation and might simply have done nothing until the courts were willing to take definite action. It is more likely that they would have done what eventually needed to be done in each community in which a desegregation decision was issued. That is, they would have organized parents and the community in order to implement the court-ordered equal funding and equal representation mandates. How might this have been accomplished?

We know that many, and perhaps most, black schools under the segregated system were quite bad. Unjust disparities in funding practically guaranteed their inferior quality. Moreover, the black schools were governed by white school systems that had no stake in improving the black schools. Thus principals in the black schools were appointed and retained according to their ability to keep order. If they managed to provide a decent learning environment, no one objected, as long as it posed no overt threat to white dominance.

We also know that the fear by blacks that segregated schools would be inferior could and did become a self-fulfilling prophecy. Du Bois explained this phenomenon in his 1935 essay, "Does the Negro Need Separate Schools?"[14] Du Bois maintained that black children needed neither "separate" schools nor "integrated" schools. They needed a good education. He noted that even then Negroes would "fight frenziedly" to end formally segregated schools. But, if the schools remained all black, they would tend simply to accept the argument that nothing of educational value can take place in black schools and "scarcely raise a finger to see that the resultant Negro schools get a fair share of the public funds so as to have adequate equipment and housing; [and] to see that real teachers are appointed."[15]

Still, not every black community nor every black schoolteacher or principal succumbed to the pressure to accept inferior black schools. In far more cases than we can document, individual teachers rose above the inadequate resources and the stifling atmosphere of the black schools to encourage excellence, to motivate ambition, and to teach the skills and self-assurance that produced scores of successful blacks in business and the professions. Some black schools earned reputations for quality that were too soon forgotten in the flood of integration-based hope that in 1954 seemed to sweep away all past experience.

It is hard for me to accept arguments that the loss of the skills and techniques developed in the best of those schools was not a devastating one. I find it even harder to imagine that such a loss would have occurred had the Supreme Court begun the school desegregation process by demanding an immediate equalization of funding and facilities and requiring proportional representation for blacks in educational policy making.

Using what-might-have-been

The most distressing aspect of school desegregation efforts – even in those southern districts where millions of children are attending desegregated schools – is the fact that the presence of both races in the same schools hardly guarantees that black children are obtaining equal access to educational opportunities. In fact, few of these desegregated districts show black scholastic achievement scores equal to those of whites or black expulsion and disciplinary rates lower than those of whites. And these grim figures do not tell the full story. Many black children continue to experience isolation, insensitivity, and outright rejection in public schools that may be perfectly balanced by race but remain dominated by whites.

Certainly, success stories exist in desegregated schools. But the number of black students who overcome the obstacles to their success represents a very small dividend indeed, given the long years and hard work invested in school desegregation. The number of truly desegregated schools and school systems, in which all black children – not just the best and the brightest – are treated according to their needs, is even smaller.

Had we civil rights lawyers been more attuned to the primary goal of black parents – the effective schooling of their children – and less committed to the attainment of our ideal – racially integrated schools – we might have recognized sooner that merely integrating schools, in a society still committed to white dominance, would not insure our clients and their children the equal educational opportunity for which they have sacrificed so much and waited so long. But from the beginning many black parents and their community leaders realized what some civil rights lawyers have not yet acknowledged. There can be no effective schooling for black children without both parental involvement in the educational process and meaningful participation in school policy making. Experience, often painful, has taught these parents and communities that neither object is brought closer merely by enrolling their children in predominantly white schools – especially if those schools are located a long bus ride from their homes and neighborhoods.

A number of black communities have determined to bring about in their public schools the high-quality schools that have always been their goal – schools such as Dunbar High School in Washington[16] and the less well-known but equally impressive Dunbar High School in Little Rock, Arkansas. Faustine Jones-Wilson of Howard University has provided a most welcome report on the latter.[17] In a number of cities, including Atlanta, St. Louis, Detroit, Milwaukee, Portland, and

Dallas, blacks have rejected plans calling for more racial balance in favor of policies that promise more control and a more equitable distribution of educational resources. In some instances, courts have recognized and encouraged educationally oriented plans – often, regrettably, over the vigorous objections of civil rights organizations still seeking relief through racial balance.

Of course, the pressures of racism may well condemn to failure any plan to educate minority children, especially the children of the poor. Surely all black parents should have the option of sending their children to predominantly white schools if they choose. But, given the tarnished record of that option nearly 30 years after *Brown*, black parents who prefer to follow a different course ought to be encouraged, not assailed.

At least these parents are trying to learn from the losses of the past. The barriers of continuing white resistance, a less than supportive Supreme Court, and the growing concentration of most poor blacks in large urban areas render continuing efforts to achieve compliance with *Brown* through racial balance plans preposterous. The chances for further progress in the 1980s lie with those who have decided that the better route to educational quality is in those schools in which black children and their parents are not treated as strangers.

Notes

1   347 U.S. 483 (1954).
2   *Green* v. *County School Board of New Kent County*, 391 U.S. 430, 442 (1968).
3   Lerone Bennett, *Before the Mayflower* (Chicago: Johnson Publishing Co., 1961), p. 189.
4   Gary Orfield, "Desegregation in the Public Schools, 1968–1980," *Focus*, a publication of the Joint Center of Political Studies. October 1982, pp. 4–5.
5   347 U.S., at 493.
6   Derrick Bell, "*Brown* and the Interest-Convergence Dilemma," in Derrick Bell, ed., *Shades of Brown: New Perspectives on School Desegregation* (New York: Teachers College Press, 1980), pp. 90–106; see also Derrick Bell, *Race, Racism, and American Law*, 2nd ed. (Boston: Little, Brown, 1980), pp. 2–51, 431–44.
7   *Plessy* v. *Ferguson*, 163 U.S. 537 (1896).
8   See, e.g., *Milliken* v. *Bradley*, 418 U.S. 717 (1974).
9   *Keyes* v. *School District No. 1, Denver, Colorado*, 413 U.S. 189 (1973) (Justice Powell, concurring in part and dissenting in part).
10 Ibid., at 240–52.
11 *Brown* v. *Board of Education*, 349 U.S. 294 (1955).
12 *Equality of Educational Opportunity* (Washington, D.C.: U.S. Government Printing Office, 1966). For one of the rare comments on this phenomenon, see Faustine C. Jones, "The Inequality Controversy." *Journal of Negro Education*, Fall 1973, pp. 537–49.
13 *Cooper* v. *Aaron*, 358 U.S. 1 (1958).
14 W.E.B. Du Bois, "Does the Negro Need Separate Schools?," *Journal of Negro Education*, vol. 4, 1935, pp. 328–35.
15 Ibid., p. 332.
16 Thomas Sowell, "Black Excellence – The Case of Dunbar High School," *Public Interest*, vol. 3, 1974, pp. 3–21; and idem, "Patterns of Black Excellence," *Public Interest*, vol. 26, 1976, pp. 26–58.
17 Faustine C. Jones-Wilson, *A Traditional Model of Educational Excellence: Dunbar High School of Little Rock, Arkansas* (Washington, D.C.: Howard University Press, 1981). An article based on the book was published in the *Phi Delta Kappan*, April 1982, pp. 540–41.

CHAPTER 15

SEXUALITY, SCHOOLING, AND ADOLESCENT FEMALES (1988)
The missing discourse of desire
Michelle Fine

Since late 1986, popular magazines and newspapers have printed steamy stories about education and sexuality. Whether the controversy surrounds sex education or school-based health clinics (SBHCs), public discourses of adolescent sexuality are represented forcefully by government officials, New Right spokespersons, educators, "the public," feminists, and health-care professionals. These stories offer the authority of "facts," insights into the political controversies, and access to unacknowledged fears about sexuality (Foucault, 1980). Although the facts usually involve the adolescent female body, little has been heard from young women themselves.

This article examines these diverse perspectives on adolescent sexuality and, in addition, presents the views of a group of adolescent females. The article is informed by a study of numerous current sex education curricula, a year of negotiating for inclusion of lesbian and gay sexuality in a citywide sex education curriculum, and interviews and observations gathered in New York City sex education classrooms.[1] The analysis examines the desires, fears, and fantasies which give structure and shape to silences and voices concerning sex education and school-based health clinics in the 1980s.

Despite the attention devoted to teen sexuality, pregnancy, and parenting in this country, and despite the evidence of effective interventions and the widespread public support expressed for these interventions (Harris, 1985), the systematic implementation of sex education and SBHCs continues to be obstructed by the controversies surrounding them (Kantrowitz et al., 1987; Leo, 1986). Those who resist sex education or SBHCs often present their views as based on rationality and a concern for protecting the young. For such opponents, sex education raises questions of promoting promiscuity and immorality, and of undermining family values. Yet the language of the challenges suggests an affect substantially more profound and primitive. Gary Bauer, Undersecretary of Education in the U.S. Department of Education, for example, constructs an image of immorality littered by adolescent sexuality and drug abuse:

> There is ample impressionistic evidence to indicate that drug abuse and promiscuity are not independent behaviors. When inhibitions fall, they collapse across the board. When people of any age lose a sense of right and wrong, the loss is not selective. . . . [T]hey are all expressions of the same ethical vacuum among many teens. . . . (1986)

Even Surgeon General C. Everett Koop, a strong supporter of sex education, recently explained: "[W]e have to be as explicit as necessary. . . . You can't talk of the dangers of snake poisoning and not mention snakes" (quoted in Leo, 1986, p. 54). Such commonly used and often repeated metaphors associate adolescent sexuality with victimization and danger.

Yet public schools have rejected the task of sexual dialogue and critique, or what has been called "sexuality education." Within today's standard sex education curricula and many public school classrooms, we find: (1) the authorized suppression of a discourse of female sexual desire; (2) the promotion of a discourse of female sexual victimization; and (3) the explicit privileging of married heterosexuality over other practices of sexuality. One finds an unacknowledged social ambivalence about female sexuality which ideologically separates the female sexual agent, or subject, from her counterpart, the female sexual victim. The adolescent woman of the 1980s is constructed as the latter. Educated primarily as the potential victim of male sexuality, she represents no subject in her own right. Young women continue to be taught to fear and defend in isolation from exploring desire, and in this context there is little possibility of their developing a critique of gender or sexual arrangements.

Prevailing discourses of female sexuality inside public schools

> If the body is seen as endangered by uncontrollable forces, then presumably this is a society or social group which fears change—change which it perceived simultaneously as powerful and beyond its control. (Smith-Rosenberg, 1978, p. 229)

Public schools have historically been the site for identifying, civilizing, and containing that which is considered uncontrollable. While evidence of sexuality is everywhere within public high schools—in the halls, classrooms, bathrooms, lunchrooms, and the library—official sexuality education occurs sparsely: in social studies, biology, sex education, or inside the nurse's office. To understand how sexuality is managed inside schools, I examined the major discourses of sexuality which characterize the national debates over sex education and SBHCs. These discourses are then tracked as they weave through the curricula, classrooms, and halls of public high schools.

The first discourse, *sexuality as violence*, is clearly the most conservative, and equates adolescent heterosexuality with violence. At the 1986 American Dreams Symposium on education, Phyllis Schlafly commented: "Those courses on sex, abuse, incest, AIDS, they are all designed to terrorize our children. We should fight their existence, and stop putting terror in the hearts and minds of our youngsters." One aspect of this position, shared by women as politically distinct as Schlafly and the radical feminist lawyer Catherine MacKinnon (1983), views heterosexuality as essentially violent and coercive. In its full conservative form, proponents call for the elimination of sex education and clinics and urge complete reliance on the family to dictate appropriate values, mores, and behaviors.

Sexuality as violence presumes that there is a causal relationship between official silence about sexuality and a decrease in sexual activity—therefore, by not teaching about sexuality, adolescent sexual behavior will not occur. The irony, of course, lies in the empirical evidence. Fisher, Byrne, and White (1983) have documented sex-negative attitudes and contraceptive use to be negatively correlated. In their study, sex-negative attitudes do not discourage sexual activity, but they do discourage responsible use of contraception. Teens who believe sexual involvement is wrong deny responsibility for contraception. To accept responsibility would legitimate "bad" behavior. By contrast, Fisher et al. (1983) found that adolescents with sex-positive attitudes tend to be both more consistent and more positive about contraceptive use. By not teaching about sexuality, or by teaching sex-negative attitudes, schools apparently will not forestall sexual activity, but may well discourage responsible contraception.

The second discourse, *sexuality as victimization*, gathers a much greater following. Female adolescent sexuality is represented as a moment of victimization in which the dangers of heterosexuality for adolescent women (and, more recently, of homosexuality for adolescent men) are prominent. While sex may not be depicted as inherently violent, young women (and today, men) learn of their vulnerability to potential male predators.

To avoid being victimized, females learn to defend themselves against disease, pregnancy, and "being used." The discourse of victimization supports sex education, including AIDS education, with parental consent. Suggested classroom activities emphasize "saying no," practicing abstinence, enumerating the social and emotional risks of sexual intimacy, and listing the possible diseases associated with sexual intimacy. The language, as well as the questions asked and not asked, represents females as the actual and potential victims of male desire. In exercises, role plays, and class discussions, girls practice resistance to trite lines, unwanted hands, opened buttons, and the surrender of other "bases" they are not prepared to yield. The discourses of violence and victimization both portray males as potential predators and females as victims. Three problematic assumptions underlie these two views:

- First, female subjectivity, including the desire to engage in sexual activity, is placed outside the prevailing conversation (Vance, 1984).
- Second, both arguments present female victimization as contingent upon unmarried heterosexual involvement—rather than inherent in existing gender, class, and racial arrangements (Rubin, 1984). While feminists have long fought for the legal and social acknowledgement of sexual violence against women, most have resisted the claim that female victimization hinges primarily upon sexual involvement with men. The full range of victimization of women—at work, at home, on the streets—has instead been uncovered. The language and emotion invested in these two discourses divert attention away from structures, arrangements, and relationships which oppress women in general, and low-income women and women of color in particular (Lorde, 1978).
- Third, the messages, while narrowly anti-sexual, nevertheless buttress traditional heterosexual arrangements. These views assume that as long as females avoid premarital sexual relations with men, victimization can be avoided. Ironically, however, protection from male victimization is available primarily through marriage—by coupling with a man. The paradoxical message teaches females to fear the very men who will ultimately protect them.

The third discourse, *sexuality as individual morality*, introduces explicit notions of sexual subjectivity for women. Although quite judgmental and moralistic, this discourse values women's sexual decisionmaking as long as the decisions made are for premarital abstinence. For example, Secretary of Education William

Bennett urges schools to teach "morality literacy" and to educate towards "modesty," "chastity," and "abstinence" until marriage. The language of self-control and self-respect reminds students that sexual immorality breeds not only personal problems but also community tax burdens.

The debate over morality in sex education curricula marks a clear contradiction among educational conservatives over whether and how the state may intervene in the "privacy of families." Non-interventionists, including Schlafly and Onalee McGraw, argue that educators should not teach about sexuality at all. To do so is to take a particular moral position which subverts the family. Interventionists, including Koop, Bennett, and Bauer, argue that schools should teach about sexuality by focusing on "good values," but disagree about how. Koop proposes open discussion of sexuality and the use of condoms, while Bennett advocates "sexual restraint" ("Koop AIDS Stand Assailed," 1987). Sexuality in this discourse is posed as a test of self-control; individual restraint triumphs over social temptation. Pleasure and desire for women as sexual subjects remain largely in the shadows, obscured from adolescent eyes.

The fourth discourse, a *discourse of desire*, remains a whisper inside the official work of U.S. public schools. If introduced at all, it is as an interruption of the ongoing conversation (Snitow, Stansell, & Thompson, 1983). The naming of desire, pleasure, or sexual entitlement, particularly for females, barely exists in the formal agenda of public schooling on sexuality. When spoken, it is tagged with reminders of "consequences"—emotional, physical, moral, reproductive, and/or financial (Freudenberg, 1987). A genuine discourse of desire would invite adolescents to explore what feels good and bad, desirable and undesirable, grounded in experiences, needs, and limits. Such a discourse would release females from a position of receptivity, enable an analysis of the dialectics of victimization and pleasure, and would pose female adolescents as subjects of sexuality, initiators as well as negotiators (Golden, 1984; Petchesky, 1984; Thompson, 1983).

In Sweden, where sex education has been offered in schools since the turn of the century, the State Commission on Sex Education recommends teaching students to "acquire a knowledge . . . [which] will equip them to experience sexual life as a source of happiness and joy in fellowship with other [people]" (Brown, 1983, p. 88). The teachers' handbook goes on, "The many young people who wish to wait [before initiating sexual activity] and those who have had early sexual relations should experience, in class, [the feeling] that they are understood and accepted" (p. 93). Compare this to an exercise suggested in a major U.S. metropolitan sex education curriculum: "Discuss and evaluate: things which may cause teenagers to engage in sexual relations before they are ready to assume the responsibility of marriage" (see Philadelphia School District, 1986; and New York City Board of Education, 1984).

A discourse of desire, though seldom explored in U.S. classrooms, does occur in less structured school situations. The following excerpts, taken from group and individual student interviews, demonstrate female adolescents' subjective experiences of body and desire as they begin to articulate notions of sexuality.

In some cases young women pose a critique of marriage:

> I'm still in love with Simon, but I'm seeing Jose. He's OK but he said, "Will you be my girl?" I hate that. It feels like they own you. Like I say to a girlfriend, "What's wrong? You look terrible!" and she says, "I'm married!" (Millie, a 16-year-old student from the Dominican Republic)

In other cases they offer stories of their own victimization:

> It's not like last year. Then I came to school regular. Now my old boyfriend, he waits for me in front of my building every morning and he fights with me. Threatens me, gettin' all bad. . . . I want to move out of my house and live 'cause he ain't gonna stop no way. (Sylvia, age 17, about to drop out of twelfth grade)

Some even speak of desire:

> I'm sorry I couldn't call you last night about the interview, but my boyfriend came back from [the] Navy and I wanted to spend the night with him, we don't get to see each other much. (Shandra, age 17, after a no-show for an interview)

In a context in which desire is not silenced, but acknowledged and discussed, conversations with adolescent women can, as seen here, educate through a dialectic of victimization and pleasure. Despite formal silencing, it would be misleading to suggest that talk of desire never emerges within public schools. Notwithstanding a political climate organized around the suppression of this conversation, some teachers and community advocates continue to struggle for an empowering sex education curriculum both in and out of the high school classroom.

Family life curricula and/or plans for a school-based health clinic have been carefully generated in many communities. Yet they continue to face loud and sometimes violent resistance by religious and community groups, often from outside the district lines (Boffey, 1987; "Chicago School Clinic," 1986; Dowd, 1986; Perlez, 1986a, 1986b; Rohter, 1985). In other communities, when curricula or clinics have been approved with little overt confrontation, monies for training are withheld. For example, in New York City in 1987, $1.7 million was initially requested to implement training on the Family Life education curriculum. As sex educators confronted community and religious groups, the inclusion of some topics as well as the language of others were continually negotiated. Ultimately, the Chancellor requested only $600,000 for training, a sum substantially inadequate to the task.[2]

In this political context many public school educators nevertheless continue to take personal and professional risks to create materials and foster classroom environments which speak fully to the sexual subjectivities of young women and men. Some operate within the privacy of their classrooms, subverting the official curriculum and engaging students in critical discussion. Others advocate publicly for enriched curricula and training. A few have even requested that community-based advocates *not* agitate for official curricular change, so "we [teachers] can continue to do what we do in the classroom, with nobody looking over our shoulders. You make a big public deal of this, and it will blow open."[3] Within public school classrooms, it seems that female desire may indeed be addressed when educators act subversively. But in the typical sex education classroom, silence, and therefore distortion, surrounds female desire.

The blanketing of female sexual subjectivity in public school classrooms, in public discourse, and in bed will sound familiar to those who have read Luce Irigaray (1980) and Helene Cíxous (1981). These French feminists have argued that expressions of female voice, body, and sexuality are essentially inaudible when the dominant language and ways of viewing are male. Inside the hegemony of what they call The Law of the Father, female desire and pleasure can gain expression only in the terrain already charted by men (see also Burke, 1980). In the public school arena, this constriction of what is called sexuality allows girls one primary decision—to say yes or no—to a question not necessarily their own. A discourse of desire in which young women have a voice would be informed and generated out of their own socially constructed sexual meanings. It is to these expressions that we now turn.

The bodies of female adolescents: voices and structured silences

If four discourses can be distinguished among the many positions articulated by various "authorities," the sexual meanings voiced by female adolescents defy such classification. A discourse of desire, though absent in the "official" curriculum, is by no means missing from the lived experiences or commentaries of young women. This section introduces their sexual thoughts, concerns, and meanings, as represented by a group of Black and Latina female adolescents—students and dropouts from a public high school in New York City serving predominantly low-income youths. In my year at this comprehensive high school I had frequent opportunity to speak with adolescents and listen to them talk about sex. The comments reported derive from conversations between the young women and their teachers, among themselves, and with me, as researcher. During conversations, the young women talked freely about fears and, in the same breath, asked about passions. Their struggle to untangle issues of gender, power, and sexuality underscores the fact that, for them, notions of sexual negotiation cannot be separated from sacrifice and nurturance.

The adolescent female rarely reflects simply on sexuality. Her sense of sexuality is informed by peers, culture, religion, violence, history, passion, authority, rebellion, body, past and future, and gender and racial relations of power (Espin, 1984; Omolade, 1983). The adolescent woman herself assumes a dual consciousness— at once taken with the excitement of actual/anticipated sexuality and consumed with anxiety and worry. While too few safe spaces exist for adolescent women's exploration of sexual subjectivities, there are all too many dangerous spots for their exploitation.

Whether in a classroom, on the street, at work, or at home, the adolescent female's sexuality is negotiated by, for, and despite the young woman herself. Patricia, a young Puerto Rican woman who worried about her younger sister, relates: "You see, I'm the love child and she's the one born because my mother was raped in Puerto Rico. Her father's in jail now, and she feels so bad about the whole thing so she acts bad." For Patricia, as for the many young women who have experienced and/or witnessed sexual violence, discussions of sexuality merge representations of passion with violence. Often the initiator of conversation among peers about virginity, orgasm, "getting off," and pleasure, Patricia mixed sexual talk freely with references to force and violence. She is a poignant narrator who illustrates, from the female adolescent's perspective, that sexual victimization and desire coexist (Benjamin, 1983).

Sharlene and Betty echo this braiding of danger and desire. Sharlene explained: "Boys always be trying to get into my panties," and Betty added: "I don't be needin' a man who won't give me no pleasure but take my money and expect me to take care of him." This powerful commentary on gender relations, voiced by Black adolescent females, was inseparable from their views of sexuality. To be a woman was to be strong, independent, and reliable—but not too independent for fear of scaring off a man.

Deidre continued this conversation, explicitly pitting male fragility against female strength: "Boys in my neighborhood ain't wrapped so tight. Got to be careful how you treat them. . . ." She reluctantly admitted that perhaps it is more important for Black males than females to attend college, "Girls and women, we're stronger, we take care of ourselves. But boys and men, if they don't get away from the neighborhood, they end up in jail, on drugs or dead . . . or wack [crazy]."

These young women spoke often of anger at males, while concurrently expressing a strong desire for male attention: "I dropped out 'cause I fell in love, and couldn't stop thinking of him." An equally compelling desire was to protect young males—particularly Black males—from a system which "makes them wack." Ever aware of the ways that institutional racism and the economy have affected Black males, these young women seek pleasure but also offer comfort. They often view self-protection as taking something away from young men. Lavanda offered a telling example: "If I ask him to use a condom, he won't feel like a man."

In order to understand the sexual subjectivities of young women more completely, educators need to reconstruct schooling as an empowering context in which we listen to and work with the meanings and experiences of gender and sexuality revealed by the adolescents themselves. When we refuse that responsibility, we prohibit an education which adolescents wholly need and deserve. My classroom observations suggest that such education is rare.

Ms. Rosen, a teacher of a sex education class, opened one session with a request: "You should talk to your mother or father about sex before you get involved." Nilda initiated what became an informal protest by a number of Latino students: "Not our parents! We tell them one little thing and they get crazy. My cousin got sent to Puerto Rico to live with her religious aunt, and my sister got beat 'cause my father thought she was with a boy." For these adolescents, a safe space for discussion, critique, and construction of sexualities was not something they found in their homes. Instead, they relied on school, the spot they chose for the safe exploration of sexualities.

The absence of safe spaces for exploring sexuality affects all adolescents. It was paradoxical to realize that perhaps the only students who had an in-school opportunity for critical sexual discussion in the comfort of peers were the few students who had organized the Gay and Lesbian Association (GALA) at the high school. While most lesbian, gay, or bisexual students were undoubtedly closeted, those few who were "out" claimed this public space for their display and for their sanctuary. Exchanging support when families and peers would offer little, GALA members worried that so few students were willing to come out, and that so many suffered the assaults of homophobia individually. The gay and lesbian rights movement had powerfully affected these youngsters, who were comfortable enough to support each other in a place not considered very safe—a public high school in which echoes of "faggot!" fill the halls.

In the absence of an education which explores and unearths danger and desire, sexuality education classes typically provide little opportunity for discussions beyond those constructed around superficial notions of male heterosexuality (see Kelly, 1986, for a counterexample). Male pleasure is taught, albeit as biology. Teens learn about "wet dreams" (as the onset of puberty for males), "erection" (as the preface to intercourse), and "ejaculation" (as the act of inseminating). Female pleasures and questions are far less often the topic of discussion. Few voices of female sexual agency can be heard. The language of victimization and its underlying concerns—"Say No," put a brake on his sexuality, don't encourage—ultimately deny young women the right to control their own sexuality by providing no access to a legitimate position of sexual subjectivity. Often conflicted about self-representation, adolescent females spend enormous amounts of time trying to "save it," "lose it," convince others that they have lost or saved it, or trying to be "discreet" instead of focusing their energies in ways that are sexually autonomous, responsible, and pleasurable. In classroom observations, girls who were heterosexually active rarely spoke, for fear of being ostracized (Fine, 1986). Those who were heterosexual virgins had the same worry. And most students who were gay, bisexual, or lesbian remained closeted, aware of the very real dangers of homophobia.

Occasionally, the difficult and pleasurable aspects of sexuality were discussed together, coming either as an interruption, or because an educational context was constructed. During a social studies class, for example, Catherine, the proud mother of two-year-old Tiffany, challenged an assumption underlying the class discussion—that teen motherhood devastates mother and child; "If I didn't get pregnant I would have continued on a downward path, going nowhere. They say teenage pregnancy is bad for you, but it was good for me. I know I can't mess around now, I got to worry about what's good for Tiffany and for me."

Another interruption came from Opal, a young Black student. Excerpts from her hygiene class follow.

> *Teacher:* Let's talk about teenage pregnancy.
> *Opal:* How come girls in the locker room say, "You a virgin?" and if you say "Yeah" they laugh and say "Ohh, you're a virgin. . . ." And some Black teenagers, I don't mean to be racial, when they get ready to tell their mothers they had sex, some break on them and some look funny. My friend told her mother and she broke all the dishes. She told her mother so she could get protection so she don't get pregnant.
> *Teacher:* When my 13-year-old (relative) asked for birth control I was shocked and angry.
> *Portia:* Mothers should help so she can get protection and not get pregnant or diseases. So you was wrong.
> *Teacher:* Why not say "I'm thinking about having sex"?
> *Portia:* You tell them after, not before, having sex but before pregnancy.
> *Teacher* (now angry): Then it's a fait accompli and you expect my compassion? You have to take more responsibility.
> *Portia:* I am! If you get pregnant after you told your mother and you got all the stuff and still get pregnant, you the fool. Take up hygiene and learn. Then it's my responsibility if I end up pregnant. . . .
> Field Note, October 23, Hygiene Class

Two days later, the discussion continued.

> *Teacher:* What topics should we talk about in sex education?
> *Portia:* Organs, how they work.
> *Opal:* What's an orgasm?
> [laughter]
> *Teacher:* Sexual response, sensation all over the body. What's analogous to the male penis on the female?

Theo:	Clitoris.
Teacher:	Right, go home and look in the mirror.
Portia:	She is too much!
Teacher:	Why look in the mirror?
Elaine:	It's yours.
Teacher:	Why is it important to know what your body looks like?
Opal:	You should like your body.
Teacher:	You should know what it looks like when it's healthy, so you can recognize problems like vaginal warts.

Field Note, October 25, Hygiene Class

The discourse of desire, initiated by Opal but evident only as an interruption, faded rapidly into the discourse of disease—warning about the dangers of sexuality.

It was in the spring of that year that Opal showed up pregnant. Her hygiene teacher, who was extremely concerned and involved with her students, was also quite angry with Opal: "Who is going to take care of that baby, you or your mother? You know what it costs to buy diapers and milk and afford child care?"

Opal, in conversation with me, related, "I got to leave [school] 'cause even if they don't say it, them teachers got hate in their eyes when they look at my belly." In the absence of a way to talk about passion, pleasure, danger, and responsibility, this teacher fetishized the latter two, holding the former two hostage. Because adolescent females combine these experiences in their daily lives, the separation is false, judgmental, and ultimately not very educational.

Over the year in this high school, and in other public schools since, I have observed a systematic refusal to name issues, particularly issues that caused adults discomfort. Educators often projected their discomfort onto students in the guise of "protecting" them (Fine, 1987). An example of such silencing can be seen in a (now altered) policy of the school district of Philadelphia. In 1985 a student informed me, "We're not allowed to talk about abortion in our school." Assuming this was an overstatement, I asked an administrator at the District about this practice. She explained, "That's not quite right. If a student asks a question about abortion, the teacher can define abortion, she just can't discuss it." How can definition occur without discussion, exchange, conversation, or critique unless a sub-text of silencing prevails (Greene, 1986; Noddings, 1986)?

Explicit silencing of abortion has since been lifted in Philadelphia. The revised curriculum now reads:

Options for unintended pregnancy:
(a) adoption
(b) foster care
(c) single parenthood
(d) teen marriage
(e) abortion

A footnote is supposed to be added, however, to elaborate the negative consequences of abortion. In the social politics which surround public schools, such compromises are apparent across cities.

The New York City Family Life Education curriculum reads similarly (New York City Board of Education, 1984, p. 172):

List: The possible options for an unintended pregnancy. What considerations should be given in the decision on the alternatives?
-   adoption
-   foster care
-   mother keeps baby
-   elective abortion

Discuss:
-   religious viewpoints on abortion
-   present laws concerning abortion
-   current developments in prenatal diagnosis and their implication for abortion issues
-   why abortion should not be considered a contraceptive device

List: The people or community services that could provide assistance in the event of an unintended pregnancy.

Invite: A speaker to discuss alternatives to abortion; for example, a social worker from the Department of Social Services to discuss foster care.

One must be suspicious when diverse views are sought only for abortion, and not for adoption, teen motherhood, or foster care. The call to silence is easily identified in current political and educational contexts (Fine, 1987; Foucault, 1980). The silence surrounding contraception and abortion options and diversity in sexual orientations denies adolescents information and sends the message that such conversations are taboo—at home, at church, and even at school.

In contrast to these "official curricula," which allow discussion and admission of desire only as an interruption, let us examine other situations in which young women were invited to analyze sexuality across categories of the body, the mind, the heart, and of course, gender politics.

Teen Choice, a voluntary counseling program held on-site by non-Board of Education social workers, offered an instance in which the complexities of pleasure and danger were invited, analyzed, and braided into discussions of sexuality. In a small group discussion, the counselor asked of the seven ninth graders, "What are the two functions of a penis?" One student responded, "To pee!" Another student offered the second function: "To eat!" which was followed by laughter and serious discussion. The conversation proceeded as the teacher asked, "Do all penises look alike?" The students explained, "No, they are all different colors!"

The freedom to express, beyond simple right and wrong answers, enabled these young women to offer what they knew with humor and delight. This discussion ended as one student insisted that if you "jump up and down a lot, the stuff will fall out of you and you won't get pregnant," to which the social worker answered with slight exasperation that millions of sperm would have to be released for such "expulsion" to work, and that of course, it wouldn't work. In this conversation one could hear what seemed like too much experience, too little information, and too few questions asked by the students. But the discussion, which was sex-segregated and guided by the experiences and questions of the students themselves (and the skills of the social worker), enabled easy movement between pleasure and danger, safety and desire, naiveté and knowledge, and victimization and entitlement.

What is evident, then, is that even in the absence of a discourse of desire, young women express their notions of sexuality and relate their experiences. Yet, "official" discourses of sexuality leave little room for such exploration. The authorized sexual discourses define what is safe, what is taboo, and what will be silenced. This discourse of sexuality mis-educates adolescent women. What results is a discourse of sexuality based on the male in search of desire and the female in search of protection. The open, coed sexuality discussions so many fought for in the 1970s have been appropriated as a forum for the primacy of male heterosexuality and the preservation of female victimization.

The politics of female sexual subjectivities

In 1912, an education committee explicitly argued that "scientific" sex education "should ... keep sex consciousness and sex emotions at the minimum" (Leo, 1986). In the same era G. Stanley Hall proposed diversionary pursuits for adolescents, including hunting, music, and sports, "to reduce sex stress and tension ... to short-circuit, transmute it and turn it on to develop the higher powers of the men [sic]" (Hall, 1914, pp. 29, 30). In 1915 Orison Marden, author of *The Crime of Silence*, chastised educators, reformers, and public health specialists for their unwillingness to speak publicly about sexuality and for relying inappropriately on parents and peers, who were deemed too ignorant to provide sex instruction (Imber, 1984; Strong, 1972). And in 1921 radical sex educator Maurice Bigelow wrote:

> Now, most scientifically-trained women seem to agree that there are no corresponding phenomena in the early pubertal life of the normal young woman who has good health (corresponding to male masturbation). A limited number of mature women, some of them physicians, report having experienced in the pubertal years localized tumescence and other disturbances which made them definitely conscious of sexual instincts. However, it should be noted that most of these are known to have had a personal history including one or more such abnormalities such as dysmenorrhea, uterine displacement, pathological ovaries, leucorrhea, tuberculosis, masturbation, neurasthenia, nymphomania, or other disturbances which are sufficient to account for local sexual stimulation. In short such women are not normal. . . . (p. 179)

In the 1950s public school health classes separated girls from boys. Girls "learned about sex" by watching films of the accelerated development of breasts and hips, the flow of menstrual blood, and then the progression of venereal disease as a result of participation in out-of-wedlock heterosexual activity.

Thirty years and a much-debated sexual revolution later (Ehrenreich, Hess, & Jacobs, 1986), much has changed. Feminism, the Civil Rights Movement, the disability and gay rights movements, birth control, legal abortion with federal funding (won and then lost), and reproductive technologies are part of these changes (Weeks, 1985). Due both to the consequences of, and the backlashes against, these movements, students today do learn about sexuality—if typically through the representations of female sexuality as inadequacy or victimization, male homosexuality as a story of predator and prey, and male heterosexuality as desire.

Young women today know that female sexual subjectivity is at least not an inherent contradiction. Perhaps they even feel it is an entitlement. Yet when public schools resist acknowledging the fullness of female sexual subjectivities, they reproduce a profound social ambivalence which dichotomizes female hetero-sexuality (Espin, 1984; Golden, 1984; Omolade, 1983). This ambivalence sur-rounds a fragile cultural distinction between two forms of female sexuality: *consensual* sexuality, representing consent or choice in sexuality, and *coercive* sexuality, which represents force, victimization, and/or crime (Weeks, 1985).

During the 1980s, however, this distinction began to be challenged. It was acknowledged that gender-based power inequities shape, define, and construct experiences of sexuality. Notions of sexual consent and force, except in extreme circumstances, became complicated, no longer in simple opposition. The first problem concerned how to conceptualize power asymmetries and consensual sexuality. Could *consensual* female heterosexuality be said to exist within a con-text replete with structures, relationships, acts, and threats of female victimization (sexual, social, and economic) (MacKinnon, 1983)? How could we speak of "sexual preference" when sexual involvement outside of heterosexuality may ser-iously jeopardize one's social and/or economic well-being (Petchesky, 1984)? Diverse female sexual subjectivities emerge through, despite, and because of gender-based power asymmetries. To imagine a female sexual self, free of and uncontaminated by power, was rendered naive (Foucault, 1980; Irigaray, 1980; Rubin, 1984).

The second problem involved the internal incoherence of the categories. Once assumed fully independent, the two began to blur as the varied practices of sexual-ity went public. At the intersection of these presumably parallel forms—coercive and consensual sexualities—lay "sexual" acts of violence and "violent" acts of sex. "Sexual" acts of violence, including marital rape, acquaintance rape, and sexual harassment, were historically considered consensual. A woman involved in a marriage, on a date, or working outside her home "naturally" risked receiving sexual attention; her consent was inferred from her presence. But today, in many states, this woman can sue her husband for such sexual acts of violence; in all states, she can prosecute a boss. What was once part of "domestic life" or "work" may, today, be criminal. On the other hand, "violent" acts of sex, including consensual sadomasochism and the use of violence-portraying pornography, were once considered inherently coercive for women (Benjamin, 1983; Rubin, 1984; Weeks, 1985). Female involvement in such sexual practices historically had been dismissed as nonconsensual. Today such romanticizing of a naive and moral "feminine sexuality" has been challenged as essentialist, and the assumption that such a feminine sexuality is "natural" to women has been shown to be false (Rubin, 1984).

Over the past decade, understandings of female sexual choice, consent, and coercion have grown richer and more complex. While questions about female subjectivities have become more interesting, the answers (for some) remain decep-tively simple. Inside public schools, for example, female adolescents continue to be educated as though they were the potential *victims* of sexual (male) desire. By contrast, the ideological opposition represents only adult married women as fully consensual partners. The distinction of coercion and consent has been organized simply and respectively around age and marital status—which effectively resolves any complexity and/or ambivalence.

The ambivalence surrounding female heterosexuality places the victim and subject in opposition and derogates all women who represent female sexual sub-jectivities outside of marriage—prostitutes, lesbians, single mothers, women involved with multiple partners, and particularly, Black single mothers (Weitz, 1984). "Protected" from this derogation, the typical adolescent woman, as represented in sex education curricula, is without any sexual subjectivity. The discourse of victimization not only obscures the derogation, it also transforms socially distributed anxieties about female sexuality into acceptable, and even protective, talk.

The fact that schools implicitly organize sex education around a concern for female victimization is suspect, however, for two reasons. First, if female victims of male violence were truly a social concern, wouldn't the victims of rape, incest, and sexual harassment encounter social compassion, and not suspicion and blame? And second, if sex education were designed primarily to prevent victimization but not to prevent exploration of desire, wouldn't there be more discussions of both the pleasures and relatively fewer risks of disease or pregnancy associated with lesbian relationships and protected sexual intercourse, or of the risk-free pleasures of masturbation and fantasy? Public education's concern for the female victim is revealed as deceptively thin when real victims are discredited, and when nonvictimizing pleasures are silenced.

This unacknowledged social ambivalence about heterosexuality polarizes the debates over sex education and school-based health clinics. The anxiety effectively treats the female sexual victim as though she were a completely separate species from the female sexual subject. Yet the adolescent women quoted earlier in this text remind us that the female victim and subject coexist in every woman's body.

Toward a discourse of sexual desire and social entitlement: in the student bodies of public schools

I have argued that silencing a discourse of desire buttresses the icon of woman-as-victim. In so doing, public schooling may actually disable young women in their negotiations as sexual subjects. Trained through and into positions of passivity and victimization, young women are currently educated away from positions of sexual self-interest.

If we re-situate the adolescent woman in a rich and empowering educational context, she develops a sense of self which is sexual as well as intellectual, social, and economic. In this section I invite readers to imagine such a context. The dialectic of desire and victimization—across spheres of labor, social relations, and sexuality—would then frame schooling. While many of the curricula and interventions discussed in this paper are imperfect, data on the effectiveness of what *is* available are nevertheless compelling. Studies of sex education curricula, SBHCs, classroom discussions, and ethnographies of life inside public high schools demonstrate that a sense of sexual and social entitlement for young women *can* be fostered within public schools.

Sex education as intellectual empowerment

Harris and Yankelovich polls confirm that over 80 percent of American adults believe that students should be educated about sexuality within their public schools. Seventy-five percent believe that homosexuality and abortion should be included in the curriculum, with 40 percent of those surveyed by Yankelovich et al. (N = 1015) agreeing that 12-year-olds should be taught about oral and anal sex (see Leo, 1986; Harris, 1985).

While the public continues to debate the precise content of sex education, most parents approve and support sex education for their children. An Illinois program monitored parental requests to "opt out" and found that only 6 or 7 of

850 children were actually excused from sex education courses (Leo, 1986). In a California assessment, fewer than 2 percent of parents disallowed their children's participation. And in a longitudinal 5-year program in Connecticut, 7 of 2,500 students requested exemption from these classes (Scales, 1981). Resistance to sex education, while loud at the level of public rhetoric and conservative organizing, is both less vocal and less active within schools and parents' groups (Hottois & Milner, 1975; Scales, 1981).

Sex education courses are offered broadly, if not comprehensively, across the United States. In 1981, only 7 of 50 states actually had laws against such instruction, and only one state enforced a prohibition (Kirby & Scales, 1981). Surveying 179 urban school districts, Sonnenstein and Pittman (1984) found that 75 percent offered some sex education within senior and junior high schools, while 66 percent of the elementary schools offered sex education units. Most instruction was, however, limited to 10 hours or less, with content focused on anatomy. In his extensive review of sex education programs, Kirby (1985) concludes that less than 10 percent of all public school students are exposed to what might be considered comprehensive sex education courses.

The progress on AIDS education is more encouraging, and more complex (see Freudenberg, 1987), but cannot be adequately reviewed in this article. It is important to note, however, that a December 1986 report released by the U.S. Conference of Mayors documents that 54 percent of the 73 largest school districts and 25 state school agencies offer some form of AIDS education (Benedetto, 1987). Today, debates among federal officials—including Secretary of Education Bennett and Surgeon General Koop—and among educators question *when* and *what* to offer in AIDS education. The question is no longer *whether* such education should be promoted.

Not only has sex education been accepted as a function of public schooling, but it has survived empirical tests of effectiveness. Evaluation data demonstrate that sex education can increase contraceptive knowledge and use (Kirby, 1985; Public/Private Ventures, 1987). In terms of sexual activity (measured narrowly in terms of the onset or frequency of heterosexual intercourse), the evidence suggests that sex education does not instigate an earlier onset or increase of such sexual activity (Zelnick & Kim, 1982) and may, in fact, postpone the onset of heterosexual intercourse (Zabin, Hirsch, Smith, Streett, & Hardy, 1986). The data for pregnancy rates appear to demonstrate no effect for exposure to sex education alone (see Dawson, 1986; Marsiglio & Mott, 1986; Kirby, 1985).

Sex education as constituted in these studies is not sufficient to diminish teen pregnancy rates. In all likelihood it would be naive to expect that sex education (especially if only ten hours in duration) would carry such a "long arm" of effectiveness. While the widespread problem of teen pregnancy must be attributed broadly to economic and social inequities (Jones et al., 1985), sex education remains necessary and sufficient to educate, demystify, and improve contraceptive knowledge and use. In conjunction with material opportunities for enhanced life options, it is believed that sex education and access to contraceptives and abortion can help to reduce the rate of unintended pregnancy among teens (Dryfoos, 1985a, 1985b; National Research Council, 1987).

School-based health clinics: sexual empowerment

The public opinion and effectiveness data for school-based health clinics are even more compelling than those for sex education. Thirty SBHCs provide on-site health care services to senior, and sometimes junior, high school students in more than 18 U.S. communities, with an additional 25 communities developing similar programs (Kirby, 1985). These clinics offer, at a minimum, health counseling, referrals, and follow-up examinations. Over 70 percent conduct pelvic examinations (Kirby, 1985), approximately 52 percent prescribe contraceptives, and 28 percent dispense contraceptives (Leo, 1986). None performs abortions, and few refer for abortions.

All SBHCs require some form of general parental notification and/or consent, and some charge a nominal fee for generic health services. Relative to private physicians, school-based health clinics and' other family planning agencies are substantially more willing to provide contraceptive services to unmarried minors without specific parental consent (consent in this case referring explicitly to contraception). Only one percent of national Planned Parenthood affiliates require consent or notification, compared to 10 percent of public health department programs and 19 percent of hospitals (Torres & Forrest, 1985).

The consequences of consent provisions for abortion are substantial. Data from two states, Massachusetts and Minnesota, demonstrate that parental consent laws result in increased teenage pregnancies or increased numbers of out-of-state abortions. The Reproductive Freedom Project of the American Civil Liberties Union, in a report which examines the consequences of such consent provisions, details the impact of these statutes on teens, on their familial relationships, and ultimately, on their unwanted children (Reproductive Freedom Project, 1986). In an analysis of the impact of Minnesota's mandatory parental notification law from 1981 to 1985, this report documents over 7,000 pregnancies in teens aged 13–17, 3,500 of whom "went to state court to seek the right to confidential abortions, all at considerable personal cost." The report also notes that many of the pregnant teens did not petition the court, "although their entitlement and need for confidential abortions was as strong or more so than the teenagers who made it to court. . . . Only those minors who are old enough and wealthy enough or resourceful enough are actually able to use the court bypass option" (Reproductive Freedom Project, p. 4).

These consent provisions, with allowance for court bypass, not only increase the number of unwanted teenage pregnancies carried to term, but also extend the length of time required to secure an abortion, potentially endangering the life of the teenage woman, and increasing the costs of the abortion. The provisions may also jeopardize the physical and emotional well-being of some young women and their mothers, particularly when paternal consent is required and the pregnant teenager resides with a single mother. Finally, the consent provisions create a class-based health care system. Adolescents able to afford travel to a nearby state, or able to pay a private physician for a confidential abortion, have access to an abortion. Those unable to afford the travel, or those who are unable to contact a private physician, are likely to become teenage mothers (Reproductive Freedom Project, 1986).

In Minneapolis, during the time from 1980 to 1984 when the law was implemented, the birth rate for 15- to 17-year-olds increased 38.4 percent, while the birth rate for 18- and 19-year-olds—not affected by the law—rose only .3 percent (Reproductive Freedom Project, 1986). The state of Massachusetts passed a parental consent law which took effect in 1981. An analysis of the impact of that law concludes that ". . . the major impact of the Massachusetts parental consent law has been to send a monthly average of between 90 and 95 of the state's minors across state lines in search of an abortion. This number represents about one in every three minor abortion patients living in Massachusetts" (Cartoof & Klerman, 1986). These researchers, among others, write that parental consent laws could have more devastating effects in larger states, from which access to neighboring states would be more difficult.

The inequalities inherent in consent provisions and the dramatic consequences which result for young women are well recognized. For example, twenty-nine states and the District of Columbia now explicitly authorize minors to grant their own consent for receipt of contraceptive information and/or services, independent of parental knowledge or consent (see Melton & Russo, 1987, for full discussion; National Research Council, 1987; for a full analysis of the legal, emotional, and physical health problems attendant upon parental consent laws for abortion, see the Reproductive Freedom Project report). More recently, consent laws for abortion in Pennsylvania and California have been challenged as unconstitutional.

Public approval of SBHCs has been slow but consistent. In the 1986 Yankelovich survey, 84 percent of surveyed adults agree that these clinics should provide birth control information; 36 percent endorse dispensing of contraceptives to students (Leo, 1986). In 1985, Harris found that 67 percent of all respondents, including 76 percent of Blacks and 76 percent of Hispanics, agree that public schools should establish formal ties with family planning clinics for teens to learn about and obtain contraception (Harris, 1985). Mirroring the views of the general public, a national sample of school administrators polled by the Education Research Group indicated that more than 50 percent believe birth control should be offered in school-based clinics; 30 percent agree that parental permission should be sought, and 27 percent agree that contraceptives should be dispensed, even if parental consent is not forthcoming. The discouraging news is that 96 percent of these respondents indicate that their districts do not presently offer such services (Benedetto, 1987; Werner, 1987).

Research on the effectiveness of SBHCs is consistently persuasive. The three-year Johns Hopkins study of school-based health clinics (Zabin et al., 1986) found that schools in which SBHCs made referrals and dispensed contraceptives noted an increase in the percentage of "virgin" females visiting the program as well as an increase in contraceptive use. They also found a significant reduction in pregnancy rates: There was a 13 percent increase at experimental schools after 10 months, versus a 50 percent increase at control schools; after 28 months, pregnancy rates decreased 30 percent at experimental schools versus a 53 percent increase at control schools. Furthermore, by the second year, a substantial percentage of males visited the clinic (48 percent of males in experimental schools indicated that they "have ever been to a birth control clinic or to a physician about birth control," compared to 12 percent of males in control schools). Contrary to common belief, the schools in which clinics dispensed contraceptives showed a substantial postponement of first experience of heterosexual intercourse among high school students and an increase in the proportion of young women visiting the clinic prior to "first coitus."

Paralleling the Hopkins findings, the St. Paul Maternity and Infant Care Project (1985) found that pregnancy rates dropped substantially in schools with clinics, from 79 births/1,000 (1973) to 26 births/1,000 (1984). Teens who delivered and kept their infants had an 80 percent graduation rate, relative to approximately 50 percent of young mothers nationally. Those who stayed in school reported a 1.3 percent repeat birth rate, compared to 17 percent nationally. Over three years, pregnancy rates dropped by 40 percent. Twenty-five percent of young women in the school received some form of family planning and 87 percent of clients were continuing to use contraception at a 3-year follow-up. There were fewer obstetric complications; fewer babies were born at low birth weights; and prenatal visits to physicians increased relative to students in the control schools.

Predictions that school-based health clinics would advance the onset of sexual intimacy, heighten the degree of "promiscuity" and incidence of pregnancy, and hold females primarily responsible for sexuality were countered by the evidence. The onset of sexual intimacy was postponed, while contraception was used more reliably. Pregnancy rates substantially diminished and, over time, a large group of males began to view contraception as a shared responsibility.

It is worth restating here that females who received family planning counseling and/or contraception actually postponed the onset of heterosexual intercourse. I would argue that the availability of such services may enable females to feel they are sexual agents, entitled and therefore responsible, rather than at the constant and terrifying mercy of a young man's pressure to "give in" or of a parent's demands to "save yourself." With a sense of sexual agency and not necessarily urgency, teen girls may be less likely to use or be used by pregnancy (Petchesky, 1984).

Nontraditional vocational training: social and economic entitlement

The literature reviewed suggests that sex education, access to contraception, and opportunities for enhanced life options, in combination (Dryfoos, 1985a, 1985b; Kirby, 1985; Select Committee on Children, Youth and Families, 1985), can significantly diminish the likelihood that a teenager will become pregnant, carry to term, and/or have a repeat pregnancy, and can increase the likelihood that she will stay in high school through graduation (National Research Council, 1987). Education toward entitlement—including a sense of sexual, economic, and social entitlement—may be sufficient to affect adolescent girls' views on sexuality, contraception, and abortion. By framing female subjectivity within the context of social entitlement, sex education would be organized around dialogue and critique, SBHCs would offer health services, options counseling, contraception, and abortion referrals, and the provision of real "life options" would include nontraditional vocational training programs and employment opportunities for adolescent females (Dryfoos, 1985a, 1985b).

In a nontraditional vocational training program in New York City designed for young women, many of whom are mothers, participants' attitudes toward contraception and abortion shifted once they acquired a set of vocational skills, a sense of social entitlement, and a sense of personal competence (Weinbaum, personal communication, 1986). The young women often began the program without strong academic skills or a sense of competence. At the start, they were more likely to express more negative sentiments about contraception and abortion than when they completed the program. One young woman, who initially held strong anti-abortion attitudes, learned that she was pregnant midway through her carpentry apprenticeship. She decided to abort, reasoning that now that she has a future, she can't risk losing it for another baby (Weinbaum, paraphrase of personal communication, 1986). A developing sense of social entitlement may have transformed this young woman's view of reproduction, sexuality, and self.

The Manpower Development Research Corporation (MDRC), in its evaluation of Project Redirection (Polit, Kahn, & Stevens, 1985) offers similar conclusions about a comprehensive vocational training and community-based mentor project for teen mothers and mothers-to-be. Low-income teens were enrolled in Project Redirection, a network of services designed to instill self-sufficiency, in which community women served as mentors. The program included training for what is called "employability," Individual Participation Plans, and peer group sessions. Data on education, employment, and pregnancy outcomes were collected at 12 and 24 months after enrollment. Two years after the program began, many newspapers headlined the program as a failure. The data actually indicated that at 12 months, the end of program involvement, Project Redirection women were significantly *less likely* to experience a repeat pregnancy than comparison women; *more likely* to be using contraception; *more likely* to be in school, to have completed school, or to be in the labor force; and twice as likely (20 percent versus 11 percent, respectively) to have earned a Graduate Equivalency Diploma. At 24 months, however, approximately one year out of the program, Project and comparison women were virtually indistinguishable. MDRC reported equivalent rates of repeat pregnancies, dropout, and unemployment.

The Project Redirection data demonstrate that sustained outcomes cannot be expected once programs have been withdrawn and participants confront the realities of a dismal economy and inadequate child care and social services. The data confirm, however, the effectiveness of comprehensive programs to reduce teen pregnancy rates and encourage study or work as long as the young women are actively engaged. Supply-side interventions—changing people but not structures or opportunities—which leave unchallenged an inhospitable and discriminating economy and a thoroughly impoverished child care/social welfare system are inherently doomed to long-term failure. When such programs fail, the social reading is that "these young women can't be helped." Blaming the victim obscures the fact that the current economy and social welfare arrangements need overhauling if the sustained educational, social, and psychological gains accrued by the Project Redirection participants are to be maintained.

In the absence of enhanced life options, low-income young women are likely to default to early and repeat motherhood as a source of perceived competence, significance, and pleasure. When life options are available, however, a sense of competence and "entitlement to better" may help to prevent second pregnancies, may help to encourage education, and, when available, the pursuit of meaningful work (Burt, Kimmich, Goldmuntz, & Sonnenstein, 1984).

Femininity may be hazardous to her health: the absence of entitlement

Growing evidence suggests that women who lack a sense of social or sexual entitlement, who hold traditional notions of what it means to be female—self-sacrificing and relatively passive—and who undervalue themselves, are disproportionately likely to find themselves with an unwanted pregnancy and to maintain it through to motherhood. While many young women who drop out, pregnant or not, are not at all traditional in these ways, but are quite feisty and are fueled with a sense of entitlement (Fine, 1986; Weinbaum, personal communication, 1987), it may also be the case that young women who do internalize such notions of "femininity" are disproportionately at risk for pregnancy and dropping out.

The Hispanic Policy Development Project reports that low-income female sophomores who, in 1980, expected to be married and/or to have a child by age 19 were disproportionately represented among nongraduates in 1984. Expectations of early marriage and childbearing correspond to dramatic increases (200 to 400 percent) in nongraduation rates for low-income adolescent women across racial and ethnic groups (Hispanic Policy Development Project, 1987). These indicators of traditional notions of womanhood bode poorly for female academic achievement.

The Children's Defense Fund (1986) recently published additional data which demonstrate that young women with poor basic skills are three times more likely to become teen parents than women with average or above-average basic skills. Those with poor or fair basic skills are four times more likely to have more than one child while a teen; 29 percent of women in the bottom skills quintile became mothers by age 18 versus 5 percent of young women in the top quintile. While academic skill problems must be placed in the context of alienating and problematic schools, and not viewed as inherent in these young women, those who fall in the bottom quintile may nevertheless be the least likely to feel entitled or in control of their lives. They may feel more vulnerable to male pressure or more willing to have a child as a means of feeling competent.

My own observations, derived from a year-long ethnographic study of a comprehensive public high school in New York City, further confirm some of these conclusions. Six months into the ethnography, new pregnancies began showing. I noticed that many of the girls who got pregnant and carried to term were not those whose bodies, dress, and manner evoked sensuality and experience. Rather, a number of the pregnant women were those who were quite passive and relatively quiet in their classes. One young woman, who granted me an interview anytime, washed the blackboard for her teacher, rarely spoke in class, and never disobeyed her mother, was pregnant by the spring of the school year (Fine, 1986).

Simple stereotypes, of course, betray the complexity of circumstances under which young women become pregnant and maintain their pregnancies. While U.S. rates of teenage sexual activity and age of "sexual initiation" approximate those of comparable developed countries, the teenage pregnancy, abortion, and childbearing rates in the United States are substantially higher. In the United States, teenagers under age fifteen are at least five times more likely to give birth than similarly aged teens in other industrialized nations (Jones et al., 1985; National Research Council, 1987). The national factors which correlate with low teenage birthrates include adolescent access to sex education and contraception, and relative equality in the distribution of wealth. Economic and structural conditions which support a class-stratified society, and which limit adolescent access to sexual information and contraception, contribute to inflated teenage pregnancy rates and birthrates.

This broad national context acknowledged, it might still be argued that within our country, traditional notions of what it means to be a woman—to remain subordinate, dependent, self-sacrificing, compliant, and ready to marry and/or bear children early—do little to empower women or enhance a sense of entitlement. This is not to say that teenage dropouts or mothers tend to be of any one type. Yet it may well be that the traditions and practices of "femininity" as commonly understood may be hazardous to the economic, social, educational, and sexual development of young women.

In summary, the historic silencing within public schools of conversations about sexuality, contraception, and abortion, as well as the absence of a discourse of desire—in the form of comprehensive sex education, school-based health clinics, and viable life options via vocational training and placement—all combine to exacerbate the vulnerability of young women whom schools, and the critics of sex education and SBHCs, claim to protect.

Conclusion

Adolescents are entitled to a discussion of desire instead of the anti-sex rhetoric which controls the controversies around sex education, SBHCs, and AIDS education. The absence of a discourse of desire, combined with the lack of analysis of the language of victimization, may actually retard the development of sexual subjectivity and responsibility in students. Those most "at risk" of victimization through pregnancy, disease, violence, or harassment—all female students, low-income females in particular, and non-heterosexual males—are those most likely to be victimized by the absence of critical conversation in public schools. Public schools can no longer afford to maintain silence around a discourse of desire. This is not to say that the silencing of a discourse of desire is the primary root of sexual victimization, teen motherhood, and the concomitant poverty experienced by young and low-income females. Nor could it be responsibly argued that interventions initiated by public schools could ever be successful if separate from economic and social development. But it is important to understand that by providing education, counseling, contraception, and abortion referrals, as well as meaningful educational and vocational opportunities, public schools could play an essential role in the construction of the female subject—social and sexual.

And by not providing such an educational context, public schools contribute to the rendering of substantially different outcomes for male and female students, and for male and female dropouts (Fine, 1986). The absence of a thorough sex education curriculum, of school-based health clinics, of access to free and confidential contraceptive and abortion services, of exposure to information about the varieties of sexual pleasures and partners, and of involvement in sustained employment training programs may so jeopardize the educational and economic outcomes for female adolescents as to constitute sex discrimination. How can we ethically continue to withhold educational treatments we know to be effective for adolescent women?

Public schools constitute a sphere in which young women could be offered access to a language and experience of empowerment. In such contexts, "well-educated" young women could breathe life into positions of social critique and experience entitlement rather than victimization, autonomy rather than terror.

Acknowledgements

This paper was originally developed during the Laurie Seminar on Women's Studies at Douglass College, Carol Gilligan, Chair, 1986. The ethnographic research was funded by the W. T. Grant Foundation. The author wishes to thank many individuals for thorough reading, comments, critique, and support: Nancy Barnes, Linda Brodkey, Richard Friend, Carol Gilligan, Henry Giroux, Carol Joffee, Rayna Rapp, David Surrey, and Sandy Weinbaum; additionally, Lori Cornish of Planned Parenthood in Philadelphia provided invaluable research assistance. These individuals bear no responsibility for the final document, but deserve many thanks for their willingness to pursue, unpack, and reconstruct the ideas with me.

Notes

1   The research reported in this article represents one component of a year-long ethnographic investigation of students and dropouts at a comprehensive public high school

in New York City. Funded by the W. T. Grant Foundation, the research was designed to investigate how public urban high schools produce dropout rates in excess of 50 percent. The methods employed over the year included: in-school observations four days/week during the fall, and one to two days/week during the spring; regular (daily) attendance in a hygiene course for twelfth graders; an archival analysis of more than 1,200 students who compose the 1978–79 cohort of incoming ninth graders; interviews with approximately 55 recent and long-term dropouts; analysis of fictional and auto-biographical writings by students; a survey distributed to a subsample of the cohort population; and visits to proprietary schools, programs for Graduate Equivalency Diplomas, naval recruitment sites, and a public high school for pregnant and parenting teens. The methods and preliminary results of the ethnography are detailed in Fine (1986).

2 This information is derived from personal communications with former and present employees of major urban school districts who have chosen to remain anonymous.

3 Personal communication.

References

Bauer, G. (1986). *The family: Preserving America's future*. Washington, DC: U.S. Department of Education.

Benedetto, R. (1987, January 23). AIDS studies become part of curricula. *USA Today*, p. D1.

Benjamin, J. (1983). Master and slave: The fantasy of erotic domination. In A. Snitow, C. Stansell, & S. Thompson (Eds.), *Powers of desire* (pp. 280–299). New York: Monthly Review Press.

Bennett, W. (1987, July 3). Why Johnny can't abstain. *National Review*, pp. 36–38, 56.

Bigelow, M. (1921). *Sex-Education*. New York: Macmillan.

Boffey, P. (1987, February 27). Reagan to back AIDS plan urging youths to avoid sex. *New York Times*, p. A14.

Brown, P. (1983). The Swedish approach to sex education and adolescent pregnancy: Some impressions. *Family Planning Perspectives, 15*(2), 92–95.

Burke, C. (1980). Introduction to Luce Irigaray's "When our lips speak together." *Signs, 6,* 66–68.

Burt, M., Kimmich, M., Goldmuntz, J., & Sonnenstein, F. (1984). *Helping pregnant adolescents: Outcomes and costs of service delivery*. Final Report on the Evaluation of Adolescent Pregnancy Programs. Washington, DC: Urban Institute.

Cartoof, V., & Klerman, L. (1986). Parental consent for abortion: Impact of the Massachusetts law. *American Journal of Public Health, 76,* 397–400.

Chicago school clinic is sued over birth control materials. (1986, October 16). *New York Times*, p. A24.

Children's Defense Fund. (1986). *Preventing adolescent pregnancy: What schools can do*. Washington, DC: Children's Defense Fund.

Children's Defense Fund. (1987). *Adolescent pregnancy: An anatomy of a social problem in search of comprehensive solutions*. Washington, DC: Children's Defense Fund.

Cixous, H. (1981). Castration or decapitation? *Signs, 7,* 41–55.

Dawson, D. (1986). The effects of sex education on adolescent behavior. *Family Planning Perspectives, 18,* 162–170.

Dowd, M. (1986, April 16). Bid to update sex education confronts resistance in city. *New York Times*, p. A1.

Dryfoos, J. (1985a). A time for new thinking about teenage pregnancy. *American Journal of Public Health, 75,* 13–14.

Dryfoos, J. (1985b). School-based health clinics: A new approach to preventing adolescent pregnancy? *Family Planning Perspectives, 17*(2), 70–75.

Ehrenreich, B., Hess, E., & Jacobs, G. (1986). *Re-making love*. Garden City, NY: Anchor Press.

Espin, O. (1984). Cultural and historical influences on sexuality in Hispanic/Latina women: Implications for psychotherapy. In C. Vance (Ed.), *Pleasure and danger* (pp. 149–164). Boston: Routledge & Kegan Paul.

Fine, M. (1986). Why urban adolescents drop into and out of high school. *Teachers College Record, 87,* 393–409.

Fine, M. (1987). Silencing in public school. *Language Arts, 64,* 157–174.

Fisher, W., Byrne, D., & White, L. (1983). Emotional barriers to contraception. In D. Byrne & W. Fisher (Eds.), *Adolescents, sex, and contraception* (pp. 207–239). Hillsdale, NJ: Lawrence Erlbaum.

Foucault, M. (1980). *The history of sexuality* (Vol. 1). New York: Vintage Books.

Freudenberg, N. (1987). The politics of sex education. *HealthPAC Bulletin.* New York: HealthPAC.

Golden, C. (1984, March). *Diversity and variability in lesbian identities.* Paper presented at Lesbian Psychologies Conference of the Association of Women in Psychology.

Greene, M. (1986). In search of a critical pedagogy. *Harvard Educational Review, 56,* 427–441.

Hall, G. S. (1914). Education and the social hygiene movement. *Social Hygiene, 1* (1 December), 29–35.

Harris, L., and Associates. (1985). *Public attitudes about sex education, family planning and abortion in the United States.* New York: Louis Harris and Associates, Inc.

Hispanic Policy Development Project. (1987, Fall). *1980 high school sophomores from poverty backgrounds: Whites, Blacks, Hispanics look at school and adult responsibilities,* Vol. 1, No. 2. New York: Author.

Hottois, J., & Milner, N. (1975). *The sex education controversy.* Lexington, MA: Lexington Books.

Imber, M. (1984). Towards a theory of educational origins: The genesis of sex education. *Educational Theory, 34,* 275–286.

Irigaray, L. (1980). When our lips speak together. *Signs, 6,* 69.

Jones, E., Forrest, J., Goldman, N., Henshaw, S., Lincoln, R., Rosoff, J., Westoff, C., & Wulf, D. (1985). Teenage pregnancy in developed countries. *Family Planning Perspectives, 17*(1), 55–63.

Kantrowitz, B., Hager, M., Wingert, S., Carroll, G., Raine, G., Witherspoon, D., Huck, J., & Doherty, S. (1987, February 16). Kids and contraceptives. *Newsweek,* pp. 54–65.

Kelly, G. (1986). *Learning about sex.* Woodbury, NY: Barron's Educational Series.

Kirby, D. (1985). *School-based health clinics: An emerging approach to improving adolescent health and addressing teenage pregnancy.* Washington, DC: Center for Population Options.

Kirby, D., & Scales, P. (1981, April). An analysis of state guidelines for sex education instruction in public schools. *Family Relations,* pp. 229–237.

Koop, C. E. (1986). *Surgeon General's report on acquired immune deficiency syndrome.* Washington, DC: Office of the Surgeon General.

Koop's AIDS stand assailed. (1987, March 15). *New York Times,* p. A25.

Leo, J. (1986, November 24). Sex and schools. *Time,* pp. 54–63.

Lorde, A. (1980, August). *Uses of the erotic: The erotic as power.* Paper presented at the Fourth Berkshire Conference on the History of Women, Mt. Holyoke College.

MacKinnon, C. (1983). Complicity: An introduction to Andrea Dworkin's "Abortion," Chapter 3, "Right-Wing Women." *Law and Inequality, 1,* 89–94.

Marsiglio, W., & Mott, F. (1986). The impact of sex education on sexual activity, contraceptive use and premarital pregnancy among American teenagers. *Family Planning Perspectives, 18*(4), 151–162.

Melton, S., & Russon, N. (1987). Adolescent abortion. *American Psychologist, 42,* 69–83.

National Research Council. (1987). *Risking the future: Adolescent sexuality, pregnancy and childbearing* (Vol. 1). Washington, DC: National Academy Press.

New York City Board of Education. (1984). *Family living curriculum including sex education. Grades K through 12.* New York City Board of Education, Division of Curriculum and Instruction.

Noddings, N. (1986). Fidelity in teaching, teacher education, and research for teaching. *Harvard Educational Review, 56,* 496–510.

Omolade, B. (1983). Hearts of darkness. In A. Snitow, C. Stansell, & S. Thompson (Eds.), *Powers of desire* (pp. 350–367). NY: Monthly Review Press.

Perlez, J. (1986a, June 24). On teaching about sex. *New York Times,* p. C1.

Perlez, J. (1986b, September 24). School chief to ask mandatory sex education. *New York Times*, p. A36.

Petchesky, R. (1984). *Abortion and woman's choice.* New York: Longman.

Philadelphia School District. (1986). Sex education curriculum. Draft.

Polit, D., Kahn, J., & Stevens, D. (1985). *Final impacts from Project Redirection.* New York: Manpower Development Research Center.

Public/Private Ventures. (1987, April). *Summer training and education program.* Philadelphia: Author.

Reproductive Freedom Project. (1986). *Parental consent laws on abortion: Their catastrophic impact on teenagers.* New York: American Civil Liberties Union.

Rohter, L. (1985, October 29). School workers shown AIDS film. *New York Times*, p. B3.

Rubin, G. (1984). Thinking sex: Notes for a radical theory of the politics of sex. In C. Vance (Ed.), *Pleasure and danger* (pp. 267–319). Boston: Routledge & Kegan Paul.

St. Paul Maternity and Infant Care Project. (1985). *Health services project description.* St. Paul, MN: Author.

Scales, P. (1981). Sex education and the prevention of teenage pregnancy: An overview of policies and programs in the United States. In T. Ooms (Ed.), *Teenage pregnancy in a family context: Implications for policy* (pp. 213–253). Philadelphia: Temple University Press.

Schlafly, P. (1986). Presentation on women's issues. American Dreams Symposium, Indiana University of Pennsylvania.

Selected group to see original AIDS tape. (1987, January 29). *New York Times*, p. B4.

Smith-Rosenberg, C. (1978). Sex as symbol in Victorian purity: An ethnohistorical analysis of Jacksonian America. *American Journal of Sociology, 84*, 212–247.

Snitow, A., Stansell, C., & Thompson, S. (Eds.). (1983). *Powers of desire.* New York: Monthly Review Press.

Sonnenstein, F., & Pittman, K. (1984). The availability of sex education in large city school districts. *Family Planning Perspectives, 16*(1), 19–25.

Strong, B. (1972). Ideas of the early sex education movement in America, 1890–1920. *History of Education Quarterly, 12*, 129–161.

Thompson, S. (1983). Search for tomorrow: On feminism and the reconstruction of teen romance. In A. Snitow, C. Stansell, & S. Thompson (Eds.), *Powers of desire* (pp. 367–384). New York: Monthly Review Press.

Torres, A., & Forest, J. (1985). Family planning clinic services in the United States, 1983. *Family Planning Perspectives, 17*(1), 30–35.

Vance, C. (1984). *Pleasure and danger.* Boston: Routledge & Kegan Paul.

Weeks, J. (1985). *Sexuality and its discontents.* London: Routledge & Kegan Paul.

Weitz, R. (1984). What price independence? Social reactions to lesbians, spinsters, widows and nuns. In J. Freeman (Ed.), *Women: A feminist perspective* (3rd ed.). Palo Alto, CA: Mayfield.

Werner, L. (1987, November 14). U.S. report asserts administration halted liberal "antifamily agenda." *New York Times*, p. A12.

Zabin, L., Hirsch, M., Smith, E., Streett, R., & Hardy, J. (1986). Evaluation of a pregnancy prevention program for urban teenagers. *Family Planning Perspectives, 18*(3), 119–126.

Zelnick, M., & Kim, Y. (1982). Sex education and its association with teenage sexual activity, pregnancy and contraceptive use. *Family Planning Perspectives, 14*(3), 117–126.

CHAPTER 16

CONTROLLING CURRICULUM KNOWLEDGE (1995)

Multicultural politics and policymaking

Catherine Cornbleth

New York, among other states in the USA, but most notably California, has been the scene of a noisy and at times acrimonious struggle over the substance of social studies education in the public schools. In New York, the focus of the on-going struggle has been "multiculturalism" or "multicultural education", a label once considered benign by some and now subversive by others. The following excerpts provide a sample of opinion on the second of two widely publicized New York State (NYS) reports, the June 1991 *One Nation, Many Peoples* (Social Studies Review and Development Committee 1991), and on multicultural education in general:

> *Multiculturalism.* That jawbreaking word has already caused huge contro-versy. The furor is sure to continue now that a committee of scholars has recommended revisions in New York State's school curriculum that would place greater emphasis on cultural diversity. But the report should be read with care and an open mind. It squarely faces a tough question: Should public schools stress the common elements that define America or the differing cul-tures that often divide it? The committee's answer is that a revised curriculum can wisely encompass both. (*New York Times,* 23 June 1991)

> The traditional notion that Columbus "discovered" America—as if before it was known to Europeans it didn't quite exist—is just one of the more appar-ent examples of what is wrong with the way schools have often taught social studies. When schools virtually dismiss the Native American culture that was here when Europeans arrived, schoolchildren get a picture of history that isn't just incomplete but misleading as well. . . . And that incompleteness is what the controversial report from a state review panel is all about. The panel's goal is to make the teaching of history and social studies more accur-ate by including the contributions of, and impacts on, non-white cultures. (*Buffalo News,* 30 June 1991)

> [*One Nation, Many Peoples*] denigrates the basic tenets of our American heritage. It is a divisive, far out, liberal sham that should be eviscerated immediately. (William Powers, New York State Republican party chairman, 14 July 1991)

> To the extent that the Report is understood—or misunderstood—to play down the significance of a common American culture and system of values,

then I think that it would be seriously flawed. Our Nation celebrates our diversity, but it depends on all of the different parts agreeing on common values and ideas that tie us all together ... the worthy aims of multicultural education are being pushed to such extremes that the casualty is common sense. (Mario Cuomo, Governor of New York, 15 July 1991)

A historic mission of the public school is to teach civic virtue and citizenship and to create a community and common culture for people of varied backgrounds. Appeals to race consciousness, group pride and a multi-racial, multi-ethnic society are socially divisive. (Diane Ravitch, former Assistant Secretary of Education, 10 September 1991)

It's no longer a question of whether we're going to have a multicultural education.... The question is whether we're going to do it well or do it badly ... [with reference to New York's plans for making social studies more multicultural] New York has often been the leader in doing things badly. (Lynne V. Cheney, former Director of the National Endowment for the Humanities, 16 December 1991)

We're in the midst of an important change in our school curriculum. By including the contributions of many different groups that have not previously been recognized, we're trying to make a multicultural curriculum that accurately reflects our society. However, some groups, including the New York State Board of Regents, which has just accepted guidelines for a new social studies curriculum, may end up sacrificing accuracy for diversity. They seem to think that, in order to give kids varied points of view, it's perfectly okay to teach ideas and theories that few or no reputable scholars accept. (Albert Shanker, President of the American Federation of Teachers, February 1992)

Efforts to understand what is happening in NYS and elsewhere with respect to multicultural education, and with what effects, might take different perspectives and examine different aspects of the struggle. Here I focus on questions of social studies curriculum *knowledge control* and examine how conflicting external pressures both delimit and are mediated by educational system actions. Three major questions frame my inquiry. First, why is control sought? Or, what is at stake? Here I address connections between curriculum and broader cultural issues. Second, who are the major combatants? What are they doing? The power of an organized voice or discourse is evident here. And third, what difference might the outcome make? Who stands to benefit? Educational policy decisions carry social and political as well as pedagogical consequences.

To focus on curriculum knowledge is to direct attention to the knowledge that is selected for inclusion in school programmes and made available to students in classroom practice. Knowledge made available to students refers to opportunities to construct, reconstruct, or critique knowledge, as well as to the more common offering of knowledge as if it were a product or object to be acquired. Curriculum knowledge might include social and world knowledge as well as so-called academic knowledge from the recognized disciplines.

Questions of multicultural curriculum knowledge are important because how we understand ourselves, others, a nation, and the world is shaped in party by that knowledge. Curriculum knowledge contributes to the shaping of identity, capacity, attitude, and action both individually and collectively. Questions of control are important because different values and interests are sustained or modified by one or another selection and distribution of curriculum knowledge. I see the question of *"whose knowledge?"* as less important *per se* than the question of *"who benefits?"* from particular knowledge selections. Further understanding of curriculum knowledge control, empirically and theoretically, would enhance understanding of larger issues of curriculum policy, practice, and change. The means of control examined here are state policy-making processes and emerging state policies and, perhaps as important, a discourse that (re)defines what is legitimate and appropriate curriculum knowledge and practice.

As the NYS case illustrates, curriculum knowledge control is neither straight-forward nor stable. It is continually contested and renegotiated (e.g. Bacchus 1986, Kliebard 1986). The necessarily partial and provisional account that I offer here draws on a continuing study of social studies–multicultural education policy in NYS since the controversial 1989 Task Force Report, *A Curriculum of Inclusion* (Task Force on Minorities 1989). Data include participant–observer fieldnotes, a range of documents, and interviews. Rather than recount either the entire NYS experience as I have come to know it or the national milieu in which NYS is enmeshed (and to which it contributes), I highlight their intersections and confrontations.[1]

Background and perspective: what is at stake?

What is taught in school, in social studies and other subjects, is necessarily only a small portion of available knowledge. Apart from the differences between the knowledge and practice of academic disciplines and their transformation into school subjects, curriculum knowledge in general and social studies in particular represents what Williams (1961: 49, 52) calls a "selective tradition". He dis-tinguishes "the lived culture of a particular time and place, only fully accessible to those living in that time and place" from the recorded culture of a period and contemporary selections from and recreations of the recorded culture, i.e. the selective tradition. He reminds us that representations of the history and culture of a society will change over time because they reflect contemporary values and special interests. These representations are "a continual selection and interpret-ation . . . a continual selection and re-selection of ancestors". For example, which authors and works of literature will students be asked to study? Which times, places, peoples, and cultures?

How, or on what basis, curriculum knowledge is selected has been obscured by the so-called, classical curriculum question, "What knowledge is of most worth?", which dates to an essay (1859) and then a book, *Education: Intellectual, Moral, and Physical*, by Herbert Spencer. Worth, for Spencer, meant contribution to the self-preservation of peoples and civilizations. While subject to various def-initions, "worth" has been widely accepted, or at least preferred, as the primary criterion for selection of curriculum knowledge. That knowledge deemed most worthy or worthwhile was, presumably, what was included in school pro-grammes. Framing the question of the selection of curriculum knowledge in this way gives the appearance of beneficence in the public interest. It deflects questions of worth for what or for whom.

Within and across school subject areas (and with respect to the subjects themselves), however, selection of curriculum knowledge has been shown to be less than coherent and more a result of tradition and politics than rational or other determinations of worth (see, e.g. Goodson and Ball 1984, Kliebard

1986, Popkewitz 1987, Reid 1990). Rather than expert determination or public consensus, curriculum knowledge, according to Kliebard (1992: 157),

> is the outcome of a complex interplay of competing values and traditions as signified by different interest groups and, at least in part, reflecting the meanings they attribute to social, political, and economic conditions . . . decisions as to what gets taught in schools are often influenced by such factors as real or alleged economic considerations, national ideals, social change, the way in which schools are structured, gender, racial, and class distinctions, as well as symbol and ritual.

And, the decisions that are made are continually contested. Victories (and defeats) are rarely complete or permanent. Despite the historical record of conflicting values, interests, and traditions in curriculum policy-making, the "most worth" question holds continuing appeal. It not only gives the appearance of wisdom and good intentions, but also carries the assumption of common interests and universality (of worth and perhaps truth) across time, place, and person.

Meanwhile, public schooling in the USA has long been an arena in which battles are fought over American values and priorities as a nation and what vision of the nation will or should be passed on to the next generation. Since the school curriculum is seen as a major vehicle of cultural definition and transmission, a goal of these battles has been control of curriculum knowledge. Curriculum knowledge and its control have been at issue not only in social studies and history but also in language, literature, and science.

In the heat of these curriculum battles, over evolutionary theory and "creation science", for example, combatants sometimes appear to lose sight of the limits of curriculum: thus, while curriculum knowledge is an important source of academic and social learning, it is one of several and is not necessarily the most influential source. Family, peers, media, and religion also are potent knowledge sources. It may be that the US traditions of local control of public schooling and faith in education to resolve societal problems as well as further individual well-being focus attention on curriculum knowledge. Family and peers, in contrast, remain private spheres, while mass media and religion seem beyond lay public control.

Curriculum policy-making in the USA is more complex and contentious now than even a decade or two ago given growing differences in social values and interests, increasing knowledge and specialization, and expanding state involvement (Cornbleth 1990: Ch. 7). This contentiousness is exacerbated by ongoing efforts to devise national standards and assessment mechanisms in the school subjects as seen in the 1989 *Summit Statement* of former President Bush and the National Governors Association, efforts reiterated in Bush's *America 2000* education strategy statement of April 1991 and again in the Clinton administration's *Goals 2000: Educate America* legislation of 1994. If curriculum knowledge is to be shaped at the national rather than at the state or local level, the stakes are raised and control is likely to be even more strongly contested.

The public, compulsory nature of schooling along with its nation-building mission makes conflict over curriculum knowledge and its control inevitable in all but the most homogeneous, traditional societies. Not solely academic or professional matters, questions of curriculum knowledge are bound up with questions of interest and equity in the larger society. Curriculum contestation becomes problematic when the debate is limited to questions and/or participants and/or outcomes determined by the individuals and groups currently in power—when the playing field is tilted so that no contest is possible. To the extent that the debate is open, curriculum stands to be reinvigorated and the public interest reaffirmed.

Actions and reactions in New York State and beyond

Periodically, US historians and geographers have reasserted the importance of their disciplines and undertaken efforts to restore what they consider to be their rightful place in school programmes. The enemies usually identified as encroaching on history are the social sciences and electives such as ethnic studies and/or social studies (see, e.g. Ravitch 1987). It is seemingly ignored that "social studies" in the secondary grades 7–12 in the USA is an umbrella term, as is "science". In most states and school districts, social studies in grades 7–12 include at least two years of US history and two years of world history (variously labelled World Civilization, World Cultures, or Global Studies). Bemoaning a lack of history in school curricula is akin to calling for "back to basics". How does one go back to what has not been left? The most recent reassertion of history, beginning in the mid-1980s, coincides with multicultural initiatives in NYS. NYS has been moving against a more conservative national tide and has been roundly criticized for doing so.

In *A Nation at Risk* (National Commission on Excellence in Education 1983: 25), social studies was identified as one of "the essentials of a strong curriculum". By 1987, with the creation of the Bradley Commission on History in the Schools (Gagnon 1989) and the publication of *What Do Our 17-Year-Olds Know?* (Ravitch and Finn 1987), the public language had changed from social studies to history. The national education goals proclaimed by President Bush and the National Governors Association at their "summit" in 1989, and reiterated in the *America 2000* education strategy outlined in 1991, recognize history and geography, not social studies.[2] The changing language not only indicates a reassertion of history but also, despite the historical scholarship of recent decades, advocacy of traditional US and western history in particular. For example, former Secretary of Education, William Bennett's proposed "James Madison curriculum" (Rothman 1988) defines social studies as history, geography, and civics, and recommends a year of western civilization, a year of American history, and a semester each of "Principles of American Democracy" and "American Democracy and the World". Bennett (in Rothman 1988: 26) states that

> The *James Madison High School* history curriculum is designed to provide a solid grounding in the European and American past ... Schools will want to offer a fourth year of history to students interested in advanced or supplementary topics (e.g., non-Western history and economics).

Meanwhile, NYS as well as several prominent universities were taking a different path and provoking the ire of advocates of traditional US and western history. In NYS, the policy-making body for education is the 16-member Board of Regents appointed by the state legislature. The Regents, in turn, appoint a Commissioner of Education who heads the State Education Department (SED) and serves at their pleasure. (The independence of the Regents and Commissioner from the Governor's Office has not been appreciated by NY governors for some time.) When the then-Commissioner of Education left in 1987 to take a position elsewhere, there was pressure to make a "minority" appointment. Bernard Gifford, the top minority candidate, turned down the opportunity to become New York's Commissioner of Education, and the Regents appointed Thomas Sobol, then a superintendent of schools in New York State.

One of Commissioner Sobol's first initiatives, partly in response to minority legislators and others unhappy with his appointment, was the creation of a Task Force on Minorities, chaired by Hazel N. Dukes, president of the New York branch of the NAACP (National Association for the Advancement of Coloured People). The dual charge to the Task Force was to review personnel policies and practices within SED and to review SED syllabi and materials to determine how well they reflect the pluralistic nature of US society. A May 1988 report addressed the first part of the charge, recommending improvement in SED affirmative action practices. Most of those recommendations have been acted upon. The July 1989 Task Force report, *A Curriculum of Inclusion*, addressed the second part of the charge, with a focus on social studies education in NYS. Its principal author was Harry L. Hamilton, then of the Department of Atmospheric Sciences, State University of New York (SUNY) at Albany.

While *A Curriculum of Inclusion* noted improvements in NYS syllabi and materials toward meeting the Regents' goal of understanding, respect, and acceptance of "people of different races; sex; cultural heritage; national origin; religion; and political, economic and social background, and their values, beliefs, and attitudes", it found that "the curricular materials do not adequately and accurately reflect the cultural experience in America" (Task Force on Minorities 1989: 16).[3] Most of the report's nine recommendations addressed materials and staff development consistent with "inclusion", which was characterized as a round table:

> European culture is likened to the master of a house ruling over a dinner table, himself firmly established at the head of the table and all other cultures being guests some distance down the table from the master, who has invited the others through his beneficence. . . . The new model is likened to the fabled Round Table of King Arthur, with all cultures offering something to be collective good, each knowing and respecting others, and each gaining from the contribution of others; no culture is master of the new table (Task Force on Minorities 1989: iv).

The furor generated by *A Curriculum of Inclusion* in both the public media and professional circles has been attributed to one or more of the following:

- its inflammatory language, e.g. 'African Americans, Asian Americans, Puerto Ricans/Latinos, and Native Americans have all been the victims of a cultural oppression and stereotyping that has characterized institutions—including the educational institutions—of the United States and the European American world for centuries" (Task Force on Minorities 1989: 6);
- the composition of the task force (16 of the 17 members were "minorities"; none were historians);
- the involvement of a controversial Afrocentric spokesperson, Leonard Jeffries, as a consultant;[4]
- the threat of social fragmentation suggested by the report's four appendices, each of which presents an analysis of NYS syllabi and other materials from the point of view of a single group—African-Americans, Asian-Americans, Puerto Ricans/Latinos, Native Americans.

A Curriculum of Inclusion was seen as an attack on historians in general, on traditional American history, and on the so-called canon of western civilization and progress in particular. It challenged the version of cultural literacy and the vision of America espoused by national figures such as former Republican administration US Department of Educational officials like William Bennett, Chester Finn, and Diane Ravitch, former (Bush administration) National Endowment for the Humanities Director Lynne Cheney, and historian Arthur Schlesinger, Jr. And it appeared at a time when the eastern bloc and Soviet Union were disintegrating, large numbers of Asian and central American immigrants were entering the USA, US students were faring poorly in international achievement comparisons, and the US position in the world economy was slipping. For those who already felt threatened by social, economic and demographic changes, *A Curriculum of Inclusion* was an anathema uncomfortably reminiscent of the 1960s. Both the supporters of the report and their critics engaged in the rhetoric of crisis, doom, and salvation. The critics, however, of this and subsequent multicultural proposals, have been much more visible than the proponents.

What had begun as an effort of the NYS Commissioner of Education to "improve" the state's education programmes for elementary and secondary school students as well as to gain "minority" support for his efforts created a maelstrom, especially in the eastern part of the state, i.e. New York City and the metropolitan area. Attacked, sometimes viciously, by neo-nativists and seemingly abandoned by others, Commissioner Sobol proceeded with a plan accepted by the Board of Regents to review the report over a period of several months before taking further action (11 July 1989 memo to Board of Regents; 28 July 1989 press release). Seven months later, in February 1990, the Board of Regents approved the Commissioner's recommendation that he and his staff develop a plan for increasing students' "understanding of the diverse groups which comprise American society today, and of the history and culture of other peoples throughout the world" (2 February 1990 memo to Board of Regents: 2).

Later that month, a five-page memo from the Commissioner, in a question-to-answer format, was widely distributed to "interested persons" in an effort to clarify and gain support for what SED had/had not done and was/was not planning to do (22 February 1990 memo to Interested Persons). In this memo, Commissioner Sobol reiterated 20 years of Regents' policy in support of "efforts to increase students' understanding of cultural diversity" and argued that further action as needed "in response to the educational, social, political, and economic imperatives of our time". He also distanced himself and the Board of Regents from *A Curriculum of Inclusion*. "The Board and I agree with the central message of that report: that we should be more inclusive in teaching about American and world history and culture. However, the Board and I do not associate ourselves with all of the language of the report, nor do we agree with every assertion and recommendation which it makes." Finally, Commissioner Sobol adamantly stated that the plan of action to be submitted to the Board of Regents in April would not result in curriculum revisions that would "rewrite or distort history", "diminish the importance of our western heritage and values", or "lead to a fragmentation of our society", as opponents claimed.

The seemingly conciliatory tenor of this memo and subsequent statements from the Commissioner's Office is captured in the following excerpt from his 22 February 1990 memo:

Recent surveys show that too many high school graduates know too little about important facts, developments, and themes in American history. Our population is becoming increasingly diverse—ethnically, culturally, and linguistically. By the year 2000, one of every three New Yorkers will be what we now call a "minority". About 90,000 people annually emigrate to New York State from other countries. New York State is home to some 40,000 Native Americans belonging to eight tribes or nations. We must make this diversity an asset, not a liability.[5]

In April 1990, the Board of Regents adopted a plan, proposed by the SED staff and the Commissioner, for social studies syllabus review and revision that would be "thoughtful, scholarly, and apolitical" (16 April 1990 "Item for Action": 1). With one major exception, a research-development-dissemination model similar to that typically used by SED was proposed. That exception was the composition and means of selection of the review committee. The NYS Social Studies Review and Development Committee ("Review Committee") would be larger than usual, include "scholars and teachers who represent the ethnic and cultural groups under consideration", and be approved by the Board of Regents.

An intricate process of selection began in May 1990. In July 1990, with the advice of the Commissioner and his staff, the Board of Regents selected a 23-member committee "of eminent scholars and educators ... distinguished scholars and teachers in relevant fields who represent a diversity of views and backgrounds" (27 July 1990 press release) from more than 300 nominees.[6] Among the best-known university scholars who attended at least one of the committee's meetings were Nathan Glazer of Harvard, Edmund Gordon then of Yale, Kenneth Jackson of Columbia, Ali Mazrui of SUNY at Binghamton, and Arthur Schlesinger, Jr. then of the City University of New York (CUNY).[7] Only 5 of the 13 university members were from public universities (i.e. SUNY or CUNY).[8]

Clearly, the creation of this second committee was intended both to continue the process of making social studies curriculum knowledge more multicultural, through more normal channels, and to ward off criticism from a range of actual and potential opponents. A "blue ribbon" committee presumably would be respected and its recommendations taken seriously. A slow, deliberate, and "apolitical" process presumably would allow time for tensions to ease and a wise course of action to emerge. Thus the educational system's policy-makers attempted to mediate conflicting demands and interests, including their own.

Neo-nativist opposition

While the course of the Review Committee's deliberations would make a lively and instructive story, I leave that to another time (Cornbleth and Waugh 1995) and turn now to the neo-nativist opposition to the Review Committee's eventual report and the subsequent recommendations of Commissioner Sobol to the Board of Regents. That opposition began prior to the committee's formation, continued throughout its 9 months of operation, and remains active.

For example, in June 1990, prior to appointment of the Review Committee, Diane Ravitch and Arthur Schlesinger, Jr. co-authored a "Statement of the Committee of Scholars in Defense of History", which was signed by 26 other scholars, in which they expressed their concern about "the proposed revision of the State of New York's history curriculum" and their intent to "constitute ourselves as a professional review committee to monitor and assess the work of the Commissioner's panel".[9] In other words, they set "scholars" like themselves as the proper authorities to judge what constitutes appropriate educational purposes for history—social studies and curriculum knowledge. We are to defer to the experts rather than involve them in a wider public debate.

The Committee of Scholars' concerns were based on their interpretation of *A Curriculum of Inclusion*, the lack of an historian among its authors, and the possibility that the then yet to be named Review Committee "might end up with only one historian". Illustrative of their interpretation of *A Curriculum of Inclusion*, the Committee of Scholars asserted:

> The report, a polemical document, viewed division into racial groups as the basic analytical framework for an understanding of American history. It showed no understanding of the integrity of history as an intellectual discipline based on commonly accepted standards of evidence. . . . We condemn the reduction of history to ethnic cheerleading on the demand of pressure groups. . . . We have further concerns: The commissioner of education's task force contemptuously dismisses the Western tradition. . . . And little can have more damaging effect on the Republic than the use of the school system to promote the division of our people into antagonistic racial groups.

The statement may well have had an influence on the selection of members of the Review Committee (four university historians were appointed, including Schlesinger who agreed to serve as a consultant to the committee, but not as a regular member). It also reflects a seeming contradiction in the position of neo-nativist critics of more multicultural history and social studies education. On the one hand, it is argued that the selection of curriculum knowledge should have historical integrity and represent high standards of historical scholarship. On the other is an urgent appeal for curriculum knowledge that unites America's peoples. This interpretation is given credence by the subsequent statements of public figures such as Diane Ravitch and Lynne Cheney cited at the beginning of this paper and others such as Schlesinger (1991: 2, 3) who warns that "The national ideal had once been *e pluribus unum*. Are we now to belittle *unum* and glorify *pluribus*? Will the centre hold? or will the melting pot yield to the Tower of Babel?" In this case, Schlesinger acknowledges that "the debate about the curriculum is a debate about what it means to be an American. What is ultimately at stake is the shape of the American future".

As I followed the professional literature and the mass media accounts of events in NYS and multiculturalism more generally, I increasingly became aware of a network of individuals, organizations, and funding agencies supporting a neo-nativist position. I use the characterization, "neo-nativist", not to disparage but to describe a position that crosscuts the conventional US liberal–conservative and political party distinctions and would contain multicultural diversity, in part, by means of a version of America and its history that emphasizes and seeks to promote a "common culture". This common culture is of Western European origin and includes democratic political ideals and institutions and, depending on the speaker, various social values and practices. The neo-nativists, few of whom are historians, staunchly support traditional versions of US history. While minority groups might be admitted to that history—a form of modest multiculturalism—their admission is to a narrative based on European immigrant experience (Cornbleth and Waugh 1993, 1995).

Several aspects of this network are noteworthy.[10] One is that a small number of highly visible individuals are associated with most of the groups. Among the most prominent are: Diane Ravitch, then adjunct professor of history and education, Teachers College, Columbia University, and former Assistant Secretary of Education for the Office of Educational Research and Improvement (OERI) of the US Department of Education; Charlotte Crabtree, professor of education and Director of the federally-funded National Center for History in the Schools and the National History Standards Project at UCLA; Paul Gagnon, former Executive Secretary of the National Council for History Education and head of the Fund for the Improvement and Reform of Schools and Teaching, OERI; and Lynne Cheney, former Director of the National Endowment for the Humanities.

A second noteworthy aspect of the network is the mix of public and private funding of the various groups. The funding groups include The Educational Excellence Network, co-founded in 1982 by Chester Finn and Diane Ravitch, with an office in Washington, DC; the Bradley Commission on History in the Schools, a programme of the Educational Excellence Network, and its successor, the National Council for History Education, both initially headed by Paul Gagnon; the National Center for History in the Schools and the National History Standards Project at UCLA, headed by Charlotte Crabtree; and the American Textbook Council in New York City, headed by Gilbert Sewall. Funders of two or more of the identified organizations included the US Department of Education and the US National Endowment for the Humanities and the Bradley, Donner, and Olin foundations.[11]

Finally, university-based individuals in the network are mostly from private universities. The organizational location of individual spokespersons lends status and authority to what they say. One speaks not for oneself but for a committee, commission, council, centre, university or federal government agency.

A relatively small group of people has created a seemingly well-orchestrated and well-funded network that has been quite successful thus far in establishing itself as the definers and defenders of legitimate history and appropriate curriculum knowledge, especially in California and at least for a period in Washington, DC.[12] Its long-run success in NYS and nationwide remains to be seen. However, it seems clear that the multicultural playing field has not been level. This is not a case of one person, one vote or voice. Some voices are heard so much more often and widely than others that they tend to drown out alternative voices. Instead of a free and open marketplace of ideas, there has been a near monopoly. There is no evidence of which I am aware of a similar, nationwide network of supporters of more multicultural history and social studies education.

The opposition to multiculturalism in general and the work of the NYS review committee in particular has taken several forms in addition to news and journal articles and public statements. For example, before the first meeting of the Review Committee in September 1990, several members, myself included, received copies of a book chapter, authored a decade earlier by a conservative British academic, that was highly critical of one committee member, Ali Mazrui. Attached to the copy was a printed card reading "Compliments of Diane Ravitch". Just prior to presentation of the NYS review committee's report in June 1991, Whittle Communications published (and distributed free of charge to review committee members) Arthur Schlesinger, Jr.'s monograph, *The Disuniting of America*, a critique of Afrocentrism and NYS's multicultural efforts.[13]

Also, under Albert Shanker's leadership, the American Federation of Teachers reprinted the "Statement of the Committee of Scholars in Defense of History" (in Shanker's paid column "Where We Stand" in the 12 August 1990 *New York Times*) and published several articles in its various publications that have been cautious about if not critical of more multicultural history and social studies education (e.g. Ravitch 1990). Media coverage of Commissioner Sobol and the NYS review committee was mixed, ranging from alarmist columns in the *New York Post* (e.g. 14 April 1990, 21 June and 17 July 1991) and John Leo in *US News and World Report* (e.g. 8 July 1991) to the evenhanded accounts provided by Debra Viadero in *Education Week* (e.g. 1 August 1990, 31 July and 16 October 1991, 8 January 1992) and supportive editorials in the *New York Times* and the *Buffalo News*, excerpts from which are cited at the beginning of this paper. Illustrative of alarmism were headings in an 14 April 1990 *New York Post* editorial, "The Sobol-Jeffries Victory": "WIDE CONDEMNATION", "BIZARRE PRIORITIES", "WASTING OUR MONEY", and "SELF-ESTEEM PABLUM". Even-handed accounts, in contrast, described documented events, presented diverse interpretations of those events, and set events in context.

Meanwhile, the NYS review committee worked to reach consensus on its review of social studies syllabi and recommendations to the Commissioner. Of the several individual commentaries included in its June 1991 report, *One Nation, Many Peoples*, only two were dissents (written by Kenneth Jackson and Arthur Schlesinger, Jr.). In July 1991, the Board of Regents (with one Regent absent) adopted, by a 12–3 vote, the Commissioner's recommendations for action, based largely on the committee report ("Understanding Diversity", 12 July 1991).

The only new state policy since 1987 directly addressing social studies curriculum knowledge was contained in the July 1991 "Understanding Diversity" document, which calls for: (a) reaffirmation of long-standing Regents policy "to promote the understanding of both our common democratic values and our multicultural origins, along with the development of a global perspective on our own and other societies' (p. 4); (b) revision of social studies syllabi; and (c) provision of support for social studies teaching and learning (e.g. teacher education, staff development, instructional materials, compatible assessment programmes). Syllabus revision was to:

- *establish balanced goals*—including "understanding and appreciation of the democratic and moral values of our common American culture", "understanding and appreciation of the history and culture of the various major ethnic and cultural groups which comprise American society", and developing "students' capacity to think critically about societal issues, drawing on historical knowledge, contemporary information, and points of view from many sources";
- *adopt sound principles*—including democracy, diversity, and economic and social justice;
- *emphasize understanding*—depth more than breadth, reasoning as well as information acquisition;
- *cultivate "multiple perspectives"*—to help students perceive and understand phenomena from different points of view;
- *teach our common traditions*—including democratic values and "the political, legal, and cultural roots of our society in England, in Europe, and in the traditions of the West" (p. 7):
  "This common tradition, the tradition which unites us and makes our diversity possible, must be taught to all our children. We must be honest, and acknowledge that we have not always lived up to our ideals— egregiously not, in some cases. And we must show how this tradition has been further shaped and enriched by Americans from all continents. But

as we make our curriculum more inclusive, we should not lose sight of what we are including people in" (p. 8);

- *include examples of the experiences of many peoples*—not an "encyclopedic list of every contribution by every person and group" (p. 8) but appropriate examples so that all students "find in the curriculum reason for believing that they and their ancestors have shared in the building of the country and have a stake in its success and . . . learn more about those who are different from themselves" (p. 8);
- *tell the whole story*—reflecting "not only our achievements, but our shortcomings; not only our triumphs, but our pain; and not only our failures, but our successes and ideals. This is not to say that all cultures or civilizations are 'equal'; but it is to say that students are capable of understanding the complexity of human nature and the human experience, and an education which does not help them do so sells them short" (p. 8);
- *maintain scholarly standards, and include up-to-date scholarship*— recognizing that history is continually reinterpreted;
- *be sensitive to language and representation*—without sacrificing accuracy;
- *avoid "hypostatization"*—"treat the issues of race, ethnicity, and culture as one way [not the only way] of understanding American history and American society" (p. 10).

Responding to criticism of *One Nation, Many Peoples* and its perceived implications, Commissioner Sobol's recommendations in "Understanding Diversity" also included the following summary of what was not being advocated "because the issue of 'multicultural education' has been subject to so much misunderstanding and misrepresentation by the public and the press" ("Understanding Diversity", 12 July 1991: 12):

NOT recommended: trashing the traditions of the West.
NOT recommended: an Afrocentric curriculum.
NOT recommended: ethnic cheerleading and separatism.
NOT recommended: distorting history.
NOT recommended: a curriculum of self-esteem.
NOT recommended: a study of American history based on ethnicity or culture alone.

His effort to gain support, however, had little impact on the critics of NYS's efforts toward more multicultural history and social studies education.[14]

Since the summer of 1991, the state-level initiative on behalf of more multicultural history and social studies has been incorporated into NYS's "New Compact for Learning", an umbrella plan for improving K-12 public schooling approved by the Board of Regents in March 1991. This has meant appointment (in December 1991 after 2 months of delay) by the Board of Regents of a Social Studies Curriculum and Assessment Committee, with 9 of 21 members, myself included, from the previous Review Committee. This committee is charged with (a) identifying desired learning outcomes for social studies education in NYS consistent with the Regent's Goals for education (1984, revised 1991) and the July 1991 policy document, "Understanding Diversity", (b) recommending "elements of a statewide programme of educational assessment" to measure progress toward desired learning outcomes, and (c) designing "a programme of state and local support [i.e. staff development] to assist teachers in preparing pupils to achieve the desired learning outcomes" (Draft Charge to the State Curriculum and Assessment Committee for Social Studies, 7 November 1991). Syllabus revision, the charge to the previous committee and the focus of "Understanding Diversity", could be part of staff development but is not explicitly mentioned since SED may no longer produce course syllabi.

Concurrently, the SED's Division of Intercultural Relations "has been given the responsibility to assist local school districts in implementing the multicultural components of the Regents Goals and the New Compact for Learning" (February 1992 memo to school district superintendents from the Division of Intercultural Relations). This responsibility, according to the memo, stems from "numerous requests for multicultural education services and resources" and will be met by development of "activities designed to assist districts and schools in their efforts to develop multicultural programmes". (That the Division of Intercultural Relations documents do not mention either the Review Committee report or the Commissioner's recommendations may be the result of the incorporation of state level multicultural policy initiatives into the "New Compact", which is mentioned, and/or the desire to distance the Division's activities from that controversy.)

Whether social studies curriculum knowledge in NYS will become substantially more multicultural in policy or practice remains to be seen. It is not clear whether incorporation into the "New Compact" means that multicultural efforts have been moved from the margins to the mainstream or that they will be dissipated within normal channels and subordinated to concerns with other social studies outcomes and assessment. Given evidence that tests do influence what is taught, making NYS social studies assessments more multicultural could have a greater impact on social studies curriculum knowledge and classroom practice than creating curriculum frameworks or revising syllabi. Making NYS social studies assessments more multicultural, consistent with the recommendations of "Understanding Diversity", however, will require that NYS continue to move beyond or against the national tide as represented by current plans for the 1994 National Assessment of Educational Progress (NAEP) US history assessment and the National Endowment for the Humanities and US Education Department funded National History Standards project at UCLA.

Uncertain benefits

Who might benefit, and how, from the continuing efforts to control social studies curriculum knowledge in NYS remains uncertain. Benefits depend, in part, on whether and how the largely symbolic policy of "Understanding Diversity" is translated into operational NYS policy regarding student assessment, social studies curriculum, and teacher education and certification. Insofar as NYS is seen as an educational leader by policy-makers in other states, wider benefits also depend on how New York's experience is interpreted and taken as a guide to action elsewhere.

For the time being at least, social studies curriculum knowledge and classroom practice may be shaped less by official state policy than by the continuing debates about history, social studies, and multicultural education—debates which have been reignited and sustained in part by the policy activity in NYS. How the debates are shaped and played our influences the perceptions and practices of policy-makers, teachers, and other school personnel whether they are active participants in or occasional observers of these debates.

Discourse matters

Life in the US in the late 20th century is so complex and turbulent that it takes a "crisis" to gain public attention. Mere problems are endemic and fail to garner much notice. Crisis rhetoric has become an integral part of our everyday political and social life (Edelman 1977). Proposals for reform are presented as antidotes to perceived crisis, and opponents of reform proposals predict crisis as a consequence of the changes they oppose. Thus, critics predict that more multicultural or inclusive social studies curricula, as recommended by *One Nation, Many Peoples* or "Understanding Diversity", could lead to fragmentation of the US and armed conflict as in Yugoslavia, e.g. Schlesinger's Tower of Babel, while proponents suggest similar consequences if the proposed reforms are not realized. As O'Sullivan (1992: 18) observes, "cultural contestation is cast as cultural crisis".

The decentralization or fragmentation of the US educational system also supports a rhetoric of crisis. Because there is no formal integration across organizational layers of the education system and no operational central authority, would-be reformers and opponents of proposed reforms must gain the attention and support of a range of audiences. Consequently nationwide efforts for or against specific changes historically have assumed a crusading religious character in contrast to less flamboyant legislative and administrative or bureaucratic actions (Meyer 1984). Thus, both proponents and critics of more multicultural or inclusive social studies present themselves as "saving" America (e.g. MacDonald 1992).[15]

Partially overlapping the larger educational reform discourse of crisis and crusade is a more specialized discourse of history, social studies, and multicultural education. One could distinguish at least three discourses: a history-as-cultural literacy discourse that excludes social studies and more than modest multiculturalism; a social studies discourse that includes various schools of history and more or less multiculturalism; and a multicultural discourse that includes both history, particularly the newer social histories, and social studies. While acknowledging that multicultural education extends beyond history and social studies and that a case could be made for three distinguishable sets of discursive practices, I treat the discourses of history, social studies, and multicultural education together and in conflict. The discourse of history-as-cultural literacy, for example, seems to have become a code for western-dominated and not multicultural or inclusive history. From the perspective of curriculum knowledge and control, the question is whether and how one discourse will achieve dominance at least for the time being—controlling curriculum knowledge by dominating the discourse.

Following Foucault (1977: 199), the discursive practices of a field are characterized and make a difference by

> delimitation of a field of objects, the definition of a legitimate perspective . . . and the fixing of norms for the elaboration of concepts and theories. Thus each discursive practice implies a play of prescriptions that designate its exclusions and choices.

Discursive practices delimit objects of the field, specifying what is to be included and what is not. What is to count as historical knowledge or history? What historical knowledge is to be selected for inclusion in social studies curriculum?

The definition of a legitimate perspective or perspectives and the fixing of norms for conceptual elaboration also can be seen to support some forms of historical and curriculum knowledge and not others. Should the so-called canon of conventional US history or school/textbook history be upheld, should a revised and more multicultural canon be instituted, or should multiple perspectives prevail?[16]

Discursive practices are not merely of academic or theoretical interest. They derive from and enter into everyday practice. Furthermore, their pervasiveness often renders them unseen and unacknowledged. Discursive practices "are embedded in technical processes, in institutions, in patterns for general behaviour, in forms for transmission and diffusion, and in pedagogical forms which, at once, impose and maintain them" (Foucault 1977: 200). Particular discursive practices are not in any sense inevitable; they are sociohistorically constructed and therefore amenable, though not easily, to reconstruction. In the current debates, not only social studies curriculum knowledge but history itself seems to be at issue. The discourse is in flux.

Self-proclaimed defenders of history (e.g. Committee of Scholars in Defense of History 1990) focus on the question of legitimate or authentic history, the implication being that it is this accredited history that is to be taught in schools. By their unspecified criteria, much if not most of the range of Afrocentric scholarship does not pass muster, and multiculturalism is defined as something other than history. In other words, their discourse delimits historical knowledge to a particular version of history and puts alternative interpretations out of bounds. It claims that a particular selective tradition is authentic and, therefore, most worthy curriculum knowledge.

In contrast to the 1990 *Statement of the Committee of Scholars in Defense of History* is the 1991 statement of the executive board of the Organization of American Historians (OAH) in support of inclusive, multicultural history and curriculum knowledge (OAH 1991). Although the OAH statement is more representative of the community of academic historians, it enjoyed less visibility than Ravitch and Schlesinger's *Committee of Scholars* statement.

Examination of the debate surrounding proposed changes in social studies curriculum knowledge in NYS that would make it more multicultural reveals additional dimensions of the discourse. One finds differences in emphasis tending toward polarization with respect to, for example, pluralism or unity, celebration or critique, political or social history. These aspects of the debate extend the discourse beyond history *per se* and academic communities of historians to a public discourse about who we are and might become, individually and collectively. As suggested earlier, questions of curriculum knowledge are not solely academic or professional matters. Evidence of polarization in the midst of crisis rhetoric, however, threatens to undermine constructive curriculum debate.

On another level, particularly striking aspects of the debates involving NYS are what might be characterized as a "discourse of derision" and the personal attacks on Commissioner Thomas Sobol. Since the Commissioner has been the key policymaker supporting NYS's multicultural initiatives, attacking him personally may be a way of pressing him to change course or resign or pressuring the Board of Regents to replace him. It also has been suggested that attacking Sobol would have made the state's governor, Mario Cuomo, more vulnerable to criticism if he had become a presidential candidate in 1992.

The "discourse of derision", a characterization borrowed from Ball's (1990) account of New Right educational politics in Britain, refers to critics' efforts to undermine multiculturalism by caricaturing and then ridiculing it. For example, multiculturalism is linked to an ethnocentric version of Afrocentrism and then both are scornfully dismissed as "ethnic cheerleading" (Ravitch), "self-esteem pablum" (*New York Post*), or leading to "the Tower of Babel" (Schlesinger). Even more strident are claims that multiculturalism is a facade for efforts "to skew the entire educational content of public education" in order to serve the perceived need of, or cater to the demands of, African Americans (e.g. Decter 1991: 29). Thus, "by setting reason against madness" (Ball 1990: 44), i.e. history against multiculturalism, critics of more multicultural curriculum knowledge attempt to dominate the discursive terrain and thereby shape curriculum policy and practice.

The absence of an equivalent, organized multicultural "voice" is significant. While explanation of such absence is beyond the scope of this inquiry, it is worth noting that "multiculturalists" are a diverse lot, with differing versions of multiculturalism and different visions of America; that, for the most part, the multiculturalists are not in positions of political prominence with easy media access nor "connected" to those who are; and that the multiculturalists have not been the recipients of substantial foundation support for their projects. It also should be noted that opposition tends to be seen as more newsworthy than support for whatever is happening, in and outside education, and that New York State *has* been moving toward a more multicultural educational policy and social studies curriculum knowledge.

Concluding thoughts

The professional and public discourse about history, social studies, and multicultural education has redirected attention to the selection of curriculum knowledge, particularly to the purposes that different selections might be expected to serve and to the criteria for knowledge selection. The attention might prompt us school districts, schools, and individual teachers to re-examine their social studies programmes and modify curriculum knowledge in multicultural directions. Until textbooks, upon which many social studies teachers depend, and mandated tests become more multicultural, however, it is unlikely that more than minor modifications will be made—except in the classrooms of a few exceptional teachers and in communities where organized interest groups continue to press for change.[17] In any event, the impact of one or another selection of curriculum knowledge will depend in large part on its compatibility with messages from out-of-school sources. But to the extent that the continuing debate tends toward polarization (e.g. pluralism versus unity), it may serve to sustain the *status quo* with respect to social studies curriculum knowledge. School leaders are mediators who try to avoid controversy and steer a middle course through conflicting demands. In the absence of state mandates or local pressures, the safest course for local educators may be to do nothing.

At the state level, policy-makers both respond to and mediate internal and external demands and interests. The interests mediated include those of the policy-makers. Mediation typically involves transforming demands that are controversial of difficult to realize into policies that are more widely acceptable and feasible to carry out. One way to do this is to route the demand(s) through normal bureaucratic channels. This tactic also slows the policy process, during which time strong feelings may fade. In this way, policy-makers and the education system attempt to maintain credibility or legitimacy, i.e. self-interest—and major change is delayed, diluted, or avoided. Whether the incorporation of multicultural policy activity in NYS into the "New Compact for Learning" becomes a case of such mediation and diminution of possible change, depends most immediately on the actions of the Social Studies Curriculum and Assessment Committee. Although movement toward more multicultural curriculum knowledge may seem slow, it is significant that NYS policy makers have not capitulated to the critics and abandoned efforts to make social studies curriculum knowledge more multicultural.

With respect to controlling curriculum knowledge, this study of policy-in-the-making strongly suggests that curriculum knowledge is multiply controlled. There appears to be no single or predominant source or means of control; there may not be any means of absolute or certain control. Teachers, textbooks, examinations, local and state policies, national policies, academic and public discourse, and experience or tradition interact in shaping curriculum knowledge. The complexity and uncertainty of curriculum knowledge control mean that curriculum knowledge will continue to be contested and renegotiated. Complexity and uncertainty also suggest that the power of curriculum policy to bring about change in classroom practice ought not to be overestimated.

Lastly, the public, political nature of curriculum knowledge is well illustrated by this case study. While learning and understanding are often quite personalized matters, part of a private sphere, curriculum knowledge and practice reside in a public sphere. Questions of curriculum knowledge require contextualized social and political analysis. They are not amenable to technocratic analysis and prescription, phenomenological individualism, or theoretical detachment.

Acknowledgements

An earlier version of this paper was presented as part of the symposium, "Multicultural education: politics and the management of knowledge" at the annual meeting of the American Educational Research Association, San Francisco, CA, April 1992. This revision has benefited in important ways from the comments of colleagues, especially those of Peter Seixas and Dexter Waugh, and the suggestions of anonymous reviewers.

Notes

1 For a juxtaposition of the New York and California experiences, see Cornbleth and Waugh (1993, 1995).
2 The US Department of Education, under the Bush Administration with Lamar Alexander as Secretary of Education and Diane Ravitch as Assistant Secretary for OERI and Counselor to the Secretary, provided funding to support the development of "voluntary" national standards in civics (to the Center for Civic Education in Calabasas, CA) as well as history and geography. The Clinton administration's April 1994 *Goals 2000: Educate America* added civics but not social studies.
3 NYS syllabi are offered as guidelines to school districts and teachers; they are not mandated. However, statewide Regents or Regents Competency tests for secondary students, based on the syllabi, are mandatory. Secondary social studies syllabi had been under revision prior to 1987; grades 7–12 social studies syllabi revised as of 1987 are labelled "tentative".
4 Leonard Jeffries, Chair of Africana Studies at the City College of New York, was one of four consultants retained by the task force, not an appointed member of author of the report as media accounts and commentators have claimed.
5 In 1988–1989, there were 2.5 million students in NYS public schools, K-12. Of these 61% were identified as white, 20% as African-American, 15% as Hispanic, and 4% as American-Indian, Alaskan Native, Asian or Pacific Islander (State Education

Department 1989: 21). The comparable percentages for the state's "big five" school districts' (New York City, Buffalo, Rochester, Syracuse and Yonkers) 1 000 000 students were: 22% white, 39% African-American, 32% Hispanic, and 7% American-Indian, Alaskan Native, Asian or Pacific Islander.

6 Prior to the review committee's first meeting, one member died and two additional members were appointed, for a total of 24.

7 Arthur Schlesinger Jr. agreed to be a consultant rather than a full member of the committee. Asa Hilliard neither attended meetings nor withdrew from the committee. Lloyd Rogler and Paul Gagnon withdrew because they could not attend committee meetings.

8 My own appointment as the only university member representing "education" probably had much to do with my being female and from western NYS. Only two of the 24 members were from western NY, and only four of the 13 university members were female (including two late appointees).

9 While Ravitch and Schlesinger were highly visible in opposition to the work of the Review Committee, I have not located oppositional statements by any of the co-signers or any further statements by the Committee of Scholars.

10 For accounts of interelationships among conservative or right-wing individuals and organizations and their activities in other arenas, see Henson and Philpott (1992) on universities, Soley (1991) on media, and Hatfield and Waugh (1992) on the foundations-think-tanks, media, state legislatures, and education.

11 For further information on individuals, organizations, and funders, see Waugh and Hatfield (1992), Cornbleth and Waugh (1993), and Cornbleth and Waugh (1995).

12 The federal funding of a National History Standards project at Charlotte Crabtree's NEH-funded National Center for History in the Schools can be seen as one indicator of success.

13 More recently, as a member of the Social Studies Curriculum and Assessment Committee, successor to the Review Committee, I received an unsolicited, free copy of the January 1992 *New Criterion* with "an article that I'm sure will interest you: Heather MacDonald's 'The Sobol Report, Multiculturalism Triumphant' ", a diatribe against *One Nation, Many Peoples* generally and Commissioner Sobol personally (personal communication from C. Carduff, Assistant Managing Editor, 30 January 1992).

14 It is significant here that Sobol is using the language of the Committee of Scholars and other critics in saying what he is *not* recommending, e.g. "ethnic cheerleading", "trashing . . .". The critics' language has been influential in shaping the debate.

15 Similar arguments about threats to "the American culture" also could be heard 75 years ago. See, for example, O'Sullivan (1992: 19) who traces "the intellectual lineage of the current opposition to 'multiculturalism' ".

16 By multiple perspectives, I mean consideration of different interpretations of phenomena (e.g. events, ideas, individuals), whether provided by participants with different vantage points or by later interpreters.

17 There are encouraging examples of local multicultural initiatives, including teachers and school districts setting goals, creating materials, organizing workshops, and networking with others within and beyond NYS.

References

Bacchus, M. K. (1986) *The Myth and Reality of Curriculum Planning* (London: Institute of Education, University of London).

Ball, S. J. (1990) *Politics and Policy Making in Education* (London: Routledge).

Buffalo News (1991) Wider curriculum lets kids discover more than Columbus: realistic history will bind, not destroy, nation. 30 June.

Cheney, L. V. (1991) Quoted in D. Viadero (1992) Two federal agencies launch project to develop national history standards. *Education Week*, 11 (16): 25.

Committee of Scholars in Defense of History, Statement of the Committee of Scholars in Defense of History (1990). *Newsday*, 29 June (reprinted in several places including *Perspectives*, October 1990, 28 (7): 15.

Cornbleth, C. (1990) *Curriculum in Context* (London: Falmer).
Cornbleth, C. and Waugh, D. (1993) The great speckled bird: education policy-in-the-making, *Educational Researcher*, 22 (7): 31–37.
Cornbleth, C. and Waugh, D. (1995) *The Great Speckled Bird: Multicultural Politics and Education Policymaking* (New York: St Martin's).
Cuomo, M. M. (1991) *Statement by Governor Mario M. Cuomo*. 15 July (Albany, NY: State of New York, Executive Chamber).
Decter, M. (1991) *E pluribus nihil*: multiculturalism and black children. *Commentary*, 92 (3): 25–29.
Edelman, M. (1977) *Political Language: Words That Succeed and Policies That Fail* (New York: Academic).
Foucault, M. (1977) *Language, Counter-Memory, Practice: Selected Essays and Interviews*. Edited by D. F. Bouchard (Ithaca, NY: Cornell University Press).
Gagnon, P. (ed.) (1989) *Historical Literacy: The Case for History in American Education* (New York: Macmillan).
Goodson, I. F. and Ball, S. (1984) *Defining the Curriculum: Histories and Ethnographies* (London: Falmer).
Hatfield, L. D. and Waugh, D. (1992) Think tanks: turning America right. *San Francisco Examiner*, 24–28 May (five-part series).
Henson, S. and Philpott, T. (1992) The right declares a culture war. *The Humanist*, 52 (2): 10–16, 46.
Kliebard, H. M. (1986) *The Struggle for the American Curriculum, 1893–1958* (London: Routledge & Kegan Paul).
Kliebard, H. M. (1992) Constructing a history of the American Curriculum. In P. W. Jackson (ed.) *Handbook of Research on Curriculum* (New York: Macmillan), 157–184.
MacDonald, H. (1992) The Sobol report: Multiculturalism triumphant. *The New Criterion*, 10 (5): 9–18.
Meyer, J. (1984) Reform and change. *IFG Policy Notes*, 5 (4): 1–2.
National Commission on Excellence in Education (1983) *A Nation at Risk* (Washington, DC: U.S. Government Printing Office).
New York Times (1991) More pluribus, more unum. 23 June: E14.
Organization of American Historians, Executive Board (1991) History education in the public schools. *OAH Newsletter*, 6 (February).
O'Sullivan, G. (1992) The PC policy in the mirror of history. *The Humanist*, 52 (2): 17–20, 46.
Popkewitz, T. S. (ed.) (1987) *The Formation of School Subjects* (London: Falmer).
Powers, W. (1991) Quoted in Associated Press, "GOP head: State report 'liberal sham' ". *Gannett Suburban Newspapers*, 14 July.
Ravitch, D. (1987) Tot sociology: or what happened to history in the grade schools. *American Scholar*, 56 (Summer): 343–354.
Ravitch, D. (1990) Diversity and democracy: multicultural education in America. *American Educator*, 14 (1): 16 20, 46–48.
Ravitch, D. (1991) Quoted in "Multicultural education: which direction?" *On Campus*, 11 (1): 7.
Ravitch, D. and Finn, C. E. (1987) *What Do Our 17-Year-Olds Know?* (New York: Harper & Row).
Reid, W. A. (1990) Strange curricula: origins and development of the institutional categories of schooling. *Journal of Curriculum Studies*, 22 (3): 203–216.
Rothman, R. (1988) Bennett offers high school's "ideal" content. *Education Week*, 7 (15–16): 1, 26–29.
Schlesinger, A. M., Jr. (1991) *The Disuniting of America* (Knoxville, TN: Whittle).
Shanker, A. (1992) Multiculturalism: don't sacrifice accuracy. *On Campus*, 11 (4): 5.
Social Studies Review and Development Committee (1991) *One Nation, Many Peoples: A Declaration of Cultural Interdependence* (Albany, NY: New York State Education Department).
Soley, L. (1991) Right thinking conservative think tanks. *Dissent*, 38 (Summer): 418–420.
State Education Department, Information Center on Education (1989) *Annual Educational Summary 1988–89* (Albany, NY: New York State Education Department).

Task Force on Minorities (1989) *A Curriculum of Inclusion* (Albany, NY: New York State Education Department).

Toulmin, S. F. (1982) *The Return to Cosmology: Postmodern Science and the Theology of Nature* (Berkeley: University of California Press).

Waugh, D. and Hatfield, L. D. (1992) Rightist groups pushing school reforms. *San Francisco Examiner*, 28 May: A–18. (Part 5 of series, "Think tanks, Turning America right.")

Williams, R. (1961) *The Long Revolution* (New York: Columbia University Press).

CHAPTER 17

"STUDENTS' RIGHT TO THEIR OWN LANGUAGE" (1995)

A retrospective

Geneva Smitherman

> *We affirm the students' right to their own patterns and varieties of language—the dialects of their nurture or whatever dialects in which they find their own identity and style. Language scholars long ago denied that the myth of a standard American dialect has any validity. The claim that any one dialect is unacceptable amounts to an attempt of one social group to exert its dominance over another. Such a claim leads to false advice for speakers and writers, and immoral advice for humans. A nation proud of its diverse heritage and its cultural and racial variety will preserve its heritage of dialects. We affirm strongly that teachers must have the experiences and training that will enable them to respect diversity and uphold the right of students to their own language.*
>
> —*Passed by the Executive Committee of the Conference on College Composition and Communication (CCCC), November, 1972, and by the CCCC Membership, April, 1974*

It has now been well over a generation since Kwame Ture (then Stokely Carmichael) issued his clarion call for "Black Power" and thus charted a new course for the Civil Rights Movement in America. But his cry, horrendous and frightening as it seemed to be to some in 1966, was not without precedent in the annals of the African American struggle. For just twelve years earlier, Richard Wright had entitled his book on the emerging independence movements in Africa, *Black Power*. And surely Rosa Parks' historic refusal to give up her seat to whites and move to the back of the bus on December 1, 1955, paved the way for Kwame Ture's "Black Power"—a bold call for new directions and strategies. These actions and events from the Black Experience symbolize the motive forces that led to the unleashing of Brown Power, Woman Power, Poor People's Power, Gay Power, and other human energy sources that fundamentally altered American power relations in our time.

The historical backdrop

As marching, fist-raising, loud-talking, and other forms of resistance marred the landscape of "America the beautiful," the power elites huddled to design reforms to acculturate the oppressed into the dominant ideology. The Unhip among researchers, scholars, and intellectuals assembled the data base upon which these reforms were built, arguing, for instance, that even though the linguistic-cultural differences of those oppressed by race, class, or gender were *cognitively* equal to those of the mainstream, they were *socially* unequal. Early on, some scholars—like James Sledd in his 1969 *English Journal* "Bi-Dialectalism: The Linguistics of White Supremacy," and me in my 1968 "Black Power is Black Language" (delivered in April, 1969 in Miami at my first CCCC Convention)—early on, such scholars tried to pull our coats (to enlighten) to the trickeration (deception) of the power brokers. They argued that it was purely academic to demonstrate, in Emersonian, arm-chair philosophizing style, the legitimacy of the oppressed's language and culture without concomitantly struggling for institutional legitimacy in the educational and public domains. If the patriarchally-constituted social and economic structure would not accept non-mainstream speech varieties, then the argument for *difference* would simply become *deficiency* all over again.

Against this backdrop, enlightened academics saw their task clearly to struggle for such legitimacy. They were not romantic idealists; indeed, many of them had been baptized in the fire of social protest and street activism. No, not idealists, but those who know that without vision, people will perish. These progressive academics began working within their professional societies and organizations to bring about mainstream recognition and legitimacy to the culture, history, and language of those on the margins. And it was not only within NCTE and CCCC that this struggle was waged, but all across the alphabetic spectrum—the APA (American Psychological Association); the ASA (American Sociological Association); the MLA (Modern Language Association); the SCA (Speech Communication Association); the ABA (American Bar Association); the ASHA (American Speech and Hearing Association); and on and on across disciplines and throughout the Academy. Though the struggle were spearheaded by Blacks, it quickly became a rainbow coalition as Hispanics, women, Native Americans, and other marginalized groups sought redress for their ages-old grievances against an exploitative system.

Let us recall that the Cause was just if the methods awkward. The Enlightened were, after all, attempting to effectuate change WITHIN THE SYSTEM. And even those of us who were more revolutionarily inclined recognized the folly of doing *nothing* while waiting for the Revolution to come.

The birth of "Students' Right"

In this socio-historical climate, in the fall of 1971, the officers of CCCC appointed a committee to draft a policy resolution on students' dialects, and thus the first "Students' Right to Their Own Language" Committee was born. After months of intense scholarly work and political struggle, both within and outside our Committee, in March, 1972, we presented the CCCC Executive Committee (of which I was also a member at the time), with the position statement which has come to be known as the "Students' Right to Their Own Language." When I say "intense struggle," it is not dramatic hyperbole; for instance, we debated for hours on the question of the student's right to *his* own language vs. *his or her* own language: remember, this was over twenty years ago.

In November of 1972, the CCCC Executive Committee passed the "Students' Right" resolution and began to pave the way to make this admittedly controversial resolution a matter of CCCC policy. They recognized that their membership, as well as other language arts professionals, would need to be educated about the current research on language variation, usage, and the history of American English. A Committee was appointed to develop a background document that would elaborate on the assertions in the brief "Students' Right" statement before presenting the resolution to the full body of CCCC and eventually to the profession at large. The background document was presented to the CCCC Executive Committee at the Philadelphia NCTE Convention in November, 1973. Subsequently, this document and the resolution itself were distributed to CCCC membership.

In April of 1974, at the CCCC business meeting in Anaheim, California, the "Students' Right to Their Own Language" became the official policy of CCCC. That fall, the complete background document was published as a full issue of CCCC's journal, *College Composition and Communication*. The "Students' Right" resolution appears on the inside cover of that issue. The document seeks to inform by presenting a set of 15 issues, in the form of questions, about language, dialect, and teaching-learning—e.g., "Does dialect affect the ability to write?" "Why do some dialects have more prestige than others?" Included also is a bibliography of 129 entries keyed to these 15 questions (CCCC, 1974).

NCTE's response to "Students' Right"

Although CCCC is politically autonomous, structurally, it is an institutional arm of NCTE, sharing some resources, headquarters, and, of course, concern for language education with NCTE. Further, many CCCC members, myself included, are members and workers of both organizations. In 1971, after the formation of what was to become the "Students' Right" Committee, CCCC leadership and its members began working within NCTE to promote the concept of the students' right to their own language. For the next three years, there was a concerted effort by CCCC to persuade NCTE to endorse the CCCC position statement. However, this did not occur. Instead, at its 1974 Convention, NCTE passed a weaker version of the CCCC's "Students' Right to Their Own Language." Although many of us on the "Students' Right" Committee and within CCCC were profoundly disappointed, we consoled ourselves by the thought that the action taken by NCTE was at least not a *negative* vote on the issue.

There are two crucial differences between the CCCC and the NCTE actions around "Students' Right to Their Own Language."

First, the NCTE resolution distinguishes between spoken and written language in relationship to students' dialects, and although it "accept(s) the linguistic premise that all these dialects are equally efficient as systems of communication," the resolution goes on to "affirm" that students should learn the "conventions of what has been called written edited American English" (NCTE Resolution #74.2, 1974). This was an issue that the CCCC "Students' Right" Committee struggled with and deliberately decided *not* to focus on. We recognized that spelling, punctuation, usage, and other surface structure conventions of Edited American English (EAE) are generally what's given all the play (attention) in composition classrooms anyway. Based on the ground-breaking linguistic research of scholars such as Chomsky (e.g., 1968), Labov (e.g., 1970, 1972), Halliday (e.g., 1973), Hymes (e.g., 1964, 1972), Dillard (e.g., 1972), Shuy (e.g., 1964, 1967), and Fishman (e.g., 1970), the CCCC background publication contends that:

> . . . dialect . . . plays little if any part in determining whether a child will ultimately acquire the ability to write EAE. . . . Since the issue is not the capacity of the dialect itself, the teacher can concentrate on building up the students' confidence in their ability to write . . . the essential functions of

writing [are] expressing oneself, communicating information and attitudes, and discovering meaning through both logic and metaphor . . . [thus] we view variety of dialects as an advantage . . . one may choose roles which imply certain dialects, but the decision is a social one, for the dialect itself does not limit the information which can be carried, and the attitudes may be most clearly conveyed in the dialect the writer finds most congenial . . . [Finally] the most serious difficulty facing "non-standard" dialect speakers in developing writing ability derives from their exaggerated concern for the *least* serious aspects of writing. If we can convince our students that spelling, punctuation, and usage are less important than content, we have removed a major obstacle in their developing the ability to write. (1974, 8)

The second crucial difference between NCTE and CCCC around the "Students' Right" issue is that CCCC committed tremendous time and energy resources to the illumination of this language issue. For several years after the passage of the position statement by the 1972 CCCC Executive Committee, CCCC committees worked to produce two documents (although one was never published) to provide guidance to teachers on the meaning and implications of the "Students' Right" position and the impact of this policy on classroom practice.

Although NCTE did not come on board with the full vigor we in CCCC would have liked, it did agree in its version of the "Students' Right" resolution to make available to other professional organizations the suggestions and recommendations in the CCCC background document and to

promote classroom practices to expose students to the variety of dialects that occur in our multi-regional, multi-ethnic, and multi-cultural society, so that they too will understand the nature of American English and come to respect all its dialects. (NCTE Resolution #74.2, 1974)

Implementation of "Students' Right"

After the NCTE action, CCCC moved into the next phase of the "Students' Right" history. To be sure, there was high interest and enthusiasm, but unfortunately, there was also lingering confusion—you know, "Well, what they want me to *do*?" Although the CCCC background document was informative in terms of theory, it did not go far enough in praxis. CCCC leadership acknowledged that there was a need for more explicit teaching materials, sample lesson plans, and a more specific pedagogy. The Executive Committee thus appointed the "Selection and Editorial Committee for Activities Supporting Students' Right to Their Own Language," on which I also served.

This Committee was charged with assembling a publication of practical classroom assignments, activities, lectures, and teaching units that would show and tell how to apply the philosophy of the "Students' Right" resolution to the day-to-day experience of teaching and learning. Many of the people who served on this Committee, as on the other "Students' Right" Committee, are well-known and active members of the profession. We spent nearly *four years* compiling and editing some excellent material, solicited from practitioners at all levels of education, only to be informed that CCCC had "reluctantly decided" not to publish the collection.

What had happened since the passage of the original "Students' Right" resolution some years earlier is that the nation was moving to a more conservative climate on the social, political, and educational fronts. It was a move which would be solidified in 1980 by the election of President Ronald Reagan. Thus the mood of CCCC, as the mood of America, had shifted from change and promise to stagnation and dreams deferred.

Product and process of "Students' Right"

We have overviewed the process; now let us look at the product in relationship to this process.

Even though earlier I generously labelled our group "progressive," we were not all of like minds about the "Students' Right" resolution, nor its implications. And we certainly were not of identical persuasion on the issue of America's linguistic ills and solutions to them. Hey, some of us even had reservations about the use of little four-letter words—not dem big, bad foe letter ones, with initial fricatives and sibilants; just the little ti-notchy ones like "damn" and "hell." (Apropos of this, I do hereby confess to being the first to introduce "cussing" into Committee deliberations, to the distinct relief of my old comrade, Ross Winterowd of the University of Southern California.) Yet despite our diverse ideologies and political perspectives, we shared a spirit of collective enlightenment on the language question.

The "Students' Right" background document is a compromise publication, born of the contradictions among radicals, moderates, and conservatives. It is, moreover, the consequence of the talented editorial hand of Richard (Jix) Lloyd-Jones from the University of Iowa and of the skillful diplomacy of late linguist Melvin Butler of Southern University, our Committee Chair, whose tragic, untimely death prevented him from witnessing the fruits of his labor. For some of us, then as now, the document is seen as equivocating; it doesn't go far enough. For others, then as now, it is perceived as too permissive.

Yet, short of totalitarianism and fascism on the one hand, or armed revolutionary struggle, on the other, compromise is what comes from working *within* the system. And so those of us who embrace the dialectical vision of history applaud the recently-renewed momentum and interest in the "Students' Right to Their Own Language," for without struggle, there is no progress.

As should be obvious to all writing teachers worth their training, the "Students' Right" document is the product of multiple writing styles. After deciding to use the admittedly wack (corny) twenty-question format of the once-popular television quiz show, we divvied up the work and the writing. Although we critiqued each other's writing and despite the admirably awesome editing job done by Melvin, and later Jix, still it must be conceded that the document is stylistically uneven. Yet the final product is preferable to what any *one* individual might have written because it reflects a *collective* response to the language question: "What should the schools do about the language habits of students who come from a wide variety of social, economic, and cultural backgrounds?" ("Students' Right," 1).

African Americans weren't the only "submerged minorities" (a term we wrestled with in Committee deliberations) forcing the question, as the "Students' Right" framed it: "Should the schools try to uphold language variety, or to modify it, or to eradicate it?" Yet, a good deal of the background document (i.e., examples, illustrations, bibliographic references, etc.) focus on *Black* speech. This is logical given not only the large numbers of African Americans among the oppressed, but also given that Blacks were the first to force the moral and

Constitutional questions of equality in this country. Further, of all underclass groups in the U.S., Blacks are pioneers in social protest and have waged the longest, politically principled struggle against exploitation.

Finally—and this is an ironic footnote in American life—whenever Blacks have struggled and won social gains for themselves, they have made possible gains for other groups—e.g., Hispanics, Asians, gays, etc., even some white folks! For instance, the nineteenth-century emancipation of African slaves in this country paved the way for the first Women's Movement, during which, in fact, Black champions for the abolition of slavery, Frederick Douglass and Sojourner Truth, for example, fought vigorously for women's rights. In similar fashion, then, *Black* students' right to *their* own language has made possible *all* students' right to their own language.

The need to recognize students' language and culture

Let me remind you that those who do not learn from the past are doomed to repeat it. In spite of recently reported gains in Black student writing, chronicled by the NAEP and higher scores on the SAT, the rate of functional illiteracy and drop-outs among America's underclass is moving faster than the Concorde. A genuine recognition of such students' culture and language is desperately needed if we as a profession are to play some part in stemming this national trend. I write genuine because, in spite of the controversy surrounding policies like the "Students' Right to Their Own Language," the bicultural, bilingual model has *never* really been tried. Lip-service is about all most teachers gave it, even at the height of the social upheaval described earlier.

You see, the game plan has always been linguistic and cultural absorption of the Other into the dominant culture, and indoctrination of the outsiders into the existing value system (e.g., Sledd 1972), to remake those on the margins in the image of the patriarch, to reshape the outsiders into talking, acting, thinking, and (to the extent possible) looking like the insiders (e.g., Smitherman 1973). In bilingual education and among multilingual scholars and activists, this issue is framed as one of language *shift* vs. language *maintenance* (see Fishman 1966, 1983). That is, the philosophy of using the native language as a vehicle to teach and eventually *shift* native speakers *away from their home language*, vs. a social and pedagogical model that teaches the target language—in this country, English —while providing support for *maintaining the home language*—Spanish, Polish, Black English, etc. All along, despite a policy like the "Students' Right," the system has just been perping—engaging in fraudulent action.

I am a veteran of the language wars, dating to my undergraduate years when I was victimized by a biased speech test given to all those who wanted to qualify for a teaching certificate. I flunked the test and had to take speech correction, not because of any actual speech impediment, such as aphasia or stuttering, but because I was a speaker of Black English. Such misguided policies have now been eradicated as a result of scientific enlightenment about language and the renewed commitment to cultural pluralism that is the essence of the American experiment.

A few years after my bout with speech therapy, I published, in the pages of this journal, my first experimental attempt at writing the "dialect of my nurture": "English Teacher, Why You Be Doing the Thangs You Don't Do?" (Smitherman 1972). Encouraged by former *EJ* editor, Stephen Tchudi (then Judy), I went on to produce a regular *EJ* column, "Soul N Style," written in a mixture of Black English Vernacular and the Language of Wider Communication (i.e., Edited

American English), and for which I won a national award (thanks to Steve Tchudi, who believed in me—Yo, Steve, much props!). In the 1977 edition of *Talkin and Testifyin: the Language of Black America*, I called for a national language policy, the details of which I had yet to work out. A decade later, I had come to realize that such a policy was needed, not just for African Americans and other groups on the margins, but for the entire country, and that the experience of African Americans could well be the basis for what I called a tripartite language policy (Smitherman 1987). Like I said, I been on the battlefield for days.

CCCC's "National Language Policy"

Over the years since 1971, CCCC has evolved its linguistic and social consciousness beyond the issue of students' right to their own dialect to encompass the students' right to multiple ways of speaking. In 1987, it established the Language Policy Committee to study the current "English-Only" Movement and to develop a position for CCCC on English-Only's call for a Constitutional amendment to make English the sole language of this country. That Committee, like its predecessor, the "Students' Right" Committee, formulated a CCCC position that has become organizational policy. In March 1988, CCCC adopted the "National Language Policy," which is as follows:

> There is a need for a National Language Policy, the purpose of which is to prepare everyone in the United States for full participation in a multicultural nation. Such a policy recognizes and reflects the historical reality that, even though English has become the language of wider communication, we are a multi-lingual society. All people in a democratic society have the right to equal protection of the laws, to employment, to social services, and to participation in the democratic process. No one should be denied these or any other civil rights because of linguistic and cultural differences. Legal protection, education, and social services must be provided in English as well as other languages in order to enable everyone in the United States to take full advantage of these rights. This language policy affirms that civil rights should not be denied to people because of linguistic differences. It enables everyone to participate in the life of the nation by ensuring continued respect both for English, the common language, and for the many other languages that have contributed to our rich cultural and linguistic heritage. This policy has three inseparable parts:
>
> 1. to provide resources to enable native and non-native speakers to achieve oral and literate competence in English, the language of wider communication.
> 2. to support programs that assert the legitimacy of native languages and dialects and ensure that proficiency in the mother tongue will not be lost; and
> 3. to foster the teaching of languages other than English so that native speakers of English can rediscover the language of their heritage or learn a second language.

The formulation of such a national language policy would mean that on *all* levels of education, every student would be required to develop competence in at least three languages. One of these would be, of course, the Language of Wider

Communication, which everyone would learn. The second would be the student's mother tongue—e.g., Spanish, Polish, Black English, Italian, Arabic, Chinese, Appalachian English. The legitimacy of the home language would be reinforced, and students' ability to function in that language would be part of their expanded linguistic repertoire by the end of twelve years of schooling. Thirdly, every student would have command of at least one totally foreign language. That language would vary, depending on the options and social conditions in local communities and schools.

"Students' Right" and new paradigm shift

In retrospect, then, the "Students' Right to Their Own Language" served its historical time and paved the way for this next evolutionary stage. We're now in the period of a new paradigm shift, from a provincial, more narrowly conceived focus to a broader internationalist perspective. We thus are being forced to address the issue of multiple linguistic voices, not only here, but in the global family. NCTE and CCCC, having grappled with these issues through the "Students' Right" era is, I think, well-positioned for a leadership role in formulating a national language policy for this nation. Not just a policy for the narrow confines of, say, composition classrooms, which was our more modest goal in developing the CCCC "Students' Right" resolution, but a language policy that would impact *all* levels of education in *all* school subjects and in *all* social and institutional domains.

This is what is needed to carry us into the next century, just six years away. I thus herein issue a call to all language arts educators and the entire NCTE membership to sign onto the CCCC National Language Policy. We—and your students—await your response.

Note

Kwame Ture, then Stokely Carmichael, first used the "Black Power" slogan in a speech in June, 1966 on a protest march in Greenville, Mississippi. The march, designed to go across the state of Mississippi, had been initiated by James Meredith, the first Black to be admitted to the University of Mississippi, who had been ambushed and shot early on during the march. Carmichael and other Civil Rights leaders had come to Mississippi to continue Meredith's march. The concept of empowerment, as well as the accompanying rhetorical strategy, had been carefully worked out by the leadership of the Student Non-Violence Coordinating Committee (SNCC), which was waiting for the opportune moment to introduce the slogan of "Black Power" into the discourse of the Civil Rights Movement. A few days before Stokely's speech, SNCC worker, Willie Ricks, had begun using the slogan in local meetings to rally the people. And it was actually Ricks who convinced SNCC leadership—and Carmichael—that this was the historical moment to drop "Black Power." In retrospect, Kwame Ture confessed that Stokely Carmichael "did not expect that 'enthusiastic response' from his audience of sharecroppers, farm workers, and other everyday Black people in Mississippi." "The Time Has Come, 1964–66," *Eyes on the Prize II: America at the Racial Crossroads (1965–1985).*

Works cited

Chomsky, Noam. 1968. *Language and Mind.* New York: Harcourt, Brace, Jovanovich.
Conference on College Composition and Communication. 1974. "Students' Right to Their Own Language." *College Composition and Communication* 25.3(Fall): 1–32.
Conference on College Composition and Communication. 1988. "National Language Policy." Urbana, IL: NCTE.

Dillard, J. L. 1972. *Black English: Its History and Usage in the United States.* New York: Vintage Books.

Eyes on the Prize II: America At the Racial Crossroads (1965–1985). 1990. PBS video series.

Fishman, Joshua A. 1966. *Language Loyalty in the United States.* The Hague: Mouton.

——. 1970. *Sociolinguistics.* Rowley: Newbury House.

——. 1980. "Bilingual Education, Language Planning, and English." *English World-Wide.* 1.1: 11–24.

Halliday, M. A. K. 1973. *Explorations in the Functions of Language.* London: Edward Arnold.

Hymes, Dell, ed. 1964. *Language in Culture and Society.* New York: Harper and Row.

——. 1972. "Introduction." *Functions of Language in the Classroom.* Eds. C. Cazden, V. John-Steiner, and D. Hymes. New York: Teachers College Press.

Labov, William. 1970. *The Study of Nonstandard English.* Urbana, IL: NCTE.

——. 1972. *Language in the Inner City.* Philadelphia: University of Pennsylvania Press.

National Council of Teachers of English. 1974. *NCTE Resolution #74.2.* Urbana, IL: NCTE.

Shuy, Roger. 1964. *Social Dialects and Language Learning.* Urbana, IL: NCTE.

——. 1967. *Discovering American Dialects.* Urbana, IL: NCTE.

Sledd, James. 1969. "Bi-Dialectalism: The Linguistics of White Supremacy." *English Journal* 58.9(Dec.): 1307–1315.

——. 1972. "Doublespeak: Dialectology in the Service of Big Brother." *College English* 33.1(Jan.): 439–457.

Smitherman, Geneva. 1972. "English Teacher, Why You Be Doing the Thangs You Don't Do?" *English Journal* 61.1(Jan.): 59–65.

——. 1973. " 'God Don't Never Change': Black English From A Black Perspective." *College English* 34.3(Mar.): 828–34.

——. 1977. *Talkin and Testifyin: The Language of Black America.* Boston: Houghton Mifflin.

——. 1987. "Toward a National Public Policy on Language." *College English* 49.1(Jan.): 29–36.

APPENDIX 1: OTHER SUGGESTED READINGS

Bernier, N. R., & Davis, R. H. (1973). Synergy: A model for implementing multicultural education. *Journal of Teacher Education, 24*(4), 266–271.

Bresnick, D. (1977). Blacks, Hispanics, and others: Decentralization and ethnic succession. *Urban Education, 12*(2), 129–152.

Bullock, C. S. (1976). Defiance of the law: School discrimination before and after desegregation. *Urban Education, 9*(3), 219–262.

Carlson, P. E. (1976). Toward a definition of local-level multicultural education. *Anthropology and Education Quarterly, 7*(4), 26–30.

Cross, D., Long, M. A., & Ziajka, A. (1978). Minority cultures and education in the United States. *Education and Urban Society, 10*(3), 263–277.

Glazer, N. (1981). Pluralism and the new immigrants. *Transaction Social Science and Modern Society, 19*(1), 31–36.

Jones, R. S. (1977). Racial Patterns and School District Policy. *Urban Education, 12*(3), 297–312.

Lee, M. K. (1983). Multiculturalism: Educational perspectives for the 1980s. *Education, 103*(4), 405–409.

Madden, N. A., & Slavin, R. E. (1983). Mainstreaming students with mild handicaps: Academic and social outcomes. *Review of Educational Research, 53*(4), 519–569.

Oakes, J. (1986). Keeping track, Part 2: Curriculum inequality and school reform. *Phi Delta Kappan, 69*(1), 148–154.

Ornstein, A. C., & Levin, D. U. (1982). Educators respond to emerging social trends with multicultural instruction. *NASSP Bulletin, 66*(450), 78–85.

Ornstein, A. C., & Levine, D. U. (1982). Multicultural education: Trends and issues. *Childhood Education, 58*(4).

Payne, C. R. (1983). Multicultural education and racism in American schools. *Theory into Practice, 54*(2), 124–131.

Sharpes, D. (1973). Residence and race in education: Conflict in courts and communities. *Journal of Teacher Education, 24*(4), 289–293.

St. Lawrence, T. J., & Singleton, J. (1976). Multi-culturalism in social context: Conceptual problems raised by educational policy issues. *Anthropology and Education Quarterly, 7*(4), 19–23.

Swadener, E. (1988). Implementation of education that is multicultural in early childhood settings: A case study of two day-care programs. *The Urban Review, 20*(1), 8–28.

Tate, W. F., Ladson-Billings, G., & Grant, C. A. (1993). The *Brown* decision revisited: Mathematizing social problems. *Educational Policy, 7*(3), 255–275.

Thurlow, M. L., & Johnson, D. R. (2000). High-stakes testing of students with disabilities. *Journal of Teacher Education, 51*(4), 305–314.

Trueba, E. T. (1976). Issues and problems in bilingual bicultural education. *NABE Journal, 1*(2), 11–19.

APPENDIX 2: JOURNAL PUBLISHERS AND CONTACT INFORMATION

Action in Teacher Education
Association of Teacher Educators
1900 Association Drive, Suite ATE
Reston, VA 20191–1502
(703)620–2110; (703)620–9530
http://www.ate1.org

American Association of Colleges for Teacher Education
1307 New York Avenue, NW Suite 300
Washington, DC 20005–4701
(202)293–2450; (202)457–8096 (Fax)
www.aacte.org

American Educational Research Association
1230—17th Street NW
Washington, DC 20036
(202)223–9485, × 100; (202)775–1824
http://aera.net

American Journal of Education
University of Chicago Press
Permissions Department
1427 East 60th Street
Chicago, IL
(773)702–6096; (773)702–9756

American Sociological Association
1307 New York Avenue, NW Suite 700
Washington, DC 20005–4701
Jill Campbell
Publications Manager
(202)383–9005, × 303; (202)638–0882
www.asanet.org

Anthropology and Education
Anthropology and Education Quarterly
University of California Press
Journals and Digital Publishing Division
2000 Center Street, Suite 303
Berkeley, CA 94704

Association for Supervision and Curriculum Development
1703 N. Beauregard Street
Alexandria, VA 22311–1714
(703)578–9600; (703)575–5400 (Fax)
www.ascd.org

Banks, Cherry A. McGee
Professor, Education
University of Washington, Bothell
18115 Campus Way NE Room UW1 244
Bothell, WA 98011–8246

Banks, James A.
University of Washington
Box 353600, 110 Miller Hall
Seattle, WA 98195–3600
(206)543–3386; (206)542–4218 Fax
http://faculty.washington.edu/jbanks

Comparitive Education Review
University of Chicago Press
Permissions Department
1427 East 60th Street
Chicago, IL
(773)702–6096; (773)702–9756

Curriculum and Teaching
James Nicholas Publishers
PO Box 244
Albert Park, Australia, 3206

Education
Dr. George E. Uhlig
PO Box 8826
Spring Hill Station
Mobile, AL 36689

Education and Urban Society
Corwin Press, Inc.
2455 Teller Road
Thousand Oaks, CA 91320–2218
(805)499–9734; (805)499–0871 (Fax)
http://www.sagepub.com

Educational Horizons
National Association for Ethnic Studies, Inc. &
American Cultural Studies Department
Western Washington University
516 High Street—MS 9113
Bellingham, WA 98225–9113
(360)650–2349; (360)650–2690 (Fax)

Educational Leadership
Association for Supervision and Curriculum Development
PO Box 79760
Baltimore, MD 21279–0760
(703)578–9600; 1–800–933–2723; (703)575–5400 Fax
www.ascd.org

Educational Research Quarterly
113 Greenbriar Drive
West Monroe, LA 71291
(318)274–2355
hashway@alphagram.edu

Educators for Urban Minorities
Long Island University Press (No longer in operation)
Eugene E. Garcia, Ph.D.
Vice President Education Partnerships
Professor of Education
Arizona State University
Eugene.Garcia@asum.edu

English Journal
1111 W. Kenyon Road
Urbana, IL 61801–1096
(217)328–3870; (217)328–9645 (Fax)
http://www.ncte.org

Exceptional Children
Council for Exceptional Children
Permissions Department
1110 North Glebe Road Suite 300
Arlington, VA 22201–5704
(703)264–1637

FOCUS
Joint Center for Political Studies
1301 Pennsylvania Avenue, NW
Washington, DC 20004
(202)626–3500

Ford Foundation
320 East 43rd Street
New York, NY 10017

Gibson, Margaret A.
Professor of Education and Anthropology
Department of Education
University of California, Santa Cruz
1156 High Street
Santa Cruz, CA 95064
(831)459–4740; (831)459–4618 (Fax)

Harvard Educational Review
Harvard Graduate School of Education
8 Story Street, 1st Floor
Cambridge, MA 02138
(617)495–3432; (617)496–3584 (fax)
www.hepg.org
+
HarperCollins Publishers
10 East 53rd Street
New York, NY 10022
(212)207–7000

Interchange
Nel van der Werf
Assistant Rights and Permissions/Springer
Van Godewijckstraat 30
PO Box 17
3300 AA Dordrecht
The Netherlands
31 (0) 78 6576 298; 31 (0) 78 6576 323 (Fax)
Nel.vanderwerf@springer.com
www.springeronline.com

Journal of Curriculum Studies
Routledge (Taylor & Francis, Inc.)
4 Park Square, Milton Park
Abingdon, Oxon OX14 4RN United Kingdom
44–1235–828600; 44–1235–829000 (Fax)
http://www.routledge.co.uk

Journal of Curriculum and Supervision
Association for Supervision and Curriculum Development
1703 North Beauregard Street
Alexandria, VA 22311–1714
(703)578–9600/(800)933–2723; (703)575–3926 (Fax)
http://www.ascd.org

Journal of Teacher Education
American Association of Colleges for Teacher Education
1307 New York Avenue NW Suite 300
Washington, DC 20017–4701
(202)293–2450; (202)457–8095 (Fax)
www.aacte.org

Journal of Research and Development in Education
Julie P. Sartor, Editor
Office of the Associate Dean for Research,
Technology, & External Affairs
UGA College of Education
(706)542–4693; (706)542–8125 (Fax)
jsartor@uga.edu

Journal of Negro Education
Howard University Press
Marketing Department
2600 Sixth Street, NW
Washington, DC 20059
(202)806–8120; (202)806–8434 (Fax)

Journal of Literacy Research (formerly *Journal of Reading Behavior*)
Lawrence Erlbaum Associates, Inc.
10 Industrial Avenue
Mahwah, NJ 07430–2262
(201)258–2200; (201)236–0072 (Fax)

Journal of Educational Thought
University of Calgary
Faculty of Education – Publications Office
2500 University Drive N.W.
Education Tower, Room 1310
Calgary, Alberta, Canada T2N 1N4
(403)220–7499/5629; (403)284–4162 (Fax)
www.ucalgary.ca

Journal of Teacher Education
American Association of Colleges for Teacher Education
1307 New York Avenue NW 300
Washington, DC 20005–4701
(202)293–2450; (202)457–8095 (Fax)
www.aacte.org

Language Arts
The National Council of Teachers of English
1111 W. Kenyon Road
Urbana, IL 61801–1096
(217)278–3621
permissions@ncte.org

Momentum
National Catholic Educational Association
1077—30 Street, NW Suite 100
Washington, DC 2007
(202)337–6232; (202)333–6706 (Fax)
nceaadmin@ncea.org

Multicultural Education
Gaddo Gap Press
3145 Geary Boulevard PMB 275
San Francisco, CA 94118
(414)666–3012; (414)666–3552
http://www.caddogap.com

National Catholic Educational Association
1077—30 Street, NW Suite 100
Washington, DC 20007
(202)337–6232; (202)333–6706 (Fax)
nceaadmin@ncea.org

National Council for the Social Studies
8555 Sixteenth Street, Suite 500
Center for Multicultural Education
Silver Spring, MD 20910
(301)588–1800 × 122;
(301)588–2049 Fax

National Educational Service
1252 Loesch Road
PO Box 8 Department V2
Bloomington, IN 47402

Negro Educational Review
NER Editorial Offices
School of Education
1601 East Market Street
Greensboro, NC 27411
Alice M. Scales (scales@pitt.edu)
Shirley A. Biggs (biggs@pitt.edu)

Peabody Journal of Education
Lawrence Erlbaum Associates
10 Industrial Avenue
Mahwah, NJ 07430–2262

Phi Delta Kappan
Phi Delta Kappa International
408 N. Union Street
PO Box 789
(812)339–1156; 800–766–1156; (812)339–0018 fax

Race, Class, and Gender
Southern University at New Orleans (No Response)
Carl contact Jean Belkhir (jbelkhir@uno.edu)

Radical Teacher
Center for Critical Education
PO Box 382616
Cambridge, MA 02238
Saul Slapikoff, Permissions Editor
slap2@comcast.net

Researching Today's Youth: The Community Circle of Caring Journal
Dr. Carlos E. Cortes
Professor Emeritus
Department of History
University of California,
Riverside, CA 92521–0204
(951)827–1487
(951)827–5299 fax
carlos.cortes@ucr.edu

Review of Educational Research
American Educational Research Association
1230—17th Street NW
Washington, DC 20036–3078

Sage Publications, Inc.
Corwin Press, Inc
2455 Teller Road
Thousand Oaks, CA 91320
(805)410–7713; (805)376–9562 (Fax)
permissions@sagepub.com

Southeastern Association of Educational Opportunity Program Personnel (SAEOPP)
75 Piedmont Avenue NE
Suite 408
Atlanta, GA 30303–2518
(404)522–4642

Teachers College Record
Blackwell Publishing
PO Box 805
9600 Garsington Road
Oxford OX4 2ZG United Kingdom
44 (0) 1865 776868; 44 (0) 1865 714591 Fax
www.blackwellpublishing.com

Teacher Education and Special Education
Dr. Fred Spooner, Editor
Teacher Education and Special Education
SPCD/College of Education
University of North Carolina at Charlotte
Charlotte, NC 28223

(704)687–8851; (704)687–2916 Fax
fhspoone@email.uncc.edu

The American Scholar
1606 New Hampshire Avenue NW
Washington, DC 20009
(202)265–3808; (202)265–0083

The Educational Forum
Kappa Delta Pi
3707 Woodview Trace
Indianapolis, IN 46268–1158

The High School Journal
The University of North Carolina Press
PO Box 2288
Chapel Hill, NC 27515–2288
(919)966–3561; (919)966–3829
www.uncpress.unc.edu

The Journal of Educational Research
Heldref Publications
1319 Eighteenth Street, NW
Washington, DC 20036–1802
(202)296–6267; (202)296–5146 (Fax)
www.heldref.org

The New Advocate
Christopher-Gordon Publishers, Inc.
1502 Providence Hwy, Suite 12
Norwood, MA 02062–4643
(781)762–5577; (781)762–7261
http://www.christopher-gordon.com

The Social Studies
Heldref Publications
1319 Eighteenth Street, NW
Washington, DC 20038–1802
(202)296–6267; (202)296–5149 (Fax)
permissions@heldref.org

The Teacher Educator
Ball State University
Teachers College
TC 1008
Muncie, IN 47306
(765)285–5453; (765)285–5455

The Urban Review
Nel van der Werf
Assistant Rights and Permissions/Springer
Van Godewijckstraat 30
PO Box 17
3300 AA Dordrecht
The Netherlands
31 (0) 78 6576 298; 31 (0) 78 6576 323 (Fax)
Nel.vanderwerf@springer.com
www.springeronline.com

Theory into Practice
Lawrence Erlbaum Associates, Inc.
10 Industrial Avenue
Mahwah, NJ 07430–2262

Viewpoints in Teaching and Learning
Indiana University
School of Education
Education Building 109
Bloomington, IN 47405

Young Children
National Association for the Education of Young Children
1313 L Street, NW, Suite 500
Washington, DC 20036–1426
(202)232–8777; (202)328–1846 (Fax)
http://www.naeyc.org

PERMISSION CREDITS

Part 3: Actions to Policy

AUTHOR INDEX

SUBJECT INDEX